IMPROVEMENT
IN ACTION

IMPROVEMENT IN ACTION

Advancing Quality in America's Schools

ANTHONY S. BRYK

HARVARD EDUCATION PRESS

Cambridge, Massachusetts

Continuous Improvement in Education
Series

Paperback ISBN 978-1-68253-499-1
Library Edition ISBN 978-1-68253-500-4

Library of Congress Cataloging-in-Publication Data
Names: Bryk, Anthony S., author.
Title: Improvement in action : advancing quality in America's schools / Anthony S. Bryk.
Description: Cambridge, Massachusetts : Harvard Education Press, [2020] |
    Includes index. | Summary: "This book presents a series of case studies of schools and
    other educational organizations that are successfully putting continuous improvement
    techniques into practice"— Provided by publisher.
Identifiers: LCCN 2020010097 | ISBN 9781682534991 (paperback) | ISBN 9781682535004
(library binding)
Subjects: LCSH: School improvement programs—United States—Case studies. |
    Inquiry-based learning—United States—Case studies. | Educational change—United
    States—Case studies. | School management and organization—United States—Case
    studies. | Organizational effectiveness—United States—Case studies.
Classification: LCC LB2822.82 .B78 2020 | DDC 371.200973—dc23
LC record available at https://lccn.loc.gov/2020010097

Published by Harvard Education Press,
an imprint of the Harvard Education Publishing Group

Harvard Education Press
8 Story Street
Cambridge, MA 02138

Cover Design: Ciano Design
Cover Image: MirageC/Moment via Getty Images

The typefaces used in this book are Minion Pro and Franca

*To those who started me some
thirty-plus years ago on a
personal journey of learning
to improve schools on the
South Side of Chicago:*

Sharon Greenberg, Sara Spurlark,
and Al Bertani

Contents

Introduction

I BEGAN WORKING on school improvement some thirty years ago in Chicago. Back then, dropout rates in the Chicago Public Schools (CPS) hovered near 50 percent, less than 30 percent of students were at grade level in reading and math, school buildings were in decay, and basic concerns about issues of order and safety were widespread.[1] The district served 90 percent children of color and 90 percent were from low-income families. In this context, improving schools meant a direct attack on institutionalized inequity by race and poverty.

Fast-forward to today: we now know that dramatic improvements have occurred in the city's schools. High school graduation rates are approaching 80 percent.[2] CPS students now achieve some of largest learning gains per year of instruction in the nation.[3] While these improvements may be exceptional, there are indications that public schools all across the country are gradually getting better. Nationally, high school graduation rates, for example, are at their highest level ever.[4] Academic standards have risen substantially.[5] Educators are working hard at trying to get better, and yet dissatisfaction with the state of public education persists.

The problem is that America's aspirations for what we want schools to accomplish today are increasing at a very fast rate. Educators now seek to embrace the goals of the Common Core State Standards and Next Generation Science Standards. They are exhorted to personalize instruction, to promote student social-emotional development, to make all students

1

technology-savvy. Educators are pressed to prepare every student for a future economy that is evolving rapidly and where the speed of technological change is outstripping the capacity of most US social and political systems to keep pace. And accompanying these larger macroeconomic disruptions, schools are often on the front line to redress an ever-expanding list of social concerns.

Given this backdrop, it is not surprising that a chasm has been widening for some time between our rising aspirations for what we would like schools to accomplish and what they are able to routinely achieve. And this gap is greatest for our most disadvantaged students and in our most troubled community contexts. This has come to be a major social justice issue for our time.

Moreover, there are indications that the economic, technological, and social forces that have been driving the growing gap between aspirations and delivery will continue to compound. This means that the expectations we hold for our educational institutions will continue to change, and likely at an increasing rate. So not only do our schools need to keep getting better, educators need to learn how to accomplish improvements faster in the years ahead.

This challenge is the organizing perspective that my colleagues and I brought to *Learning to Improve—How is it that America's schools can get better at getting better?*[6] Put simply, in that volume we argued that we need answers to two big questions:

- How can our educational organizations *continuously get better at what they do?*
  And recognizing the quickening pace of change,
- How do we *accelerate learning to improve?*

In this volume, I, with contributing authors, offer six stories of educational organizations that have stepped up to the challenges of "getting better at getting better." These organizations span the nation from north to south and east to west; their work is alive in urban and rural contexts. *Improvement in Action* brings forward the visions, aspirations, and concrete moves that these educators have made to vitalize improvement.

These stories *inform how* other educators might embark on similar activities. They also *inspire why* working in these pioneering ways really matter for the children, the families, and the communities that educators aim to serve.

Before sharing the six stories, I recount below a bit of recent educational reform history. It sets the context for where the discipline of improvement science and working in structured improvement networks takes root.

AN ASPIRATION IN SEARCH OF A METHOD

In response to the forces of change noted above, policy leaders and reform advocates have been pressing an increasing number of new ideas into America's educational systems. Unfortunately, these ideas often arrive without the expertise and practical know-how to make them work. Reformers and policy makers then get frustrated that educators cannot seem to turn their "great" ideas into effective execution; and the commitment of educators gets called into question.[7]

W. Edwards Deming, the improvement guru whose writings and research have inspired productive change across many different industries and sectors, said that education is a field characterized by "miracle goals and no methods."[8] He made this observation in 1991, as policy leaders touted national education goals that pledged, among other things, for the US to be first in the world in math and science by 2000. Deming's characterization of "miracle goals" was apt then, is equally true looking back now on No Child Left Behind (NCLB), and remains salient as we move into the era of Common Core Standards.

Performance Management
Important initiatives have been developing over the last two decades that seek to tackle Deming's methods question. One such effort is the performance management strategy embraced by NCLB and now found in many school and teacher evaluation systems. A strength of this approach is that it has focused educators' attention on data. As a result, there is much greater transparency today around student outcomes, including disparities in

these outcomes among groups. This transparency is a new, important phenomenon. I think back to one of my first efforts in Chicago in the late 1980s to analyze systemwide student achievement data broken down by racial-ethnic subgroups. Everyone knew there were large disparities in student attainment, but back then there was little published data on this point. As our tabulations began to shed light on this issue, we initiated conversations with system and community leaders about making these data public. Some of them feared, however, that our findings would be read as blaming the victim and cautioned against releasing them.[9] In the end, the need for data transparency won out, but is took an argument to accomplish this. Today, the commitment to transparency about results is settled, and this development is central in allowing improvement science to spring forward in the education context.

In somewhat simplified form, the basic logic operating in performance management systems is as follows: policy makers set the targets, create incentives, provide schools with data dashboards, and then hold individuals accountable for reaching the established targets. This is a plausible strategy if you think that the missing ingredient is effort, or the problem is that educators are just not focused on the right objectives. However, if you think that improving outcomes is principally a problem of educator learning—of not knowing how to do better—then performance management as the primary strategy is lacking in a critical regard. Specifically, there is no detailed working theory embedded in this strategy about *how* to actually improve practice. Instead, educators are told the goals; they are told to work harder and figure out how to reach them; and they are put on notice that failing has consequences for them and their schools.

The Evidence-Based Practice Movement

Evidence-based practice represents a second response to Deming's methods problem (see figure I.1). This movement has been prevalent in medicine for over fifty years, and it began to take hold in education in the early 2000s. In the ideal scenario, a researcher in an academic institution—or perhaps a commercial educational products firm—has some research-based ideas about new educational materials, programs, or tools. Systematic design and

FIGURE I.1 A process map for evidence-based practice

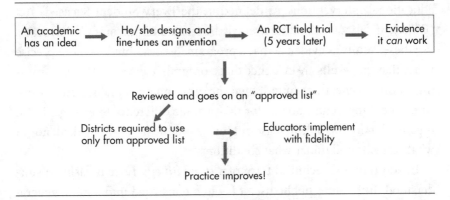

initial testing occur in a controlled context orchestrated by the researcher, and a proof of concept emerges. A small field trial, which is also directed by the researcher, takes place; this is followed up with a larger, often multiyear randomized control trial (RCT). The final results are eventually reviewed by the What Works Clearinghouse (WWC—part of the US Department of Education's Institute of Education Sciences (IES)). If the intervention is judged successful, then typically seven or eight years after the initial research inquiries began, it is added to a list of effective programs that districts are encouraged to buy and implement with fidelity.

The strength of this evidence-based movement is that it has brought increased conceptual and analytic discipline into education. This is a much-needed antidote in a field where supporting evidence has often been an afterthought. This attention to bringing empirical evidence to bear, and to drawing on more basic social and psychological research findings to undergird change, is another grounding tenet of improvement science.

But the primary focus in the evidence-based practice movement is on estimating a program's *standard effect size*. Basically this is just the *average difference* between a group of students, classrooms, or schools that received the intervention and another group that did not. At present, the focus on average outcomes is so deeply embedded in policy and practice contexts that educators tend to lose sight of what this perspective obscures. Even the large-scale RCTs, which sit at the apex of the four tiers of evidence for educational interventions, as defined in the Every Student Succeeds Act (ESSA), are about estimating average differences in outcomes.[10] Advocates use these results as evidence that a program "works," but it is more precise to say that the results are evidence that a program *can* work. That is, assuming a positive effect was found, then the program presumably had to work somewhere for some students for this average difference to emerge. But it is generally not possible to tease out for whom the program worked, nor in what contexts and under what conditions.

In addition, the technical term of a *standard effect size* is easily misunderstood. In broader public use, it is often construed into a more general claim, leading lay audiences to think that the standard effect size is what routinely occurs and what should reliably result—that is, the standard— but it does not mean that.

There is now a growing body of evidence that almost all interventions actually have highly variable effects, working well in some places and not at all in others.[11] Researchers report that the standard deviation in the size of an intervention's effects is as large as, and sometimes even larger than, the average effect. This means, again, that while these studies provide rigorous causal inferences that the intervention *can* work (i.e., the statistical evidence about the average difference), these interventions often have not worked in a quarter to a third or more of the sites where they have been attempted. Moreover, there are reasons to believe that the results, which occurred under the controlled conditions of an RCT, likely underestimate the propensity for the null effects that will occur if the intervention were to scale more broadly.[12]

In essence, the education field is relearning observations that date back to the 1970s—and are documented in the evaluations of programs such as Planned Variation Head Start, Follow Through models, and the television series *Sesame Street*. Interventions produce wide variability in outcomes. Moreover, this variability in effects is especially important when the aim is to address long-standing disparities in educational outcomes, because these null effects tend not to be randomly distributed. Rather, the most disadvantaged students and contexts are often the ones left behind.[13]

Finally, at the most basic level, the overall corpus of work in the WWC remains modest. This contrasts with health care, where clinical trials have been supported at multiple orders of magnitude greater than in education, and where the knowledge base has been building for over half a century.[14] To put this difference in perspective, in 2010 alone, some twenty-seven thousand clinical trials were published in medicine. Contrast this with education, where after more than a decade of effort, there are about one thousand entries in the WWC. In short, the overall body of program effectiveness evidence available to educators is very limited. These studies may afford a useful starting point for improvement for some educators on some problems, and in some contexts; but realistically, if our aim is to close the aspirations chasm described earlier, this evidence base will not take us very far anytime soon. We need to look beyond this for improvement guidance.

School-Based Learning Communities

Forming school-based learning communities represents a third strategy for advancing improvement. In some ways, this approach represents the polar opposite of the evidence-based practice movement. As noted above, field trials tend to focus on evaluating programs such as a new curriculum, a pedagogic practice, or a technology. Since the emphasis is placed on average results, the influences of local contexts fade into the background. Communities of practice, in contrast, take local context very seriously. They direct attention to the day-to-day problems that educators experience in their own classrooms, schools, and districts.

A strength of this strategy is that it directly engages practitioners as problem solvers—identifying issues they care about addressing—and recognizes them as active agents of change. Learning communities break down the work silos and norms of private practice that have long characterized teaching.[15] In their stead, collaborative coaching, walkthrough processes, and collective inquiry cycles have been building in many schools and districts since the 1990s. These developments, like performance management and evidence-based practice, represent real progress. And they reinforce another core theme in improvement science—that those engaged in the work are central to its improvement.

But the research-base and empirical grounding of communities of practice is often unclear and sometimes absent. Most important, these communities have weak mechanisms for articulating what they are learning,
and then testing and refining it under more diverse conditions. As a result,
what gets learned in many such communities tends to live and die with
the individuals who have learned it. There is no established mechanism
for developing a practical knowledge base that might more readily support
improvements at larger scale.[16]

To sum up, then, each of these three approaches has distinctive strengths,
but none alone or even in combination will help to close the aspirations
chasm. Instead, as educators, we need to draw on the best of what these
strategies offer and join to them the best of what has been learned about
improvement in other sectors and by pioneers in our own field, some of
whose stories are recounted here. Moving toward such a synthesis is where
the improvement paradigm, introduced in *Learning to Improve,* took its
inspiration.

A BRIEF REVIEW OF THE IMPROVEMENT PARADIGM

The paradigm shared in *Learning to Improve* is organized around the six
principles highlighted in figure I.2. The first principle—*to be problem-
centered and user-specific*—is anchored in a deceptively simple question:
"What is the specific problem or problems you are trying to solve?" The
critical word here is *specific.* Educators typically know what outcomes
they want, but often do not know exactly what they need to change to
achieve them.

In the past, as concerns arose about some educational problem, educators often moved quickly to implement reforms. Typically they did so by
drawing on a standard set of solutions such as adding a new curriculum,
offering more professional development, hiring more staff, or introducing
another new program. In contrast to just jumping on solutions like this,
improving organizations take time to analyze and understand better the
actual problems they have to solve. And they go about this analysis of root
causes in a very specific way—by being user-centered. Improvers try to

FIGURE I.2   The six principles that form the improvement paradigm

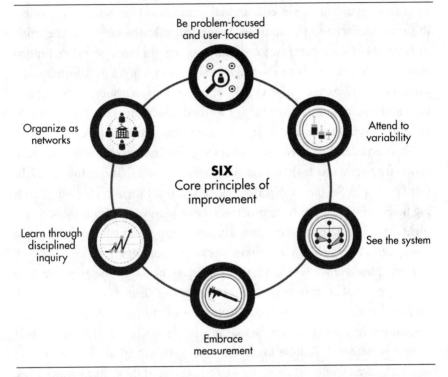

see the problems through the eyes of the students whom they serve and the adults who work with and for them: "What are those people actually experiencing and how do they make sense of the environment that embeds their work?"

This examination of the root causes of specific problems leads to the second principle: *Attend to the variability* in the outcomes regularly observed. Education is complex work. Studies demonstrate that whenever organizational complexity exists, wide variability in performance typically accompanies it.[17] As noted above, addressing this concern requires moving beyond knowing that something can work on average to learning *how* to achieve improved outcomes *reliably* for different subgroups of students and their teachers, and in the many different organizational and community contexts in which they work.

This is part of why the improvement paradigm is especially well suited for attacking disparities in educational outcomes. The focus on variability in performance, and the sources creating it, is at the center of the work. This stands in stark contrast to all that remains hidden in standard reports about mean differences and average trends, even when this information is presented for separate racial, ethnic, or linguistic subgroups. These reports may well document the existence of a broad educational concern, but they generally offer little insight as to how one might actually solve it.

This consideration drives improvers to zoom in on seeing how their educational systems create these unsatisfactory outcomes. This brings us to the third principle: *See the system.* This principle directs attention to understanding more fully the underlying processes, norms, and organizational arrangements that produce unacceptable outcomes. Improvement teams then use this systems knowledge to develop a working theory of improvement.

Principles 4 and 5 turn to the empirical heart of the improvement paradigm. First in this regard is to *embrace measurement* (principle 4). As noted earlier, educators today have a lot of student outcome data and consequently a much better handle on the variability in these outcomes than ever before. But these measures tend to be global in content and are generally available only after the work is done. Standardized test scores, for example, arrive after the academic year is over. For this reason, they are referred to as *lagging indicators.* Improvers, in contrast, typically need more timely and finer-grained information that gets down into the actual work processes, the roles people enact and the prevailing norms that shape their work, because, as noted above, this is where the observed outcomes actually take root. Such *leading* indicators provide signals as to what is and isn't working on the ground and help educators to identify where the next round of changes should focus.

Now, on balance, the measurable aims targeted for improvement are often expressed in terms of standard lagging indicators. But even here, to inform improvement efforts, teams may need to organize these data in new ways to help them see more clearly the problem they are trying to solve. For example, rather than only looking at overall year-by-year outcome results for high school graduation, several of the teams whose stories we tell tracked longitudinally the progress of individual students and sub-groups of students toward graduation over time. They also created new measures explicitly focused on the specific changes in practice that they were trying to effect.[18] Developing these practice-based measures is one of the ways that improvement science builds on the spirit of performance management, but goes well beyond it.

Likewise, as is characteristic of evidence-based practice, improvement teams *learn through disciplined inquiry* (principle 5). At the core of improvement research are rapid iterative cycles of testing possible changes against data, and then typically revising, retesting, and refining these change ideas to work well across diverse conditions. Throughout these cycles, improvers are constantly questioning: "Are the proposed changes actually happening as envisioned? Are we seeing the immediate process outcomes expected from these changes? And where process improvements are occurring, is there evidence that this is actually moving us toward the measurable aims we seek?" The kind of causal thinking embedded here will often lead improvers to stepping back a bit to ask still other, often more fundamental, questions: "What are we assuming that we may need to revisit? What else do these results suggest we might need to work on?"

Improvers are opportunistic and pragmatic in the design of their inquiries. The plan for improvement cycles may take many different forms, ranging from lesson study protocols, to small RCTs, to interrupted time series analysis (often visualized as run charts), to qualitative field observations, and more. At base is the question, "How can I efficiently learn about the problem at hand and whether the change I am introducing is actually an improvement?" In this regard, the method of inquiry is simply a servant to improvement learning.

As will be seen in several of the narratives that follow, improvement cycles often aim to create good routines that scaffold how educators might better do their work. Importantly, these routines are being developed with, by, and for educators. In this regard, improvement activity mirrors the social dynamic of school-based learning communities. In moving beyond this local learning, as new protocols take on the status of tested routines—things we know *can* work—improvement teams recognize that these routines are likely to need some adaptation in order to be taken up and used well by other colleagues and in other settings. So the process of spreading an effective change idea is itself a "learning to improve" problem.

Equally important, research-based evidence gets woven throughout the processes of continuous improvement. This is where the conceptual frameworks and statistical methods that develop from more basic research add value to how these practice-based efforts are carried out. Cast as improvers, practitioners and researchers bring distinctive knowledge and expertise to the table and collaborate in practical problem solving. This is very different from the traditional models that see researchers as the expert and educators as the implementers of their external knowledge.

Finally, as educators tackle larger and more difficult problems, they *organize as improvement networks* (principle 6). These are necessary because contemporary educational systems, and many of the problems embedded within them, are now so complex that few educators can solve them alone. Addressing these concerns requires coordinated, collective action. Whether this networked activity occurs within a single organization or in a deliberately structured cross-organizational arrangement, certain commonalities are evident:

- Each network is organized around a specific problem.
- Participants' efforts are disciplined by a shared working theory of improvement that is anchored in seeing how their system generates the unsatisfactory outcomes targeted for change.
- The network develops and uses common measures and inquiry tools so that members can learn together and quickly share whether the changes they are testing are actually moving their system in the right direction.
- These intentionally formed networks draw together diverse sources of expertise from practitioners, school leaders, researchers, designers, technologists, and, depending on the problem, often families and students as well.
- Participants are deliberate in consolidating the practical knowledge developing from their efforts and making it quickly accessible to still

others who may further refine it as they seek to integrate it effectively in their particular contexts.

These are the core mechanisms through which a networked improvement community accelerates learning to improve.

Embedded in the improvement paradigm is a key shift from telling educators *what* to do to fostering a social learning environment where everyone is learning about the *how* and *why* of making schools work better. Creating broad agency for improvement is a core idea in Deming's work on how organizations continuously improve. Writing seventy years ago, Deming understood the dysfunction that was rampant in industry—where a small number of people thought about the design of the work while the vast majority labored as replaceable parts. In Deming's mind, when corporations disregarded their workers, they were throwing away most of the social intelligence and goodwill resident in their organizations that could advance improvement. Such behavior was both morally unconscionable and would ultimately undermine corporate goals. Deming's insights remain equally salient today as we seek to improve our nation's schools.

SINCE THE PUBLICATION OF
LEARNING TO IMPROVE

In writing *Learning to Improve*, my coauthors and I sought to bring together a compelling set of ideas, with accompanying tools and practices, about how educators might engage in new and different ways to make real progress. The volume drew heavily on our early experiences at the Carnegie Foundation in initiating two networked improvement communities (NICs). Three big questions motivated the launch of these NICs:

- What would it take to move from a compelling set of ideas—the six improvement principles—to execution?
- Would anyone, anywhere, agree to work with us in these new and different ways?
- If they did, could we assemble a body of evidence that such work truly advanced measurable improvements?

We sought to learn fast about how, and whether, we might be able to move this set of promising ideas into practical action.

The first, and by far the larger NIC, was the Carnegie Math Pathways (CMP); the second was the Building a Teaching Effectiveness Network (BTEN). In each case, we tackled a problem that had previously seemed insurmountable: the abysmal failure rates in developmental math instruction in community colleges and the low rate of retention among new and early career teachers, respectively. Both were high-leverage problems. Developmental math courses in community colleges operated as the gatekeeper to opportunity for large numbers of students, especially students of color and from poverty. As for new teachers, they often encountered an incoherent and largely dysfunctional human resource development system that produced the same outcomes year after year—predictable failure rates and high churn, cohort after cohort. Getting new teachers better, faster and holding on to them could change student outcomes for a generation to come.

In terms of our own internal learning goals, the Carnegie Math Pathways provided us with an entry into working with ideas about a deliberately structured improvement community. In a complementary fashion, BTEN was our first test bed for engaging improvement science on the ground in schools.

These two initiatives created the base of practical experience that we shared in *Learning to Improve*. As we concluded that book, we noted that the idea of continuous improvement might be easy to say but harder to do (well). Subsequently, we have now heard this same sentiment expressed by others who have become excited about these principles, tools, and methods and have shared with us their earlier experiences in trying to make them work. So the rationale for *Improvement in Action* emerged—to make more visible how those seriously engaged in improvement actually do the work.

When *Learning to Improve* was first published, staff at the Carnegie Foundation for the Advancement of Teaching knew that there was interest in the field to learn more, but we did not anticipate the intensity of this interest, nor how quickly it would grow. Five years later, we are excited that efforts at continuous improvement and working in improvement networks have moved to the center of educational reform. The Every Student Succeeds Act, for example, has devolved significant resources and authorities to states and districts with strong guidance to be evidence-based and to engage in continuous improvement. Philanthropic institutions are committing increasing resources to initiating and growing improvement networks around targeted educational problems. Participation in Carnegie's annual Improvement Summit on Education expands each year, and the project proposals submitted for consideration continue to strengthen in depth of detail.

In short, a movement is gaining force, but it has also surfaced a critical new question: "What does it actually take to move this promising set of ideas into quality execution?" As noted above, the results of our own first efforts were encouraging, but this just raised a next question: "Could other educators working on different problems and in varied contexts make the improvement principles work for them as well?" Realistically, we knew that variation in the use of the improvement principles, tools, and methods was likely to manifest as engagements in continuous improvement spread. Some groups might make good use of these resources but others would take them in less effective directions. So a concern for *quality* in the enactment of improvement came into view.

A FOCUS ON *QUALITY* IN
CONTINUOUS IMPROVEMENT

Over the three decades that I have been involved in school improvement efforts, I have seen a lot of good ideas, and a few not-so-good ones, come and go. Throughout, I have remained hopeful about the possibilities for improving our nation's schools. But I am also a critical realist, and my realist voice reminds me that the history of educational reform is replete with good ideas that got taken up in superficial ways.[19] Leaders often embrace these new ideas precisely because they are new and doing so casts them as reformers. A frenzied spate of activity typically follows, but productive improvements prove harder to find. As the next leader takes the reins of the organization, that person champions other new ideas, and the process just continues to churn. The academic literature refers to this phenomenon as a form of *ritualized rationality*.[20] As a very experienced and somewhat haggard Chicago teacher once told me as she rolled her eyes, "This, too, shall pass."

I worry that this same phenomenon might torpedo the current embrace of continuous improvement. Educators are increasingly using terms like *improvement science* and *networked improvement communities*. They tell me they are implementing new routines like root cause analysis and conducting Plan-Do-Study-Act (PDSA) cycles, but sometimes it is not clear that the fundamental changes in thinking and action that the improvement paradigm demands are actually taking place. Let me offer a couple of examples to make this more concrete.

Over the last few years, I have had opportunities to interact with a number of different groups who have heard about improvement science and networked improvement communities. Sometimes I am told, "Oh, we're already doing that."

"Really?" I ask.

"Oh yes, at the end of every year, we look at our accountability data and we talk together as a faculty about it and then we figure out some new things that we might try next year."

In short, the annual school improvement plan has become "continuous improvement"—a new label for an old practice.

In other places, I have witnessed constructive first steps taken toward continuous improvement. Professional development programs focused on improvement have been added either at the district level or through some regional intermediary, such as a county office. These sessions introduce educators to the basic tools and methods of improvement science. Teachers then are encouraged to do PDSA cycles, but then often left largely on their own to figure out exactly how to design and carry out these cycles. More problematic, the source of change ideas may be parochial and the research base doubtful. Additionally, the data necessary to evaluate whether a changes is actually an improvement may be missing altogether, or take the form of, "Well, what does your gut say?" Other key shifts in practice, such as bringing the users' perspective into the work and identifying the specific sources of variation in performance that need to be addressed, may also be weak or absent.

Likewise, organizational leaders supporting these efforts may not recognize how the shift into improvement affects their own work. They continue to view their responsibilities as providing services to schools and districts rather than operating as full learning partners in the improvement efforts. I have seen administrators counting the number of PDSAs that have been completed in schools and encouraging more activity. How all of this local activity consolidates into collective progress, however, remains unaddressed. Likewise, the role of improvement leadership, as orchestrating a set of social learning processes, has not yet been activated. Instead, improvement efforts look a bit like performance management: administrators offer training, monitor activity levels, and then hold others accountable for change. The focus isn't on what is being learned, but rather on how much is being done.

On balance, the transformation for any organization into a continuously improving one is no small endeavor, and the tendency to fall back on old ways of thinking and doing is understandable, and even to be expected. The six improvement principles represent a fundamental change and a major challenge to the ways of thinking and acting for both practicing educators and for those who partner with them, including educational researchers and commercial vendors. Helping to illuminate this shift into *quality* in continuous improvement is the central purpose of the cases that follow in this volume. In these stories, I use the term *continuous improvement* in reference to a broad range of activity aiming to advance educational outcomes through iterative cycles of change over time. I distinguish this term from the *improvement paradigm*, which constitutes a transformation in the ways educators think and act as they advance such activity. The improvement paradigm is about living the six principles, about bringing agency to frontline educators as improvers while also fusing research knowledge, and the expertise of researchers and others, more productively into these processes.

INTRODUCING THE SIX STORIES

Learning to Improve offered a vision of practitioners and researchers fusing their domains of expertise to make a difference for all students. This volume, offered five years later, is testimony to moving beyond a vision. The chapters that follow provide accounts of a diverse set of improvement efforts in action. The stories open up some of the many ways that the six improvement principles are being used by different educators in different organizational settings and with different resources, but in each instance to pursue ambitious change efforts. Although each of the organizations used somewhat different labels for the roles, routines, and structures that they put in place to orchestrate their change efforts, for simplicity, I refer to all of these developments as the work of an *improvement hub*.

At one level, the chapters are a collage of improvement narratives. Each describes impressive work in a different educational context. Two detail the efforts of traditional school districts, Fresno Unified School District and Menomonee Falls. Two other chapters tell the stories of highly innovative charter management organizations, Summit Public Schools and High Tech High. And two more are accounts of intermediate organizations that work with large networks of schools, New Visions for Public Schools and the National Writing Project.

Chapter 1 chronicles the improvement efforts of Fresno Unified School District, located in California's Central Valley. This chapter introduces the metaphor of a leaky pipeline as a heuristic device, not only for the work in Fresno, but also for the efforts of New Vision for Public Schools, Summit Public Schools, and High Tech High (chapters 2, 3, and 4, respectively). At multiple steps in the journey from high school entry to matriculation into college, Fresno students were falling through the cracks. Improving high school graduation and college-going rates required Fresno educators to carefully orchestrate a series of efforts at every juncture where the pipeline leaked. The Fresno team kept their eyes on seeing the system—on understanding how a set of processes that students experience as they move through high school created the overall outcomes they were observing. Their problem-solving took them into thinking about data in new ways, creating new data tools and processes for their use, and putting in place the staffing and professional development supports necessary for practitioners to turn useable evidence into productive action. The Fresno story also introduces a theme that will be repeated in subsequent accounts: how insights from relevant research and the inclusion of researchers as partners can inform productive change.

The New Vision for Public Schools case presented in chapter 2 introduces the organization and role of an analytic hub of a networked improvement community. New Visions' efforts took the organization deeply into how basic administrative systems around student absenteeism, course-taking, grades, credits earned, and, in New York, the number of Regents exams passed, contributed to the graduation problem they wanted to solve. On the surface, the functioning of routine administrative data systems like these might seem mundane and uninteresting. But the breakthrough at New Visions was to realize that embedded within the operations of these systems was a complex array of taken-for-granted ways of working that needed to be understood more deeply, and then challenged, to advance better outcomes. Like Fresno's leaders, the hub at New Visions focused on building good data systems and tools that aimed to provide the right information to the right people and at the right time. Hub staff collaborated with educators in their network of schools to field-test and refine a key change idea, that they eventually came to call the Strategic Data Check-Ins process. The breakthroughs affected by New Visions are now moving out across the entirety of the New York City Public School System.

The portrait of Summit Public Schools in chapter 3 opens up a window into what it means for a system of schools to function as a learning organization. Started some fifteen years ago as a single school, Summit has grown into a charter management organization that now operates a network of schools in California and Washington. As part of this organizational growth, Summit embraced an extraordinarily innovative agenda for high school reform. It aimed to give students more choice in the work they do and to move at their own pace toward well-articulated learning outcomes. In Summit's vision of a good school, teachers function as mentors and advisers supporting students to take charge of their own learning. Figuring out how to actualize these aspirations—every day, for every student, and in every learning context—proved a huge challenge. And it was this challenge that led Summit to develop its own internal capacity to undertake and advance continuous improvement. The organization invested in building improvement capabilities among school staff, in assembling expertise in a central hub to facilitate and support these activities, and in building analytic capacity to inform and guide these efforts. Summit also drew on research and nurtured relationships with applied researchers whose knowledge and skills could help them on their journey to improve.

High Tech High (HTH), the focus of chapter 4, offers a story of improvement science going deep in a most unexpected place. The progressive educators who founded HTH harbored a fundamental skepticism about data, and this sat alongside a strong commitment to individual teacher autonomy. These are not conditions in which one might expect to find a ready embrace of either improvement science or organizing as improvement networks. HTH educators, however, recognized that even though everyone was working hard, their organization was coming up short on its core aspiration: preparing every one of its students to graduate high school and succeed in college. This recognition propelled them to explore new ways of trying to get better. Successes in a modest initial improvement project expanded interest among HTH educators to learn more about improvement science and generated momentum for its increased use. An organic process of organizational development emerged with transformative effects. Today, High Tech High operates multiple networked improvement communities across its system of schools. It has developed a strong cadre of teacher leaders who support these improvement efforts, and has woven improvement science into its new graduate school of education. Having reached these milestones, it has also moved the goal line. The aim now is to make this approach normative in the way their educators do their own work and to enable the spread of these practices to a next generation of teachers and other educational professionals.

In the course of learning how to do improvement, each of the four organizations mentioned above developed expertise and considerable practical know-how to advance real progress on improving high school graduation and college-going rates. These problems have functioned for too long as gatekeepers to opportunity, and especially for students of color and low income. The lessons that we can learn from their stories opens up possibilities for scaling these successes more broadly.

Chapter 5 ventures into the domain of improving classroom instruction. Efforts to engage the principles, tools, and methods of improvement science and organize as instructional improvement communities are more recent than the work cited above. This chapter offers a first look at a distinctive set of challenges that improvers confront as they turn their attention in this direction. The problem that the National Writing Project (NWP) took on was motivated by a new emphasis on argument writing that surfaced as part of the Common Core standards. The NWP story documents how the organization drew on the expertise of consulting teachers and the established relationships of trust that were resident in its national network of local research-practice sites to mobilize and quickly advance measureable improvements in students' writing. To form this networked improvement community, NWP focused on: *what to teach* (i.e., the community developed text sets to enable instruction around the writing of arguments), *how to teach it* (i.e., consulting teachers offered local professional development on core pedagogical practices), and *how to know* whether the teaching and learning was actually improving (i.e., for this purpose a new instrument, the Using Sources Tool, was developed to inform NWP's continuous improvement efforts). The case offers a glimpse into what educators can accomplish in improving instruction when they organize as a professional scientific community solving a problem together.

Finally, the work of the School District of Menomonee Falls (Wisconsin), taken up in chapter 6, is quite different from the others. It is not a story that begins with a specific problem to be addressed, but rather with an ambitious organizational aim—the transformation of a whole school district into a continuous improvement organization. Menomonee's district leaders aimed to reorient the work of everyone in the school system in this direction. In support of this goal, literally every person in the district—teachers, auxiliary staff, operations personnel, board members, the leadership team, and students—was trained in continuous improvement methods, and improvement projects were launched all across the system. The chapter offers a detailed account of an evolving set of leadership actions carried out over several years—first to catalyze these changes and then to institutionalize them in how the school system does its work.

Interestingly, chapter 6 can be read comparatively with the narratives of Summit Public Schools and High Tech High. Like Menomonee Falls, these other two cases can also be read as stories of transformative leadership, although the courses they followed were quite different. Both Summit and HTH began with a modest improvement project that grew into a gradually expanding set of projects. The success of the initial projects, and the know-how developed and energy generated among those first participants, quickly brought more colleagues into the work. Sustained support from organizational leaders enabled improvement efforts to expand and eventually transform their organizations over time. Taken together, these three cases offer considerable fodder for conversations about the role and actions of leaders in advancing continuous improvement deeply into how educational systems operate.

While each of the six cases tells a different story, important themes repeat across the cases that are worthy of note at the outset. To launch their efforts, educators in all six contexts examined extant data to better understand how their systems operated to produce their current unsatisfactory outcomes. All turned to extant research evidence and drew on external research expertise to both deepen their understandings about how their systems worked, and to identify possible change ideas. And all continuously monitored the progress of their improvement efforts as the basis for fueling subsequent tests of change.

Additionally, each organization committed to developing its hub capabilities to support improvement. They created specialized staff positions and new organizational roles. Hub staff facilitated and supported local improvement teams. They invested broadly in developing improvement knowledge, skills, and dispositions among staff within their respective organizations. Along the way, hubs developed new data resources and processes that sought to inform local change efforts in a more timely fashion.

Lastly, all of these contexts also benefited from stable leadership and supportive institutional governance environments that made it possible for efforts to germinate and grow. In some cases, the organizing leaders were new to their contexts (chapters 1 and 6); in the others, the leadership for transformation had been present for some time and only the ideas were new.

For this book, my colleagues and I worked closely with leaders in each organization to learn about their distinctive improvement journeys. We provide our take on their respective stories as a way to illustrate, amplify, and teach key improvement ideas in action. In some instances, we studied these organizations from outside; in others, we offered direct support as they launched and advanced their improvement efforts. Regardless, we acknowledge that the full range of work occurring in each of these organizations is much more extensive than our accounts, constrained to chapter length and a specific focus, permit.

Although each case stands on its own as an account of action for possible discussion among a group of readers, the chapters together show how the same principle, concept, or tool was applied by different teams and in different educational contexts. Seeing it at work across multiple and diverse contexts creates opportunities for these resources to be understood more flexibly and deeply than any one telling would allow.

Finally, each of the organizations has made real progress toward its improvement aims. It is notable that even given their documented successes, their organizational leaders remain humble about their improvement journeys. They acknowledge that they still have much more to learn and many miles still to go. In this sense, the chapters are dynamic portraits of improvement in action. I am deeply grateful that these six organizations have allowed us to share some of the *what*, *how*, and *why* of their efforts. They afford all of us an opportunity to see the extraordinary in the ordinary day-to-day work of getting better. Now, on to their stories.

1

Attacking Inequities in Postsecondary Opportunities

Fresno Unified School District

AT A TIME when postsecondary education was becoming essential for all young people, the Fresno (California) Unified School District (FUSD) took on the challenge of ensuring that more students were prepared for college, that they had more and better choices about which college to attend, and that they matriculated into institutions more likely to advance their educational goals. At the start of Fresno's improvement work, the desired outcomes were clear, but the team really did not know what it would actually take to achieve them.

In organizational terms, Fresno was confronting a *leaky pipeline* problem. To expand the flow of students graduating high school and attending college would require a carefully orchestrated series of efforts at every juncture where the pipeline leaked and students fell through the cracks. The team kept their eyes on seeing the system—how a set of processes organized students' experiences through high school and ultimately yielded unsatisfactory outcomes. They then tackled these one by one.

Fresno's efforts pushed its improvement team to think about how they might provide more useable and timely data that would better advance the actions of students, parents, school-based educators, and central office staff. This in turn required the development of new data tools and routines for their use, adding more college advising staff and supporting their professional development. Lastly, running as a through-line in the Fresno story is the value of access to relevant research and researcher expertise in informing the district's efforts to address a long-standing equity concern.

THE FRESNO CONTEXT

Located in the agricultural Central Valley of California and home to many farmworkers, Fresno has one of the highest poverty rates in the nation. It also has some of the lowest rates of educational attainment; only 75 percent of adults in Fresno County have a high school diploma, and only 20 percent have a bachelor's degree or more.[1] Almost 90 percent of Fresno's students are eligible for free and reduced-price lunch.[2] A fifth of the district's 73,455 students are English learners.[3] The income gap between college-educated and high school–educated workers has widened sharply in the past several decades, and district leaders knew that a high school diploma no longer assured a successful future.[4] The challenge in front of them seemed huge.

Moreover, the organizational context for improvement was far from ideal. The district had been plagued by poor management for years. As one central office administrator put it, "We'd had revolving superintendents for several decades. It was complete dysfunction."[5] A community task force convened in 2004 found fiscal problems, poor management structures, and major weaknesses in the district's academic programs. The task force called for wide-ranging reforms in district operations, including an overhaul in financial management; new human resources policies and practices; a restructuring of the central office to shift more resources to school sites; and stronger community and family engagement.

IT STARTED WITH LEADERSHIP

The most basic function of a board of education, and arguably its single most important responsibility, is to hire a good superintendent and support that person's actions. Fresno's board was challenged by the task force report to "do the right thing." They sought to end the pattern of revolving-door superintendents and pledged sustained support when they hired superintendent Michael E. Hanson in 2005. Hanson was a politically savvy educator who was deeply committed to the local community and to addressing its educational needs. He also brought a strong analytic orientation to the work, believing that good data and research evidence should inform their improvement efforts. From the start of his tenure, Hanson worked closely with the school board to forge a united front in addressing the issues raised in the task force report.

The same year Hanson was hired, the University of California opened its first campus in California's San Joaquin Valley at Merced. An explicit part of its mission, as set forth by its founding chancellor, Carol Tomlinson-Keasey, was to expand college access for students in the valley, and more broadly to bring the university's assets to bear to improve their prospects. This commitment carried forward through UC Merced's third chancellor, Dorothy J. Leland (2011–2019), who observed, "Given the complexity of the challenge, neither K–12 nor higher education by itself can make the necessary changes that will result in increased postsecondary opportunities for students." These institutions would need to work together. Accompanying Leland's personal commitment to this issue was a sense of institutional humility:

> To make these partnerships a success, it is incumbent upon the higher education community to better understand the culture [and organizational conditions] of K–12, and to learn how the knowledge and research expertise resident in our faculty can engage more productively with that of our colleagues in K–12. I know that working together in these new ways we can increase postsecondary opportunities for more and more students, especially those who have been previously underrepresented in colleges and universities.[6]

The shared leadership commitments at both FUSD and UC Merced created an opening for practice improvement research partnership—named *Equity and Access*—to emerge. Even prior to the official opening of UC Merced, campus leaders had established a Center for Educational

Partnerships. Associate Vice Chancellor and the center's founding director, Jorge Aguilar, quickly embraced the partnership with FUSD as a major community engagement initiative on the part of the university. To cement the partnership, the university granted Aguilar a leave of absence so that he could personally join FUSD as an associate superintendent and special assistant to Hanson. Hanson, in turn, invited Aguilar to head up a new unit in the district's central office, also called Equity and Access, to spearhead their efforts to improve postsecondary access.

SEEING THE SYSTEM AT WORK

In California, students must pass a prescribed set of courses, known as the A–G curriculum, to qualify for admission into either the University of California (UC) or California State University (CSU) systems. So the first challenge for the Equity and Access team was to ensure that students were taking the right courses to qualify. To get a handle on the scope of the problem, Aguilar brought in a longtime colleague and programmer from UC Merced, Rei Suryana, who, together with a team of FUSD personnel, assembled and organized student-level data on their academic programs. Hanson and Aguilar knew that Fresno had a history of systematic inequities in student course-taking: students of color and from low-income families were less likely to achieve the A–G requirements. But the team did not have ready access to information about which students were failing to meet which specific requirements, nor did they know where these breakdowns were most likely to occur. In other words, the problematic overall outcomes were clear, but there were no extant analyses of students' pathways through instruction and therefore little insight as to where students might be falling through the cracks.

A Leaky Pipeline Problem

The first analyses carried out by Suryana revealed a myriad of issues. Importantly, it enabled district leaders to see how their system was essentially tracking students out and away from postsecondary opportunities.

Although Equity and Access leaders in FUSD and UC Merced were just becoming acquainted with improvement science, they grasped its core principles. Rather than just moving quickly to implement some new program, they knew that they needed to take the time to understand more deeply the problems they had to solve. As they engaged in their analysis of root causes, it became obvious that multiple factors produced the unsatisfactory outcomes observed. To matriculate into a postsecondary institution, students had to successfully navigate a series of steps from the time they entered high school through the time they actually arrived at college. At multiple points along the way, students were slipping through the cracks, and once they fell off the college-going track, it was difficult—and in some cases, nearly impossible—for them to get back on course.

From the student side, progressing through high school and moving on to college was akin to running the high hurdles. With each hurdle cleared, you get to jump one more, but stumbling at any point might take you out of the race. As Suryana's analyses clarified, the hurdles included taking the A–G sequence of courses, passing all of them with sufficiently high grades, taking and scoring well on the SAT and ACT, identifying appropriate colleges to apply to, drafting personal statements and completing other application requirements, filling out and submitting the Free Application for Federal Student Aid (FAFSA), and many other steps. As one former administrator put it:

> None of this [analysis] solved anything. In fact, it created more problems for us, but in a good way. We recognized more gaps in what we were doing. It's kind of a pain, right? You might think you're OK at something, and then you realize you're really not. These challenges have always been there. It just wasn't brought to light. Equity and Access pushed us to a place where we couldn't be comfortable any more. That I think is important.[7]

Specifically, the data showed that only a quarter of Fresno students were completing the A–G requirements. Fewer than 70 percent graduated. Of those who did, only two-thirds applied to any institution of

FIGURE 1.1   Addressing a leaky pipeline problem: An orchestrated set of
              improvement efforts

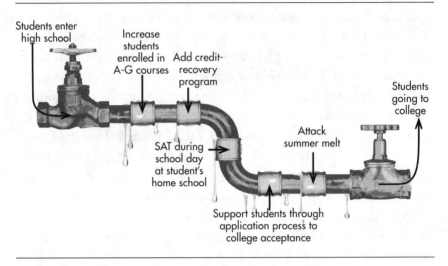

higher education; and only two-thirds of that group filled out the FAFSA—
although many more were eligible for postsecondary financial aid. Even
these limited and initial findings showed that the problem had multiple,
complex roots. No single, simple solution would suffice. Rather, expanding the flow of students graduating with the credentials needed to attend
college would require a set of improvement efforts playing out over time.
Figure 1.1 illustrates the multiple initiatives that Fresno developed to stem
the leaks in their pipeline.

INFORMING SYSTEM-LEVEL POLICY CHANGES

The systemwide data analyses triggered a number of changes that could
be addressed through direct district-level actions. For example, the data
revealed that one of the major hurdles in attaining A–G credits was meeting a foreign language requirement. To address this problem, the district
added a University of California–approved Spanish course for native speakers. Prior to this, English learners, who were already proficient in Spanish,

were being placed into French or other language classes. This substantially raised the hurdle for these students to meet this particular A–G requirement and at times worked against their attaining mastery of English as well. Similarly, Equity and Access leaders realized that further back in the pipeline, some of Fresno's middle schools did not offer foreign languages, and that this was the start of the problem for other students. So the district added foreign-language courses at every middle school.

The data also showed that many students missed the A–G requirements because they did not earn a grade of C or better in one or more of these courses. In response, the district added a summer school credit recovery programs to enable students to move back on track. Complementing this, they also added Advanced Placement courses in every high school to give more students opportunities to take higher-level coursework.

The district had also learned through looking at their data that some qualified students were not taking the SAT admissions test. Still another hurdle had been identified. In response, the district struck an agreement with the College Board so that the exam would be administered at the students' home school and during the school day rather than on the weekend in some strange and less welcoming environment.

As these initial hurdles were being cleared, the Equity and Access team identified further problems to address. Analyses had illuminated for central office staff the leaks in the pipeline, but how could they make these same data easily accessible and actionable out in the schools? In principle, the policy changes mentioned above opened up opportunities for more students to succeed, but whether the students actually progressed really depended on what was happening in their schools. Fortuitously, an initiative to build an integrated student data system and data dashboards was already under way in FUSD, and the Equity and Access team was able to piggyback onto it. Ironically, a scandal had provided the impetus for upgrading the data system. The 2004 task force report had revealed that many Fresno students inappropriately received passing grades despite numerous absences. The extant data system was simply not tracking this information. In response to this scandal, resources had already been appropriated to improve the district's data infrastructure. As is the case in many school districts, Fresno's first efforts focused on traditional end-of-year account-ability indicators. But the challenges being taken up by the Equity and Access team demanded more fine-grained information. Fresno's new system quickly evolved to include indicators on key processes that advanced students toward postsecondary enrollment, such as their progress on A–G course-taking and whether or not they filled out and submitted the FAFSA.

The Equity and Access team also wanted to get these kinds of data out to school-based educators in a more timely fashion. The system should alert school staff as problems were emerging—if, for example, a student was not enrolled in a required A–G course, or was in danger of failing such a course—so that school staff could respond quickly. As the Equity and Access team phrased it, "[so that school staff] could change conditions in the present." If staff could see such problems in real time, and if they could intervene to help a student make the necessary adjustments, the team reasoned, huge payoffs might follow. Ultimately, the design of a data system with this functionality became a primary driver in FUSD's working theory of improvement, and it led to the development of a number of different data tools for counselors and other school-based educators. These provided real-time information, student by student, as to who was on track, who was off track, and where interventions might be needed.

REACHING EVERY STUDENT, IN EVERY SCHOOL: DATA PLUS PERSONALIZATION

The system-level changes discussed above plugged several leaks in the pipeline. But as the Fresno team deepened its understanding of the problems they needed to address, leaders recognized that a big issue still remained: How would they actually make their system better support *every student*? That was the million-dollar question. Introducing new programs and processes is one thing; getting intended results to occur reliably is quite another. To do this would require new data tools that put the right information into the right hands in a timely way so that better interventions could occur. This would also necessitate hiring more counselors, who were better trained and supported than before, to make all of this come alive.

One of the first data tools that the Equity and Access team developed and deployed was the A–G Course Monitoring Tool. It provides information on each student's progress on A–G coursework, including grades and credits earned. With this tool, counselors were able to see in real time which students are advancing toward meeting the A–G requirements and who might be falling out. Counselors' roles also were reshaped to recognize the importance of advising students and monitoring their progress through applying to college. Developing counselors' capabilities to take on these new responsibilities became still another improvement target.

Attention also focused on the development and support of school leaders. With access to new and more timely information on student progress, they too could now see where students were more likely to be stumbling and where particular problems might be occurring in their school. This new capacity for supporting site-based action encouraged high school principals, for example, to expand the number of sections in key A–G courses and adjust school schedules to make it possible for more students to meet the requirements.

The next tool developed by the Equity and Access team was called the Higher Education Student Dashboard. The impetus for its development was when the team, working with school-level counselors, learned that more fine-grained information on each student's academic record would be helpful. This tool brought together attendance and behavior data; a checklist on students' progress in meeting the matriculation requirements for California colleges and universities, such as taking admissions and placement tests; tracking data on the colleges that students had applied to and where they were denied admission or accepted; and the reasons why they might have opted out of attending particular institutions. Counselors needed this information in an easy-to-use form to guide more students from high school entry to matriculation. To advance this objective, the Equity and Access team engaged in a series of iterative processes to create specific data visualizations. They also collaborated with school-based educators to design good work routines for how counselors might productively use this new information.

The impact of the Student Dashboard was palpable. As one counselor stated,

> When I talk to [people in other districts], it's like, "You don't know which kids are on A–G track and which kids are not, and you have to do transcript analysis?" I don't. I just push a button, and it pulls it up for me and tells me which kids, which classes, under which category. They're like, "Yeah, that takes us hours." I'm like, "It takes me five minutes." I can do it by high school; I can do it by district; I can do it by foster youth; I can do it by whatever I want. They've seen it, and everybody that I've shown a few of the tools to are extremely jealous because they're, like, "You don't understand how many hours and hours and hours we have to spend manually doing this."[8]

In short, the early analytic efforts that the Fresno team had undertaken to reveal the nature and extent of the problems to be solved also proved informative as they transitioned to developing data tools to keep students moving forward. The Equity and Access team learned that getting the right data into the right hands at the right time was essential to vitalizing their improvement aims. But alone, this was still not enough. To get these tasks done also takes people with the right skills, the right dispositions, and reasonable workloads. So Aguilar and Hanson together persuaded the school board to fund the hiring of more counselors. (Fresno now has one counselor for every 350 students, which is a much lower ratio than previously, and lower than the state average of one counselor for every 500 students.) Fresno also trained all of its counselors, both veteran and new, in conversational protocols to scaffold how they might engage more effectively with students and their families around these data.

NOTICING THE UNDERMATCHING PROBLEM

As a result of the changes described above, Fresno was now moving many more students toward meeting A–G requirements and progressing toward college. So far, so good—well, almost. Along the way, they uncovered still one more leak in the pipeline—the "undermatching" problem.

Higher education in the United States is extremely stratified. At the top level are the selective colleges, often private, where admission is competitive. In the middle are less-selective four-year institutions, which admit virtually every applicant. In most states, these tend to include all but the state's flagship national research institutions. Lowest in the lineup are community colleges. Notwithstanding the higher published tuition costs for selective colleges, students enrolling in these institutions often "get more for less," Carnevale and Strohl write.[9] That is, students will often actually wind up paying far less for their education in more-selective institutions because these colleges can offer more extensive financial aid. These students also are more likely to graduate, and in less time.[10] Moreover, students who graduate from the most selective institutions tend to go into managerial and professional occupations that pay high salaries; those in less-selective institutions tend to end up in rank-and-file professions, such as health care technician.[11] Thus, the stratification across higher education institutions operates as a significant mechanism for reproducing long-standing inequities in social and economic opportunities for students, especially along race and class lines.

Other research has documented that a large number of low-income students and students of color could enroll in more-selective colleges and universities, but many fail to apply to them; that is, students who have attained the academic credentials to earn acceptance into a selective institution often apply only to less-selective places. This phenomenon is known as *undermatching*, and it is widespread.[12] Disadvantaged students are more likely than affluent peers to *substantially undermatch*—that is, to enroll in colleges that are at least two levels below the selectivity level they could qualify for.[13]

Aguilar was familiar with this research and brought it to his team's attention. Even though Fresno's college-going rate was improving, Aguilar worried that students might not be taking advantage of all of the benefits available to them. Referring to the information that the new data systems were making visible, he said, "We are now seeing cases where student academic profiles indicate that they could have applied to more selective colleges and universities than they actually did."[14] By connecting Fresno

educators to research on undermatching, Aguilar helped district colleagues grasp the significance of this problem. Moreover, the research he
shared with them documented that substantial improvements in this area
had been realized in other districts and might be possible in Fresno as well.
These research-based insights became both a guide and an inspiration to
the Fresno team as they explored this problem in their own context.

When district staff began to look more closely at the nature and extent
of their undermatching problem, they engaged the logic of the Pareto
principle.[15] Based on empirical findings from improvement efforts across
widely different organizations and sectors, the Pareto principle tells us that
80 percent of the variation in outcomes is often associated with just 20
percent of the causes. This is an encouraging finding, because in complex
organizations such as large urban school districts, many different targets
for improvement typically exist, but no district can work on all of them
at once. The Pareto principle directs improvers to try to identify the small
number of issues, typically three to five, that might be "high-leverage" to
solve—meaning there is reason to believe that the targeted 20 percent is
responsible for the lion's share of the problems. Undermatching was clearly
an important concern in Fresno. But prior to the new data systems, no one
really knew how prevalent this problem actually was, nor did they understand its specific contours in their context. Absent a clearer sense of the
problem's dimensions, it was hard to know what to target as an improvement priority. Likewise, without a deep understanding of the problem,
identifying the most promising change ideas would be largely guesswork.
This is a place where good data analysis is an invaluable guide to productive action. Without good data, the power of the Pareto principle remains
largely muted.

Fresno's analyses of its undermatching problem was enabled by the data
resources that the improvement team had been building for some time,
plus additional information that they integrated from the National Student Clearinghouse.[16] Specifically, using historical data, the Equity and
Access team created academic profiles for a large number of Fresno students that included course-taking patterns, course grades, and test scores.
They then matched each student profile with a list of colleges that likely

would accept a student with similar academic characteristics. Next, they compared those profiles with the actual decisions these students had made. The results confirmed their suspicions: large numbers of Fresno students undermatched. Many could have won admission to a UC or CSU outside the county, but they had not applied. Often, students with strong academic credentials were applying to only one institution, and it was usually Fresno State University.

Vincent Harris, then the executive officer for district accountability and improvement within the Equity and Access office, said that the district's goal should be to expand opportunities for all students and support them so that they could make more informed choices about college-going possibilities. "This was not done from the standpoint that [applying only to Fresno State] is wrong," he said. "But we're seeing that many students are eligible for other institutions [in the UC and CSU systems] and yet are not applying. We can and should be able to do better." This analysis, of course, led to still another round of questions: "Exactly why aren't students applying to more places?" "What are the actual causes of our undermatching?"[17]

Looking for Root Causes

To figure out possible causes, the team decided to take a closer look at the multiple processes in the pipeline that shaped a student's awareness of available colleges, application processes to those colleges, and decisions to matriculate. The team was drawing on a core idea embedded in the first principle of the improvement paradigm: *Be user-centered.* How were students actually experiencing these processes? Who and what was influencing their thinking, and how did these influences in turn shape their critical next steps? Similarly, how were counselors engaging with students, and what was shaping their thinking and actions? To get started, the team conducted an initial round of interviews with a small number of students and counselors. At this juncture, they just wanted some quick insights about what might be causing the problematic behavior they were seeing. Based on these initial inquiries, the team then crafted a survey for each group. The surveys helped the team to assess the prevalence of some of the issues voiced in the earlier interviews, and to gain more extended information on how these processes actually played out for different students and across varied school contexts. The hope was that this larger source of data would help the team decide which problems might be most important to tackle.

The inquiries did not disappoint. One thing the team learned, as Harris recounted, "There were a lot of proud and successful Fresno State alumni working in our system."[18] Not surprisingly, a big part of the reason that so many students were heading toward Fresno State was because counselors were recommending the college they knew best and felt a personal connection to. In addition, survey responses revealed a diverse array of logistical considerations. Applying to selective colleges was time-consuming for both the students who applied and the counselors whose job it was to support them. Drafting a personal statement was a daunting challenge for many students, and sometimes it did not get completed as a result. Moreover, much of the application process occurred online, and some students did not have adequate internet access at home. As the team's inquiries proceeded, they kept finding more places where students were falling through the cracks and where educators failed to notice and intervene. The students were trying and the counselors were well-intentioned. But many students, and their hopes for the future, were being derailed.

The Equity and Access team was now meeting "all the time" to try to pull together everything they were seeing and learning. Three major root causes stood out:

- School staff and counselors did not have detailed knowledge about institutions of higher education outside of the Fresno area because most had attended local colleges themselves.
- Even though the workload for school counselors had been reduced, their time to meet individually with students to discuss college plans remained limited.
- Students and their parents too had little knowledge about institutions of higher education outside of the area. They also lacked crucial information about financial aid, application waivers, and other policies designed to help low-income students.

Identification of these root causes set the stage for the Equity and Access team to shape a working theory of improvement.[19]

The team now confronted a theory of action problem: How and where should they start to intervene? What were possible routes for moving forward? In general, a form of dialogic thinking often shapes this process. Depending on the nature of the problem, the desired, deep changes may take multiple years to enact and possibly even more time for measurable improvements to emerge. Recognizing this fact is important because it directs improvers to also consider its complement: "Where is the low-hanging fruit?" "What might we be able to influence readily and where might early improvements be realized?" Achieving quick wins is important politically in maintaining external support and important internally in reinforcing the commitments of the people engaged in the work ("We are making progress; let's keep at it"). In addition, it also serves a tactical objective in affording cover for some of the deeper changes mentioned above that may be harder to advance and where achieving success may take longer to accomplish.

So, realistically appraising constraints and identifying possible resources that might be deployed in problem-solving is at the heart of developing a viable course of action. In this regard, the Equity and Access team recognized, for example, that counselors' time was a binding constraint, and any proposed changes—at least in the immediate term—would have to work within this constraint. As mentioned above, the district had already increased the number of counselor positions, so more staff allocations here seemed unlikely. Consequently, the team zeroed in on the idea that a workable solution—some low-hanging fruit—might be found in responding to the last root cause: Students and parents were unaware of their realistic college options.

Testing and Iteratively Refining a Change Package

With this perspective now in their sights, the Equity and Access team began to brainstorm possible change ideas.[20] They considered, for example, taking students on college visits and offering parent workshops. Both would be costly, however, and would make extensive demands on district staff. Eventually, the team settled on a relatively simple, quick, and low-cost change to try: mailing individually tailored information packets about college eligibility—which they called "I Am Ready" packets—to each high school senior. Aguilar was aware of recent research that suggested that a change along these lines might work.[21] Using data assembled on each student's A–G coursework, grades, and SAT and ACT scores, they matched each student against the academic profiles of students whom they knew had previously been accepted at various CSU and UC campuses. The data systems they had previously built, and the earlier analytic work that they had undertaken made these analyses, and the mailings to individual students and their parents, feasible. As Harris recounted, "We found more power through the US Postal System than anything we could quickly leverage through district staff."[22]

The team also undertook some quick small tests of change to settle in on the information that needed to be included in the I Am Ready packets. Each packet was based on the student's academic profile and suggested colleges he or she might consider applying to. Informational materials reminded students that they could apply to up to four colleges using fee waivers. The packet also included a form for setting up an appointment to discuss college options with their school counselor.

Complementing the I Am Ready packet and informational materials was a carefully designed professional development initiative to help guide counselors in their advising sessions with students. For many counselors, both the content of the packets and how to have good conversations with students about the process represented new work. To prepare counselors, the Equity and Access team, with the assistance of Trish Hatch, a counseling expert from San Diego State University, designed a scenario-based training initiative in which actors posed as students to simulate college advising conferences. The sessions stressed the importance of showing students all of their potential postsecondary options. It encouraged them to approach the task as one of exploring options over the course of an application process that takes several months. In terms of tone, the simulations modeled a collaborative conversation that would help students think through their best choices. "Students don't have to make a high-pressure decision in September," said Harris. "It's a process—where to apply, how to apply for financial aid, deciding where is a good fit. They don't have to jump immediately. There are steps along the way."

Lastly, the Fresno team developed another tool to add to the data system. The Cycle of Continuous Improvement Learning and Competency (CCILC) tool made it possible for counselors to easily track students as they engaged the process: when they set up appointments; whether they used the form provided in the mailed packets; the specific college(s) each student applied to; and their reasons for not applying to colleges whose eligibility criteria they met. It also generated dynamic data for the Equity and Access team to monitor how each of these new processes was working, and to learn from this initial trial about what further adjustments might be needed in the future.

Through these steps, the Fresno team was in the process of developing, testing, and refining a change package. Rarely do improvement efforts involve a single change. Rather, an interrelated set of processes—some newly created, others existing but in need of improvement—are often targeted for change. In this instance, the change package consisted of: (1) the I Am Ready Packet and related information materials mailed to students' homes; (2) a form to facilitate (and encourage) students to schedule an appointment with their counselor; (3) specifically designed professional development for counselors around a conversation protocol to engage their students; and (4) the CCILC tool to assist counselors in managing the workflow and to inform the Equity and Access team on how to further improve the intervention system that they were creating. This working theory of improvement is illustrated in figure 1.2.

RESULTS

The results from the change package were dramatic. The number of eligible Fresno students who applied to a CSU or UC campus beyond Fresno State rose from 382 to 578 between 2015–2016 and 2016–2017, a 51 percent increase. In that time, the number of eligible African American students applying increased by 56 percent, and the number of eligible Latino/Hispanic students applying to CSU and UC campuses rose by 71 percent.

FIGURE 1.2   Fresno's theory for improvement: under-matching problem

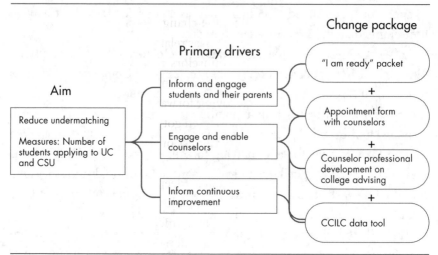

Undergirding this work focused on undermatching were the earlier improvements in the proportion of FUSD students completing the A–G courses, which had risen from 32.1 percent in 2009 to 47.8 percent by 2014; the proportion applying to institutions of higher education, which had increased from 68 percent to 84 percent in that period; and the proportion completing the FAFSA, which jumped from 67.2 percent to 87.7 percent.

On balance, Harris acknowledged that the team could not make a strong causal inference that it was the undermatching change package per se, as distinct from other activities, that influenced students' behavior. "In a pure experimental design, once you send a letter to four thousand students, nobody else should talk to students about college," he explained. "The letter is the treatment. But nobody can stop a parent from talking to a student about UC Davis or taking their child to UCLA for a weekend. We'll never know whether it's the visit to UCLA or the I Am Ready packet [that influenced the student to apply]. And we don't care."[23] What was important to these practitioners, and likely to any practitioner who wants to help students get into the best possible college, is that the results were changing rapidly and moving in the right direction.

CONCLUDING COMMENTS

After Fresno had tested and refined the change package described above, the effects were large; the intervention was relatively low-cost; it integrated fairly easily into the work life of counselors and other school staff; and general reactions were positive all around. Under these circumstances, it is perfectly sensible to just keep moving forward. If the results continued to replicate year after year, and ideally even got better, Fresno would surely know that they were making good progress on advancing more equitable student outcomes.

Along the way, the Fresno team had deepened their understanding about which processes were important to address. Similarly, they continued to refine what constituted actionable information to improve postsecondary enrollments. Importantly, as they went down this road, they increasingly embraced the mindsets of improvers—continuously asking, "Why and how is this happening?" To answer these questions, they turned to extant research and data where available, and initiated new local inquiries where necessary. Through these processes, they got better at seeing the root causes that kept many Fresno students from graduating and matriculating at college, and this knowledge, in turn, guided their efforts to solve problems.

While traditional accountability reports gave them a view of unacceptable district outcomes, the improvement tools and information they developed served a very different purpose: they aimed to get the right data into the right hands to inform timely actions that would keep more of their students flowing through the pipeline to college. Embedded here is an important larger lesson. Data on its own is inert; it does not drive. It is people with a passion for solving a problem, with a passion for using these new resources, and with adequate time and support, who turn data into information that guides productive action.

A Next Problem to Solve

Continuous improvement is just that, continuous. Even as the Fresno story depicted here was drawing to a close, the team was launching yet another improvement project. It turned out that one more leak needed to be addressed—"summer melt." In tracking each student's progress from application to matriculation, the team had noticed that many students, and particularly low-income students, were not arriving in college in the fall even after they had been accepted and indicated their intention to attend that previous spring.

Here again, their own data, combined with published research, alerted the team to another potential hurdle to college-going.[24] And although the problem was different, the process for solving it was largely the same. The team would again be guided by the improvement principles and draw eclectically on tools and methods of improvement science in addressing this new concern. To better understand summer melt, they would undertake a study of root causes. Empathy interviews with students and their parents would enrich their understandings. They would brainstorm possible change ideas and develop a working theory of improvement. Through PDSA cycles, they would quickly test and refine the most promising of these change ideas. With each success and failure, a still deeper understanding of their system would emerge. As data documented initial successes and failures, they would continue to learn about what more might be needed.

In short, improvement is not an endpoint; it is a journey. As a team moves down this path, they engage a learning-to-improve spirit: *We can do better*. The drive to get better and to continue to become the best at getting better—this is the ethos and the ethic of living continuous improvement.

A Few Larger Lessons

Pipeline problems, such as those encountered in Fresno, are actually common in education, but they are infrequently seen as such and consequently rarely addressed as needed. Just as Fresno learned that getting students into college required attention to the multiple hurdles they would confront along the way, so does, for example, ensuring that students read proficiently by the end of third grade or that they all students pass algebra in middle school. The reform tendency is to focus on solutions at the end of the pipeline—for example, providing additional time and better teachers for reading instruction in grade 3. But the "third-grade reading problem" does not begin in grade 3. It has important antecedents earlier in the pipeline: weak instruction in the earlier grades; Response to Intervention (RTI) systems that fail to accelerate the progress of struggling readers; chronic absenteeism for some students; and summer learning loss for others are just a few examples. For still other children, presenting concerns may reach all the way back to exposure to trauma and toxic stress in their experiences prior to school. The general point is that at multiple places along the way, a child's development can be affected, but our educational systems will fail too often to see problems when they first manifest and act on them in a timely fashion. As a result, these systems will continue to produce unsatisfactory and inequitable results year after year after year. In contrast, as the Fresno experience shows, by seeing the system as its actually works, multiple key breaks in the pipeline were identified and district leaders were able to advance substantial improvements.

This case also sheds light on how fusing the expertise of practitioners and researchers can be foundational in vitalizing improvement efforts.[25] Jorge Aguilar brought distinctive expertise that assisted practitioners to better understand the problems they wanted to address. His engagement also contributed valuable insights about plausible change ideas. Most local school problems are not unique. Chances are that someone has already worked on it somewhere, and relevant research knowledge may exist that can be useful as a starting point for local adaptation. Part of Aguilar's role was to make more of this extant knowledge accessible inside the FUSD. In a complementary fashion, researchers who work in collaboration with local K–12 educators develop a deeper and more nuanced understanding of conditions on the ground. This, in turn, helps them see what might actually be involved in taking a promising idea and detailing it into a practice that can be executed reliably and improve outcomes across varied school contexts and student populations. These developments aligned well with what Chancellor Dorothy Leland had in mind for UC Merced's partnerships with school districts when she first encouraged her faculty to engage the collaboration. The fruits of practice improvement research partnerships of this sort hold great potential for building a robust professional knowledge base about advancing progress on targeted problems that educators really care about solving.

Finally, foundational to Fresno's successes was a civic leadership that created a stable, supportive, and resourced environment for improvement to occur. Building institutional capacities, such as data systems and good tools and processes for their use, takes time and resources. So does developing staff capabilities, such as hiring and developing counselors to work with new tools and in new ways. Consequently, the existence of stable leadership in the superintendent, the board, the Fresno-UC Merced partnership, and the Equity and Access team were also central to this account. It allowed the processes of improvement to go forward and stay the course so that meaningful changes might emerge.

In closing, each of the three themes explored here—seeing the leaky pipeline, forging supportive research-practice connections, and sustaining leadership for change—represents a powerful mechanism in systems improvement in school districts. One of the functions of a first chapter in a book like this is to open up some of these larger themes. I return to each of these three themes, and introduce some others as well, in the stories ahead.

2

Supporting Improvement
Through an Analytic Hub

New Visions for Public Schools

with Sharon Greenberg

OVER THE PAST THIRTY YEARS, New York City has undertaken multiple efforts to redesign its high schools. Challenged by stagnant and low graduation rates, and also recognizing that many students felt anonymous and disengaged in large comprehensive high schools, the nation's largest school district dismantled many of these schools, breaking them up into smaller schools, often organized around a specialized theme. The district also introduced dozens of charter schools for similar reasons. While many of these new schools proved successful, large numbers of New York City students still failed to earn a high school diploma.

New Visions for Public Schools (New Visions) took on the challenge of improving high school graduation rates. Working as the hub for an improvement network that included more than seventy New York City high schools, it adopted an improvement science-based approach. They recognized that they needed to understand better how poor results persisted despite many people's best efforts. Why did so many students, including some who otherwise appeared to be on track, fail to graduate? Where and how were students falling through the cracks? Would it be possible to identify vulnerable students sooner and for school staff to intervene more productively when issues were emergent rather than after they had consolidated as stubborn failures? As the New Vision story unfolded, it became clear that there was a wide variety of causes. In fact, seeing the multiple factors driving the disparity in outcomes proved critical to actually making progress on the problem.

New Visions' investigations took it deeply into a study of how basic administrative systems around student absenteeism, course-taking, grades, credits earned, and, in New York, the number of Regents exams passed, contributed to the graduation issues they wanted to solve. These administrative systems were originally designed to meet district-level reporting and accountability needs, but New Visions came to think about them differently, and over time this led to a distinctive working theory of improvement. It focused on building good data systems that would enable more productive school-based actions. As part of this effort, the New Visions hub, collaborating with its network of schools, also learned how to orchestrate better data conversations among educators. These new ways of engaging with data would open up productive school-site discussions rather than the "Gotcha!" judgments that frequently close them down.

THE NEW VISIONS CONTEXT

New Visions has been part of New York City's education landscape since 1989. Launched as a reform organization that partnered with neighborhood schools in all five boroughs, it was at the heart of the city's efforts to create small, themed high schools. More recently, it has opened and operates its own charter schools.[1]

Bob Hughes became president of New Visions in 2000. A civil rights lawyer by training and a self-described student of improvement science, Hughes focused New Visions' attention on closing the achievement gap and ensuring that all students had opportunities to do intellectually challenging work and were supported to succeed. This equity commitment was expressed in New Visions' "80/50" aim—to help its network of schools graduate 80 percent of their students on time, and for 50 percent or more of those students to be college ready.[2]

It was under Hughes's leadership that New Visions began building an analytic hub to complement its internal education support group, which was composed primarily of successful district teachers and administrators who were deeply knowledgeable about conditions in the city's schools. Within the New York City Department of Education (NYCDOE) context at that time, New Visions operated as a Partner Support Organization (PSO). PSOs came into existence under Chancellor Joel Klein's administration, making it possible for schools to forgo support from their community district office if they thought that a PSO might better meet their needs.[3] Unlike the standard reporting line in large public school districts, however, PSOs did not exercise any formal authority over affiliated schools.[4]

New Visions' specific focus on improving administrative data systems took center stage when Hughes recruited Mark Dunetz to become Vice President for School Support and Operations in 2013.[5] Dunetz had been a high school teacher and then the founding principal of a non-selective Queens public high school, the Academy for Careers in Television and Film. The Academy graduated 94.8 percent of its first class of students. Over the next few years, that rate climbed to 98 percent and has stayed around there ever since.

As principal, Dunetz recognized that amid the multitude of seemingly routine administrative processes occurring every day in his school, there were many different ways for students to fall behind. To understand the problem, he and his staff needed to better see and support every student's journey, beginning with daily attendance and including appropriate course enrollments and grades, credit accumulation, and Regents exam results. This directed their attention to a novel focus: how the basic administrative data systems embedded in these processes actually worked. These systems are so baked into the operations of a modern high school that few educators give them much attention other than noting that collecting and reporting these data take a lot of time and are prone to error.

Dunetz's move to New Visions gave him the opportunity to focus on these issues at a much larger and more varied scale than being principal of a single school allowed. And New Visions' rapidly expanding analytic hub, coupled with its extensive network of professional educators and schools, afforded a team with the necessary human and social resources to attack this problem.

GETTING STARTED

New Visions' effort to improve student data systems was a multipronged effort. Dunetz's experiences in leading an NYC high school guided the team to focus on three core processes: improving student attendance; students' timely progress through courses of study and credits accumulated; and, in the New York context, enhancing students' preparation for and passing of Regents exams. Up to this point, no one had attended much to how the information embedded in these systems might actually function as an improvement driver. Dunetz had some ideas about what might be possible, but he also knew that the New Visions hub team needed to start with "eyes wide open." They would have to assemble an integrated data system, explore patterns in the data to test their hunches, and simultaneously begin to engage with these problems firsthand in the schools, including initiating small-scale tests of change.

Working on Improvement in One School

The principal of the High School for Advanced Math and Science (AMSII) was eager for her school to serve as an early context for some of this work. She considered improving daily attendance as "important to help keep her students on track and help the school reach the upper bound of its graduation threshold." AMSII had achieved a 94 percent average daily attendance rate the past year—a high number. But absenteeism was nevertheless a problem. The principal and the New Visions team recognized that absenteeism was not a matter of each student being absent a few days here and there—for some students, it was a chronic concern. And a stream of research had already established that chronic absenteeism was a powerful leading indicator for subsequent school failure.[6]

To the untrained eye, reporting attendance seems simple and bureau-cratic. The first hint of its complexity is that the reporting systems actually tracks more that just "attendance"; it also monitors late arrivals or tardi-ness, and incidences of class-cutting. Gathering the information engages a multitude of people across a high school—usually an attendance coor-dinator; all of the classroom teachers who take attendance, mark students late, and sometimes make calls to parents; counselors and social workers (if the school has them); and often the dean or whomever is in charge of discipline. Additionally, the system utilized by the NYCDOE involved a number of reporting forms that got handed off from one person to the next, and these processes were time sensitive. So in operation, attendance-taking is a complex system of multiple interlocking processes, tools, and people. And as is generally the case in systems improvement work, as the number of people, processes, and transitions or hand-offs rise, so too do the opportunities for mistakes and breakdowns.

Seeing the System in Action and Some First Tests of Change

Susan Fairchild, who was New Visions' Director of Knowledge Manage-ment and chief of staff at the time, set out to see how the attendance system actually worked at AMSII. Fairchild's first act was to crunch some numbers. AMSII had a roster of 546 students, and the majority were programmed for seven periods a day.[7] This meant there were 3,822 daily opportunities for students to be absent, arrive late, or cut a class, which added up to almost 688,000 opportunities per year. Yet despite that daunt-ing challenge, Fairchild also saw opportunities for learning to improve. Each day, and each class period within the day, represented a potential occasion for a small, fast test of change.

Fairchild started her observations by shadowing Chris Roberts, the school's attendance coordinator.[8] Roberts's morning routine was to col-lect attendance information from classroom teachers, record it, report it to NYCDOE, and then, if there was time, call parents of absent students to alert them that their child had not come to school. Fairchild's initial plan was to record how long this process took, but as soon as she started observing, she added columns to her data sheet to track how often Roberts was interrupted and how much time each interruption took. With interruptions, the logging took about three hours (190 minutes) that first day.[9] This meant that Roberts had time to call only a handful of parents before it was necessary to switch to other duties.

While the principal did not formally call her next move a PDSA cycle, it had all the makings of one. As soon as she and Fairchild discussed these data, a testing cycle emerged: (1) There was a change idea she wanted to try out; (2) a prediction was made about what it might accomplish; (3) a time and place to try it was set out; and (4) a measure identified by which they would judge whether the change was actually an improvement. The next morning, the principal moved Roberts from the main office to a more private, quiet space on another floor. She thought this might minimize interruptions and reduce the time it took to log the morning's attendance. This small, quick change brought interruptions down from over forty to a handful. The logging time, in turn, dropped from 190 minutes to about 70 minutes the first day and stayed fairly constant as she and Fairchild continued to check in on this new process on subsequent days. In schools where time is the most precious resource, this newly achieved efficiency, saving two hours of work time each day, meant that Roberts could call many more parents and also document each of her calls.

Working together, the principal and Fairchild had made a measurable improvement, but there was more to do. The principal was concerned that the count of students entering the building each morning was often lower than the counts coming from classrooms throughout the day. This mattered because these different counts had to be reconciled for reporting and funding purposes, and the reconciliation was itself a frustrating and time-consuming process. To once again literally "see" this process, Fairchild arrived early one morning and set a chair next to the security station where students used their identification cards to swipe in. The station was located in front of the main office, which seemed like a reasonable spot to ensure compliance, but it also was ninety feet from the entry door. Most students swiped in, but Fairchild also mapped various routes by which some students managed to bypass the checkpoint entirely.

Fairchild's mapping of student flows prompted the principal to test another change idea. She relocated the check-in point to a new spot about twelve feet from the main door, and also reorganized the entry flow so that now each student had to swipe in as he or she entered the building. As a result, the accuracy of this count improved and the time needed to reconcile discrepant counts decreased.

Fairchild continued to observe periodically at AMSII over the next several months.[10] She eventually mapped six essential tasks that comprised the lived attendance system:

- Preparing and distributing attendance forms for the day and otherwise setting up the student entry system
- Monitoring students' actual entry in the morning and throughout the day
- Verifying attendance reports (e.g., reconciling the classroom attendance data, generated throughout the day, with building entry data to determine daily attendance)
- Processing data (e.g., uploading the data into NYCDOE data systems, retrieving attendance files)
- Reporting internally about attendance to staff throughout the school
- Calling parents and documenting the calls[11]

Fairchild also noted that these six tasks involved eleven reporting forms that were completed by different people, mostly by hand, and then manually reconciled.[12] Each person and form created multiple opportunities for error. Moreover, what was perhaps the most important part of AMSII's attendance system—calling parents—was also the most frequently compromised. Before the principal and Fairchild began their improvement work, calls were sporadic, and even when parents were called, there was rarely any record as to what interventions, if any, had occurred.

Data Analytics on the Flows of Students over Time

Complementing the fieldwork occurring at AMSII, the New Visions hub was simultaneously examining extant student data for overall patterns in student attendance over time.[13] The team recognized that there were many occasions between the start of freshman year and graduation when students' attendance problems could go unrecognized for far too long. The analyses they undertook here opened up a second angle of view into the root causes for this problem.

When a problem is complex and resources are constrained, as was the case here, data-based insights can help improvers discern where to target their efforts. Among all of the considerations that *could* be the focus for change, New Visions had to decide which smaller subset might offer the greatest potential to improve student attendance and ultimately their larger aim of improving graduation rates. While conversations among school-based and hub staff may generate lots of plausible explanations for problems and possible targets for change ("*flaring*" conversations), looking at data can inform improvers as they hone in on the best places to start addressing them (*focus* conversations). Similar to the Fresno story, the Pareto principle was at work guiding the efforts of the New Visions team.[14]

Some of the hub's first studies were "snapshots" of AMSII's current attendance data. The team was curious to learn if attendance varied by days of the week, before or after a holiday, before or after lunch, by season, by month, and perhaps between younger and older students. The team also looked at related behaviors of class-cutting and tardiness to see if these varied by subject, by class period, by teacher, and so on. While absence, tardiness, and class-cutting are three distinct behaviors, they all represent time out of class—and when that time cumulates for whatever reason, it can put a student at risk.[15]

These first analyses confirmed patterns that were easily recognizable, such as depressed attendance at the beginning and end of the week, and on the bookends of holidays. Additionally, the New Visions' analytic team saw a higher incidence of tardiness and class-cutting after lunch and assemblies. The principal also learned that "senioritis," where students start to disconnect from school prior to graduation, afflicted juniors as well as seniors in the spring. Although commonly regarded as an innocent seasonal malady, for some juniors it had potential to derail their path to graduation. Each of these "hot spots" was a piece of the attendance puzzle.

The New Visions team then shifted to look at their student data in a different way, aiming to understand better the actual flows of students over time. If the team could "see" students' journeys as they progressed through the four years of high school, they might have new insight about when and where different groups really began to struggle. This information about variation in students' behavior over time and contexts was largely hidden in the event-based snapshots of data that they had been looking at so far.

The hub returned to AMSII's historical data, this time to look for patterns in student attendance over the school year. Because New Visions had already begun to build an integrated data base around individual students' course-taking, credit accumulation, marking period and semester grades, and the number of Regents exams passed, they were able to create designations for each student as on track to graduation, almost on track, or off track. This made it possible to look at the attendance data relative to each of these categories.[16] Interestingly, the hub examined two different indicators: average daily attendance and the percentage of students attending more than 90 percent of the time. This second measure focuses directly on the incidence of chronic absenteeism, and it is here that they found the most noticeable differences. Many of the students with histories of chronic absenteeism were already off track for graduation early in their high school careers. And when the hub examined these data month-by-month across the year, they were able to pinpoint where serious attendance problems had emerged for students in the past and were most likely to emerge for current and future students as well.

AIMING FOR A HIGH-RELIABILITY SYSTEM

Through New Visions' diverse set of school-based and data analytic inquiries, a view of a reimagined attendance system was taking form. Prior to the collaboration with New Visions, attendance interventions at high schools like AMSII were mostly limited to the attendance officer making calls to parents when she had time. This was anything but systematic and, as noted above, few calls were made. Compounding the problem was NYCDOE policy. As is the case in many districts, students in New

York City automatically fail a course if they miss too many classes, and in the most egregious cases, truant offers are deployed. But these processes kick in late and the behavioral consequences are serious, punitive, and compliance-oriented.

In contrast, New Visions was focusing on a different kind of system comprising two interdependent functions. The data analytics of the new system would keep track of behavior patterns and also identify potential problems as soon as they occurred. Complementing this would be an intervention capability to support students and their families to successfully address attendance problems early. Importantly, rather than a single blunt policy applied to all students regardless of circumstances, the high-reliability system that New Visions envisioned would be able to detect differences between students' attendance patterns and personalize the response. The system also would identify and support the school staff assigned to carry out specific tasks and activities, and it would develop and refine clear protocols and processes by which that work would get done. This included documenting what happened and noting where further efforts might be needed. And these processes would now regularly generate data to inform further improvements to the system itself.

This vision became grist for the hub's initial working theory of improvement.[17] The New Visions team shared what they were learning with school-based colleagues at principals' meetings and other forums. It also became a focus of the one-on-one coaching conversations they had with their network principals. Over a short period, a small group of "early adopter" principals emerged who were intrigued by this new approach to getting better. They were eager to bring their voices into the conversation about the problems and to brainstorm possible change ideas to test in their schools. Importantly here, the New Visions team did not impose their ideas as outside experts. Rather, by taking on the real conditions in schools and bringing practitioner voices to the fore, they were deliberately building agency for change, which is key to effecting meaningful improvements. In essence, the New Visions team was embracing the taproot of the improvement paradigm: *Involving those engaged in the work is central to its improvement.*

The intervention components of this new system did not develop overnight. Rather, through trial and error, school staff—supported with improvement coaching from members of the New Visions' hub—figured out what constituted risky behavior for individual students and different student groups, and then set criteria for those groups so that the appropriate administrator or staff would be notified and prompted to act accordingly whenever a threshold was breached.[18] Like all improvement work, it took many PDSAs for the network to "learn their way" into developing both new tools for analyzing and displaying data, and good social processes for using these new forms of information to identify the right problems, alert the right people, and then prompt them to respond in a timely and personalized manner.[19] There were fits and starts, and successes and failures, along the way. But what resulted was a succinct triage system that calibrated school-based educators' responses to different attendance patterns and did not let anyone—neither the student whose behavior was of concern nor the adults who were tasked with responding—fall through the cracks.[20]

In essence, the aim of this improvement work was to transition from a dysfunctional "old" system into a high-reliability "new" one.[21] This was done knowing that the big failures that we witness far too often in education typically emerge out of a series of smaller events hiding in plain sight. For example, being suspended or expelled from high school often has its seeds in earlier incidents of being absent, class-cutting, tardiness, and other forms of acting out. Similarly, the ultimate failure of dropping out is usually the cumulation of a host of problems, including chronic absenteeism, low grades, failed classes, and other academic and disciplinary problems that were not successfully resolved much earlier on. Part of the challenge in redressing these problems then, is to drill down into these processes and disrupt that chain of events to avert catastrophic failure for the students involved.[22] This requires being "obsessively vigilant about performance and by driving the attention of each individual to the details of predictable failures and how they evolve out of various day-to-day processes."[23] Needless to say, the New Visions' staff consider "obsessive vigilance" a virtue, and a behavior that they strive to cultivate in their school partners.

BROADENING SCOPE AND PREPARING FOR SCALE

As noted in the introduction to this chapter, in addition to improving student attendance systems, the New Visions hub was actively targeting two other key processes: students' progress through courses and credit accumulation, and enhancing students' preparation for and success on Regents exams. The hub posited that improvements across all three of these administrative processes was necessary to achieve their overall 80/50 aim. While the initial efforts to improve attendance were under way, work was simultaneously progressing on the other two processes. In addition, a spread strategy had emerged: from starting work in one school to engaging a more diverse array of early-adopter schools, and from that learning how to move this out across the entire New Visions network. In essence, the New Visions hub was designing, testing, and refining a set of data tools and conversation processes that would ultimately support the work at scale.

From the beginning, New Visions had been intrigued by research from the Consortium on Chicago School Research (CCSR) which had demonstrated that starting and staying on track in ninth grade was an essential step in the pathway to graduation.[24] Informed by this research, New Visions suggested to their early-adopter principals that a fruitful improvement might be to focus on ensuring that all ninth-graders got off to a strong start and were supported to stay on track to graduation. But New Visions also asked the principals to share their perspective: *What was their most pressing problem to solve?* In response, principals pointed to a different concern that was much more urgent for them. In each of their schools was a group of juniors and seniors who had seemed to be on track to graduate but were suddenly in jeopardy of not doing so. What could be done for them?

Getting Juniors and Seniors Back on Track to Graduate in Four Years

In response to the principals' feedback, New Visions put the idea about ninth-graders and early indicators on hold and focused instead on the performance of upper-grade students in terms of courses taken, credits accumulated, grades, and Regent exams. While Mark Dunetz viewed this initiative as a form of crisis management, he also knew that helping schools graduate more of these at-risk students could build good will for broader and more complex improvement efforts down the road.

This is another instance where the New Visions hub did not just jump in with solutions. Rather, they again adopted the perspective of learning their way into the problem and into possible productive changes. The traditional end-of-year accountability reports on dropout rates and breakdowns in these data by various racial-ethnic, language, and other ascriptive sub-groups shed little light on the problems to be solved. The breakthough for the New Visions team came with seeing how to explicate what was hidden in these traditional accountability reports.

The analytic team at the New Vision hub explored historical data on indi-vidual student progress to graduation, and an important insight emerged from one analysis in particular. A fair number of students started their senior year having passed some Regents exams and having acquired an appropriate number of course credits, yet they would not graduate the fol-lowing spring. How could this be? Moreover, when these data were broken out school by school, marked variation in outcomes was observed. Figure 2.1 presents this analysis.

The graph indicates that some rising seniors had already passed four of the five required Regents exams. In most network schools, virtually all of these students were graduating. But in a quarter or so of the schools, as many as 20 percent or more of these students did not graduate. This varia-tion between schools was even wider when the hub looked at rising seniors who had passed only two or three Regents. Results were especially variable for students who had passed only two. In a few schools, these students still managed to graduate at a high rate. In over half of the schools, however, the graduation rate for such students dropped to less than 50 percent. New Visions had uncovered big disparities in educational outcomes between schools that were now visible for all to see.

To explore why these graduation rates might be so different, New Visions organized a quick field study of high- and low-performing schools on this measure (i.e., rising seniors who had passed two or three Regents exams). They needed to understand what was happening in these different

FIGURE 2.1 Graduation rates varied substantially across schools (based on number of Regents passed prior to senior year)

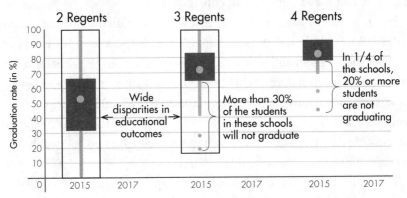

Note: The range in graduation rates found among the middle 50 percent of schools is captured inside the box. The line heading up from the box represents results from the top 25 percent (i.e., the results for the schools with the best graduation rates). The line dropping down from box represents the outcomes in the weakest 25 percent of schools The dots below the lines are results for individual schools that were exceptionally low (i.e., outliers).

schools—similar students succeeding in some places but not others. They also were curious to learn how local educators made sense of their own results. To Dunetz's surprise, variation in terms of the specific supports available to students did not seem to affect results very much. Operating here were much more basic considerations: Did the school have viable supports in place? Were students actually taking advantage of them? and Did school administrators keep track? "What stood out," Dunetz told us, "was that the schools that were achieving better results carefully tracked the progress of each of their students. If a student was designated for a support activity, they also knew whether that student had signed up and was actually attending."

This finding was echoed in Dunetz's personal conversations with school administrators. "In the schools with better results, if you asked the principal, 'Show me who is in danger of failing this term, and what are you doing about it?' she would show you the rosters and the classes [for remediation]." In a low-performing school, by contrast, Dunetz noted, "If I asked the same questions, you get a list of activities such as 'We do Saturday school, [and] we do tutoring.' But they were not focused on who was actually enrolled and attending regularly." In essence, the better-performing schools were acting with the obsessive vigilance characteristic of a high-reliability organization. These schools monitored every student's progress, knew if and when someone went off track, intervened early and with a range of progressively more intensive supports, and then kept watch to ensure that the student took advantage of the support offered. In short, educators in these schools had figured out what to do, how much to do, for whom, and when. These insights lent further credence to New Visions' theory that a redesigned system of administrative data and student support services might indeed bring about substantial improvements in high school graduation and college readiness.

To further probe the variation they observed, the hub again turned to an analysis of extant data as a source of guidance. They wanted to know how students were progressing through each of the performance gates that led up to graduation and where systems might be breaking down. Among the current group of vulnerable juniors and seniors, what were the specific obstacles blocking their pathways to success?

To get struggling junior and seniors back on track, the New Visions hub took aim at how schools tracked, monitored, and supported students' accumulation of course credits.[25] In general, high school students need to accumulate a certain number of credits to graduate, and the credits need to be distributed among subjects in specific ways to meet state-established requirements. But several problems were obvious when New Visions took a systematic look at these data. For many juniors and seniors, there was a gap between what was needed to graduate and the courses they were currently programmed to take. Another group had sufficient credits, but the course distribution was wrong. A third group appeared to have a credit gap, but on closer examination, their course information had just been entered incorrectly. Thus, the operating problems were multifold. There was "noisy" data that the system did not catch; tracking systems that failed to ensure that every student had the opportunity to earn the necessary credits; and monitoring systems that did not routinely call out problems when they first emerged. Additionally, schools' efforts in each of these areas were often idiosyncratic depending on an individual counselor's time, access to (good) data, and whether a staff member(s) there had a personal passion to sustain attention to these students. All of these factors conspired to keep students from graduating.

It was late in the game to help juniors and seniors, but New Visons knew that attacking this problem was important to their principals. In a sense, this was a critical early test for New Visions toward establishing credibility for its larger improvement agenda. Staff at New Visions believed that they could make a difference here, even if some important root causes occurred much earlier on.

The hub's first move was to clean the data to ensure that credit gaps were not based on errors in course coding—an issue that was exacerbated by the absence of standardized course codes across the NYCDOE.[26] In tandem with this, they developed new data-collection and -entry protocols to make these processes more efficient and minimize errors going forward, much as they were doing with the attendance data. This work was time- and resource-consuming, but relatively speaking, cleaning the data and developing collection and entry protocols was the easy part.

Much more daunting was what to do for the students whose programs were not going to yield the right course distribution or number of credits to graduate. The remedy for at least some of them was to encourage counselors to immediately change or add to these students' programs so that they could make up the credits. Another option was to enroll students into summer school and other extra or online credit-recovery programs. In these different ways, students might still be able to earn credits needed to close the gap and graduate on time.

To make progress on these fronts, the hub knew that just sharing the data with educators would be insufficient. School administrators would have to initiate difficult conversations with students and families—to tell them that the student's courses of study had not been programmed properly and explain how everyone had to act with immediacy and purpose to set things right. Learning how to open up and carry out these difficult conversations posed a challenge for all involved. In response, New Visions began some tests with network educators to examine new protocols that might enable more productive conversations with the students and parents affected. They tested out a variety of different conversation prompts and process flows. In addition, New Visions developed its internal staff to coach and then support school-based educators as they learned to examine their local data, analyze students' progress, and then, based on that analysis, make informed decisions and plans. The care with which New Visions developed and tested each of these supports contrasts sharply with more typical school district efforts, where a one-time workshop might be offered, but then it is left to individual educators to figure out, largely on their own, how to actually make things work.

Developing Supportive Data Tools and Processes for Their Use

In addressing the problems associated with student attendance and with juniors and seniors off track for graduation, New Visions had already begun a broader initiative to develop an integrated set of tools and processes to access, analyze, interpret, discuss, and then act on information about students at risk for failure. New Visions came to call this overall ensemble of activity *Strategic Data Check-Ins* (SDCs).[27] One of the principals involved in this early work noted "*Data* is a difficult word for many teachers. In my previous schools, we called it 'death by data'—we would have a lot of conversations about the data, but that's it. But it's not just conversation. You need to analyze it. You need to come up with interventions for students and have conversations about what you have to change to meet students' needs." Early in the work, New Visions had come to conclude that they needed to design, test and refine: (1) dynamic data tools that made concerns about student progress clearly visible; (2) strategic check-in routines that drew on these data and that schools could use routinely to identify and address student needs; and (3) appropriate supports personalized to each student. Over time, the New Visions hub would expand their suite of tools and refine their SDC process.

Similar to the effort described earlier to improve attendance, New Visions' work to close credit gaps for juniors and seniors began with a small network of early adopter principals and their schools. As hub staff learned their way into improvements in this initial set of schools, they made their processes and tools available to all New Visions district and charter schools. Many took advantage of the offer, and Dunetz kept a running chart of the number of credit gaps found in each one. The hub also tracked the number of gaps that the school was able to close each month with its SDC process, and the number still pending.

Over time, an increasingly refined change package was emerging through the collaborations of the New Visions hub with partner schools. Together, they were learning how a smart, comprehensive data system and tools for its use, coupled with effective interventions, could disrupt the chains of events that had previously led to student failure. Developing easy-to-use data tools that could track and visualize an expanding array of measures, coupled with strategic school-based processes for examining and acting on these data, became the core work for the New Visions hub. This work culminated in a coherent system supporting improvements in attendance, course-taking, grades, credits, and Regents exams. Now, in every participating network school, each student's progress is tracked and monitored across all of the measures; historic and current data across all of these measures are accessible; data collection and entry procedures are standardized and automated wherever possible; and the data are refreshed in close to real time. Appropriate adult(s) are alerted at the first sign of difficulty; and those adults are cued to intervene in ways proven responsive to the presenting problems. Adults are also reminded to document what happened and follow up as needed.

Taken together, New Visions invented new sets of processes that provided the right information to the right people when they needed it to catalyze more productive conversations and timely actions with individual students and families, among educators within schools, and across its network. In the course of this work, the New Visions hub assembled an up-to-date, integrated, individual student information system that also now made it possible to investigate which interventions worked, for whom, and under what conditions. This meant that the interventions themselves could now be systematically tested, refined, and detailed so as to better support schools to embrace an evidence-based practice, rather than operating in the more idiosyncratic ways of the past.

Starting and Staying Strong in Ninth Grade

Once the work described above was well under way and principals were seeing measurable improvements, the hub was able to bring their initial problem concern—ensuring a stronger start to high school for every ninth grader—back to the table. New Visions was now in a better position to tackle this problem because, as part of the work described above, the improvement team had pioneered the use of new visualization tools including something called a *stock and flow*.[28] These displays show both the *stocks*—where students are at any fixed point in time; and the *flows*— their progress or movement during high school. New Visions used this tool to help its school-based partners see students' progress, and pinpoint when and where student subgroups might stumble in their path to graduation.[29] Looking at student progress data in these ways made it possible to see when freshmen (and other students) got into trouble, and then what happened to them subsequently.

New Visions collaborated with another of its network schools, the High School for Telecommunication Arts and Technology (Telly) on this investigation.[30] The hub started by analyzing Telly's historic data for patterns and identified seven distinct conditions characterizing student progress over the four years of high school (see figure 2.2). The hub labeled these: on track to graduation and college-ready; on-track to graduation; almost on-track (further subdivided into high, medium, and low); off-track; and dropped out. On the far right-hand side are the end results, ranging from an Advanced Regents diploma to not graduating in four years or dropping out. Students' status designation upon entry to high school also is indicated on the far left-hand side.

Telly's stock and flow indicates that the school graduated almost 80 percent of its students with some form of a Regents diploma. While these overall results are impressive by NYCDOE and national standards, the analysis also made visible an improvement challenge for the school. The percentage

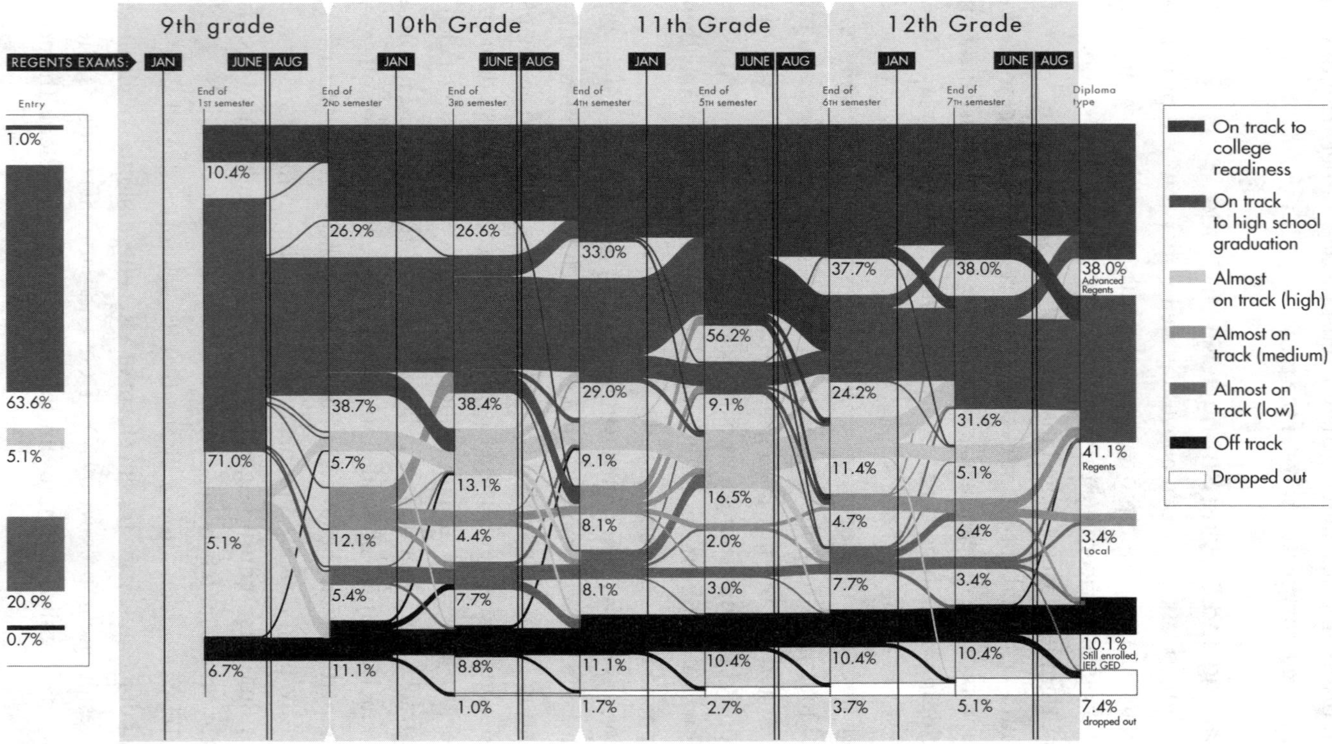

FIGURE 2.2   A stock and flow visualization of the progress of students through high school

of students at-risk at entry to ninth grade closely resembles the percentage who were either off-track or had dropped out by the end of senior year. The flow of students down into the off-track group gradually increased over time and the flow back up was virtually nonexistent. In other words, students who were strong when they entered Telly did fine, but weaker students did not. In essence, predictable failures were visible in the data at entry to ninth grade, but because this had not been recognized early on, little was being done to close the performance gap for those most in need.

Interestingly, prior to initiating their improvement effort, Telly, like many urban high schools at that time, held off on providing supports to struggling students at the start of high school. Educators opted instead for a "wait and see" approach to how students adjusted to high school, whether they would have disciplinary issues, and whether they passed or failed (or even attended) their first-semester classes. Telly waited until these grades and other performance measures were in and analyzed—which was often February—before recommending students for any type of support or intervention.

The evidence that was building around the power of early warning systems, however, argued for a more proactive stance. Rather than letting some students struggle for a semester and lose more ground, the team sought to disrupt this pattern and accelerate students' progress by offering supports that would begin on the first day of high school. Initially, the New Visions hub used middle school test scores to help the school anticipate who might struggle, and the first intervention that Telly offered to students whose scores indicated potential problems was a supplemental reading program. The hub also started to track students' real-time performance on a variety of measures. At the start of the year, these were limited to attendance, class-cutting, and tardiness data, but by the end of the first quarter there also were test scores, end-of-quarter marks, as well as teacher recommendations about who might benefit from academic or social support (or both). The hub wanted to understand more fully who was struggling and also the specific challenges each student faced. These analyses would help schools identify more students who might benefit from support, and also the expanded range of supports (beyond a supplemental reading class) that they might need.

The intervention system that evolved follows the logic of New Visions' earlier work: interventions were targeted to subgroups of students; they were offered as soon as problems materialize; and the supports intensified as needs manifest.[31] In addition, the hub checked to see which students actually took advantage of the supports once they were invited in, since earlier work had demonstrated that regular attendance was key to improvement. The SDCs guided school personnel to work with each student and family to identify the student's "best-case" graduation date and diploma type. They then monitored courses actually taken, as well as grades and credits earned to avoid credit gaps. And they analyzed course sequences in relation to the Regents exam schedule so that students were better prepared to pass the associated tests.

Here again, to increase the odds that schools would see the problems that the stock and flow visualizations revealed, and to build a suite of tools that would eventually become the New Visions Data Portal (a web-based application that allows for the comprehensive management of student planning and progress monitoring), the hub worked from the ground up.[32] New Visions asked its network of schools to serve as beta testers based on what they had learned through their earlier partnership with Telly. This expanded co-development process gave school leaders the opportunity to express their opinions about what was most important and how user-friendly various versions of the tools were. "We gave feedback on the creation of the Data Portal," said one principal. "They watched me and a few other principals go through the Portal. On some things, we struggled; on others we had an easy time. [New Visions] learned what the user experience was really like" and then modified the Data Portal to meet school leaders' needs. This is another instance where New Visions was living the first improvement principle: *Be user- and problem-centered.*

In broad strokes, the end product that New Visons developed looks like a product that a district might go out and buy—in this case, a student learning-support management system. But how it developed the tools that support this system and the social practices for their use—the improvement process—was quite different. In reflecting back, Dunetz commented, "The multiple iterations simply produced a better product. Had we come in six years ago and spent $50 million to procure a massive software app, we would have failed miserably. Instead, our Portal and Strategic Data Check-in systems, based on [these] iterative co-development efforts with schools, are now on the ground working in hundreds of schools."

Dunetz's observation is reminiscent of reports about the sustained, superior results achieved by Toyota Industries.[33] Analysts have wondered for years why Toyota allows even its competitors to visit and why it so freely gave away what others might consider proprietary information. The answer is that improving productivity at Toyota is not solely in its work processes, but also in the way those processes are developed and the culture that sustains them—something outsiders typically found harder to replicate. The day-to day life in the Toyota organization enlivens an improvement and coaching *kata*; that is, all involved in the work are engaged as improvers of the work, and it is the responsibility of managers at every level to coach improvement efforts. Better processes do matter, but it is this organizational culture of improvement that is truly the secret sauce. Tools can be transported easily from place to place, but making them work in a new environment often involves considerably greater nuance than the familiar directive to "implement with fidelity."

New Visions' end product seems straightforward—graduation planning as a set of standard processes used throughout the high school years—but it is actually a truly innovative development. Dunetz put it this way: "There are few standard operating procedures related to much of the core work of schools. That work [typically] is done in idiosyncratic ways by individuals who carry it out in total isolation and with little transparency. That accounts for the tremendous variation we see." To reduce that variation, New Visions collaborated with school-based educators to develop quality work processes and an evidence base that gave warrant to "this is how it should be done." In so doing, they embraced a paradigm that was quite different from how school systems have traditionally operated, where reforms are often seen as arbitrarily imposed on school-based staff from outside or above. Not only did New Visions and its network of schools develop a better and more standard way to support graduation planning, but they also deployed a better set of processes to get there.[34] The network had come together around a shared problem. The New Visions hub engaged school-based participants as active agents in problem solving. They needed and respected the knowledge and expertise that these educators brought into the activity. Additionally and importantly, New Visions blended this with extant research evidence and analytic expertise assembled in the hub. "What we could do, from an external vantage point, is to lessen the burden on schools," said Dunetz. "It's not realistic that schools on their own can solve basic infrastructure issues like this. We could contribute by doing the work of getting information out of the district's antiquated systems, organized it around the decisions and tasks schools are engaged in, and then giving local educators useable tools to manage it."

Too often in impassioned discussions about reform, advocates paint a picture that is either black or white, up or down. Pronouncements are made: it is all about teacher empowerment and buy-in, or districts must implement more evidence-based practices, or strengthening accountability is the answer, and so on. Most of these reform claims offer an important insight into more productive educational problem solving, but each, taken alone and to its logical end, will routinely fail.

In contrast, the New Visions story shows how productive improvement requires the careful orchestration of multiple forms of expertise and knowledge. This is where the critical role of the hub of an improvement network comes to the fore. A vital hub must assemble the measurement and analytic capacity for the network; draw in research knowledge relevant to the presenting problem; and blend these with the practical insights from those actually doing the work. In fact, much of the overall vitality of an improvement network hinges on the efforts of a hub to assemble the necessary sources of expertise and to integrate them into a coherent set of resources for problem-solving.

RESULTS

Three years after the New Visions hub began their learning journey, clear and measurable improvements had emerged for those rising seniors who in years past might have failed to graduate the following spring. Notably,

FIGURE 2.3   Substantial improvements in graduation rates two years later

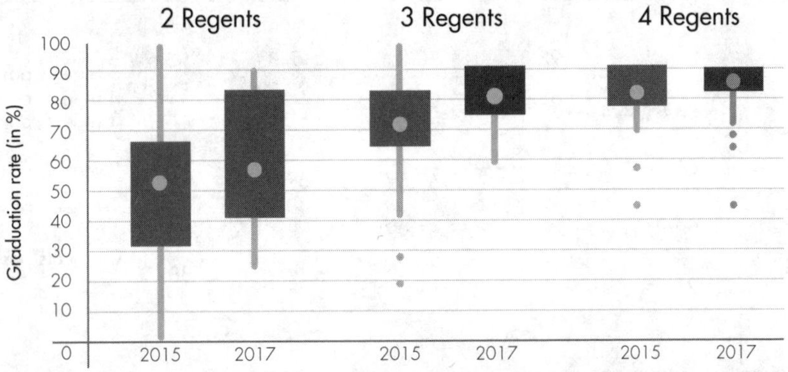

Note: The range in graduation rates found among the middle 50 percent of schools is captured inside the box. The line heading up from the box represents results from the top 25 percent (i.e., the results for the schools with the best graduation rates). The line dropping down from box represents the outcomes in the weakest 25 percent of schools The dots below the lines are results for individual schools that were exceptionally low (i.e., outliers).

improvements were occurring in schools where the most negative results had previously been posted. This is illustrated in figure 2.3, where the lower tails of the box plots have been truncated while the overall graduation rates (the grey circles) have risen. This is precisely the kind of result desired in any effort to attack disparities in educational outcomes—a closing of the gap as the mean outcome rises. This stands in sharp contrast to other educational reforms, where the mean may rise, but inequities in outcomes expand at the same time.[35]

Overall, graduation rates in New Vision's schools improved from 74.7 percent in 2015 to 83.1 percent in 2017, and college-readiness rates rose even faster, from 23.3 percent to 43.9 percent over the same period. As figure 2.4 indicates, students who had previously passed four or five Regents exams continued to graduate at high rates. Most important, large improvements were registered for students who had passed fewer Regents exams on entry to their senior year and were at risk for failure. The graduation rate for students who entered their senior year having passed just one Regents exam, for example, rose from 27 percent in 2015 to 56 percent in 2017; and

FIGURE 2.4 Closing the gaps in graduation rates by regents passed prior to senior year

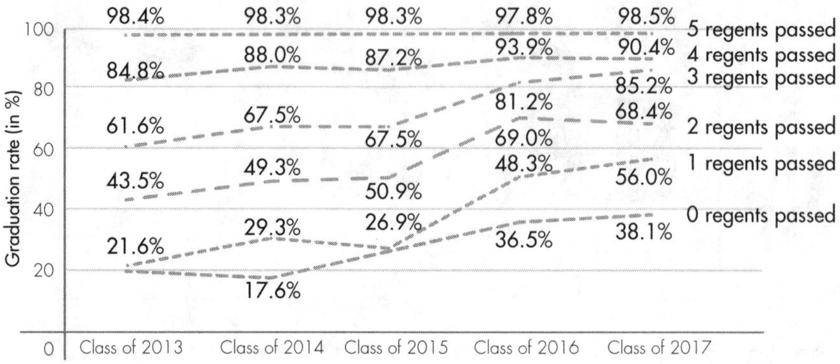

for those entering senior year having passed two Regents exams, the rate increased from 51 percent to 68 percent.

Importantly, in concert with these overall gains, gaps in graduation rates between racial and ethnic groups also narrowed (see figure 2.5). For the class of 2015, the graduation rate for white students was 85.1 percent, while the rate for African American students was 76.5 percent, and the rate for Latinos/Hispanics was 75.1 percent—a gap of 8.6 and 10.0 percentage points, respectively. By 2017, the graduation rate for all groups had risen, and the gap between graduation rates for whites and for African Americans and Latinos/Hispanics had narrowed to 6.3 and 6.4 percentage points, respectively.

These improvements continued with New Visions schools' overall graduation rate reaching 85.6 percent by 2019. This marked the third consecutive year that New Visions' network of high schools had exceeded what initially had been perceived as a very ambitious goal (an average of 80 percent).

Regardless, New Visions believed more could and should be done. Although it had made substantial progress by 2017 on its second goal of improving students' college-readiness rate (43.9 percent), more work was needed to reach the original goal of 50 percent or beyond. Having now

FIGURE 2.5   Closing the gaps in graduation rates by race and ethnicity

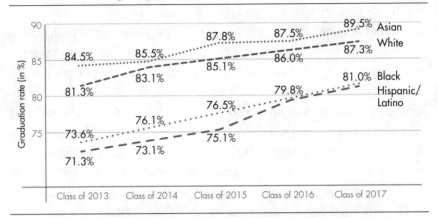

steadily surpassed the 80 percent graduation target as *an average across the network*, New Visions next aspired to bring *every school to a minimum* of 80 percent. This is the nature of continuous improvement; as accomplishments are achieved, aspirations continue to rise. In 2013, only 37 percent of schools had a graduation rate of 80+ percent; by 2019 this had now risen to 75 percent.

Looking forward to 2020 and beyond, efforts are now under way to move the data tools and processes developed and refined within the New Visions network out to all public high schools in New York City. This is a remarkable story of an improvement efforts starting small and learning fast as the basis for learning how to scale well—in this case out across the entirety of the largest public school system in the United States.

CONCLUDING COMMENTS

As noted in the concluding chapter of *Learning to Improve* and returned to in more detail in the concluding chapter of this book, the hub of an improvement network plays multiple roles. Among its central functions, a hub provides guidance around what we call the *charter* for the network. The charter represents a shared set of understandings among participants about the root causes of the problems to be solved, an exposition of a working theory of improvement, an explicit statement of aims, and a system of measures for informing the work as it proceeds. Once a charter has been developed, the hub coaches participants as they carry out PDSA cycles. It maintains an analytic capacity to inform the network's continuous improvement efforts and accesses research knowledge relevant to the focal problem. The hub is also on point for consolidating knowledge as it is emerging in practice, and ensuring opportunities for broader social learning across the network about these insights. It advances a culture of improvement both out in schools and up into school system leadership. At a basic operations level, it facilitates productive face-to-face meetings and ensures the vitality of virtual connectivity in between. While the New Visions case is principally a story about the analytic efforts of a network hub, inklings of these other key functions of a hub are apparent throughout.

The New Visions case offers strong guidance as to what an information infrastructure to inform improvement actually looks like. Three elements stand out. First is the power of examining data as a way to more deeply understand the actual problems to be solved. Doing this typically involves moving well beyond the standard year-by-year reports on lagging student outcomes such as the annual dropout rates. To be sure, these are important data—they are the "big dot" outcomes that we seek to improve. These data confirm that there is a problem to address and offer guidance about the variation in problematic outcomes between schools and between different student subgroups. But if we want to understand the causes of the observed outcomes, it will often be more informative to look at data that follows students longitudinally over time (as in the simple box plots in figure 2.1 and in the more sophisticated stock and flow visualizations such as in figure 2.2). Such analyses open up the system for examination in ways that traditional data reports obscure.

Second, insightful analyses, as carried out by New Visions, depend on a deep understanding within the analytic team of the actual work occurring in schools. Having good data and powerful data tools is essential, but they do not answer improvement questions. As noted throughout this book, data does not drive, but in skillful hands it may inform. To do this, improvers needs insights about the factors that shape work lives on the ground, because these insights suggest where and how to look at the data to probe the system further. This, in turn, necessitates a weaving together of the diverse forms of expertise resident in the analytic hub, in expert practitioner staff, and in the hearts and minds of participating school educators. This is a vital networked improvement community at work.

Finally, turning insightful visualizations into constructive action entails structuring a set of processes respectful of all of the participants involved. And it depends on the development of a safe and trusting environment for the difficult conversations about problems that these data may surface. Additionally, it means transforming mindsets—establishing new norms— so that these new ways of working are "indeed what we should do."

In sum, what on the surface may have looked a simple and uninteresting problem facing the New Visions hub—the routine functioning of traditional administrative data systems—actually had embedded within it a complex array of taken-for-granted ways of working. These needed to be understood more deeply and then challenged in a very disciplined and systematic fashion to advance effective improvements.

3

Becoming a Learning Organization

Summit Public Schools

SUMMIT PUBLIC SCHOOLS, a network of charter schools in California and Washington State, has embraced an innovative agenda for high school reform. The organization aimed to move away from the traditional course and classroom structure of schooling toward a competency-based framework where students would exercise choice in the work they do and move at their own pace to achieve well-articulated and measurable learning outcomes. Teachers would no longer be front and center in classrooms. Instead, they would serve as roving mentors and advisers supporting students to become active agents of their own learning.

Summit's pursuit of this agenda meant a total reinvention of how work was to be carried out in its schools for both students and teachers. The idea of personalizing students' experiences was inspiring; but figuring out how to make this happen every day for every student and in every learning context was a huge challenge. There was no blueprint to follow. Summit's leaders would have to learn how to do this by trial and error.

This orientation toward continuous improvement was in Summit's DNA from day one. As founding director Diane Tavenner put it, "Everything for us is a work in progress." Early on, she and her leadership team had read Eric Ries's book *The Lean Startup*, which had encouraged them in this direction.[1] "Intuitively, it all made sense," reported Tavenner. However, it was not until they were exposed to improvement science, first through an Explorers' Workshop at the Carnegie Foundation for the Advancement of Teaching and then by reading *Learning to Improve* as a group, that they began to see how some of the different pieces that they had initially started to work on cohered together as a fundamentally different way of thinking about and acting toward their goals.

Summit's ethos of continuous improvement was formally spelled out in a 2017 vision statement: "[O]ur thinking continues to evolve each day. We remain open to (and hungry for) new ideas and new insights that challenge our thinking."[2] Embedded here, and perhaps most daunting, is the need to live day-by-day with a profound tension between strongly held beliefs about the power of their innovative ideas and the reality of what was and was not actually happening for students in their schools. Summit's work was a very personal version of the improvement mantra, "definitely incomplete and possibly wrong." Tavenner's general orientation in this regard had been strongly shaped by her graduate studies at Stanford, and in particular her mentorship with Larry Cuban. He challenged her to align her leadership actions to her thinking about good schools, good learning environments for students and adults alike, and a productive work culture to support all of this. Summit would seek to live the credo "We are a learning organization."

THE SUMMIT CONTEXT

Summit opened its first high school in Redwood City, California, in 2003, with the mission of ensuring that every student in its diverse student body graduate with the skills and habits necessary to lead the lives they wanted to live. The network has since expanded to eleven schools in California and Washington State, serving three thousand students, of whom 44 percent are Latino/Hispanic, 20 percent are white, 11 percent are Asian, and 6 percent are African American.[3] Half the students are eligible for free and reduced-price lunches, and 11 percent are English learners.

Beginning with its very first cohorts, Summit succeeded in graduating virtually all of its students and enrolling them in college. However, many of these students subsequently failed to thrive in college. Although a lot of attention had been paid to instilling a solid underpinning of students' basic knowledge and skills, Summit leaders concluded that they also needed to strengthen students' sense of personal agency for their own learning as this seemed key for students to respond more productively to challenges in college and beyond. Out of these early experiences, a press to personalize learning emerged as the cornerstone in Summit's instructional system.

Summit's first steps in this direction involved developing an annual personalized learning plan (PLP) with each student. The idea was that teachers would meet with students and their families in the fall to discuss personal goals for the year ahead and then periodically review progress toward them. After a couple of years, school officials conceded that their initial efforts were coming up short. The PLPs were print documents that often ended up in file drawers or trash cans. "They weren't living, breathing things in kids' lives," said Adam Carter, Summit's chief academic officer.

Summit had stumbled into the first big problem in any effort to personalize learning. The work of high schools is conventionally organized around processing groups of students through standard courses of instruction conducted at a common pace. It is carried out by teachers in classrooms using published curricular materials and lesson plans. Vitalizing more individualized forms of instruction meant innovating on the nature of the instructional resources available in every school. It would also require new tools for tracking individualized programs for students and monitoring their progress through what would now be more varied and complex instructional pathways. In principle, these changes would give students much greater control of their own opportunities to learn. However, teachers would still need to ensure that the PLPs developed for each student met standards for graduation, and they would need to be able to track how well students were advancing toward this goal. This personalized learning system would also require new and more dynamic ways to assess learning outcomes. It quickly became clear that personalized learning demanded a more sophisticated technology to support work of both students and teachers than that found in conventional learning management systems, which are typically organized around courses, homework assignments, tests, exams, class grade and attendance data.

So beginning in 2011, Summit embarked on its journey to design this personalized learning environment. One early effort included the development of an online system in partnership with Illuminate Education. It bridged on-demand assessment information and learning resources so that students could direct their learning based on what they knew and did not know. Another involved a Summit-orchestrated partnership with Khan Academy and Dr. Jo Boaler at the Stanford School of Education to support students' personalized pathways through the "gatekeeper" subject of ninth-grade mathematics. After piloting these efforts in two schools in San Jose, California, in 2011–2012 and 2012–2013, Summit launched a new academic model across its entire school network in 2013–2014. The anchor for this new model was an initial version of an integrated online learning platform. It was based on their experiences from 2011–2013, and developed by an in-house software engineer in collaboration with Summit leaders, teachers, students, and community members.

In 2014, Summit formed a partnership with Facebook to build a more robust and personalized learning platform for free use by Summit's school network as well as interested partner schools. In this new jointly developed web-based system, each student maintains a "playlist"—an online record of the work completed and the tasks that are still ahead. Based on common standards for each grade level, students identify the core knowledge and skills they need to learn. They also track their progress on performance tasks that make up the bulk of the curriculum. The performance tasks are graded according to a common rubric that was developed by Summit in partnership with the Stanford Center for Assessment, Learning, and Equity. Complementing these performance tasks are sets of online instructional units focused on the basic conceptual knowledge and skills that students needed to acquire. Progress on these is checked through multiple choice tests. This student learning support and information system, subsequently called the Summit Learning Platform, made it possible for teachers to see where students were succeeding and where they might need additional help. These data reports, in turn, facilitated "checkpoint conversations" between students and their teachers to determine whether the student could move forward or might need to stop and regroup.

THE ORIENTING PROBLEM: REDUCING INCOMPLETES

Not long after they started this work, the improvers at Summit encountered a problem within their innovative structure—student incompletes. Student progress in Summit schools is based on a grading system consisting of two factors: 70 percent of grades derive from scoring rubrics associated with the specific projects that students undertake; the remaining 30 percent is based on multiple-choice tests of students' knowledge about key concepts and skills. Per its mission, however, Summit does not fail students. Rather, if a student does not demonstrate adequate performance on the basic knowledge and skills assessments or the project-based rubrics, his or her progress is simply marked as "incomplete." The student is then encouraged to work at the problem again, retake the on-demand assessments and/or revise and resubmit the project. Again, developing students' sense of agency and responsibility for their own success is an important formative goal at Summit and the grading system was designed with this educational goal in mind.

In principle, all students were expected to complete their work by the end of the academic year, but in a system where students move at their own pace, some inevitably fell far behind, and this put them at-risk for high school graduation and their goals beyond. So two valued organizational aims—developing each student's sense of agency and ensuring that all students succeed—now stood in tension with one another. Summit educators were eager to find a way to resolve this problem. They turned to improvement science to do so.

BEGINNING THE IMPROVEMENT JOURNEY

In 2014, a small group of teachers came together with Summit leaders to form an initial improvement team. They found the core ideas of improvement science and improvement networks intriguing, but they also quickly recognized that moving these ideas into action entailed much more than reading *Learning to Improve* together and participating in an introductory workshop. Extended support for the Summit team came through joining with teams from several other districts assembled at the Carnegie Foundation for the Advancement of Teaching as part of its Student Agency Improvement Community (SAIC).[4] In addition, Summit staff consulted individually with Caitrin Wright at the Silicon Schools Fund, Anna Kawar at the Carnegie Foundation, and Joan Grebe, an experienced improvement adviser who had trained and previously worked with the Institute for Healthcare Improvement. Through the professional learning opportunities that these coaches provided, the initiating improvement team came to recognize that Summit staff would need to learn a new form of professional practice if the team's ambitious aims were to be realized. Summit leaders were truly embarking on a learning journey, and it is a journey that continues to this day.

According to Tavenner, when she and her team first tried to understand why students were not succeeding, they were "flying blind." At this juncture in their development as a charter management organization, all of Summit's resources had been committed to the schools. Consequently, although Summit had a small central office, there were neither the data systems nor the analytic staff to inform improvement work. To fill this analytic gap, Tavenner and her team took a first step toward developing an improvement hub by appointing Kyle Moyer to a new position of Manager of Continuous Improvement. Moyer had been a founding faculty member at Summit's second school, Everest, and he had joined Summit's Academics Team as an instructional coach and program manager in 2013. Experienced Summit teachers, including Katie Goddard, Jimmy Zuniga, and Megan Toyama, also joined the improvement team to attack the incompletes problem.

One of Summit's first improvement inquiries was to review extant data on student performance. Like many educational improvement efforts, Summit's initial focus was on end-of-year student outcomes. Indeed, its concern about student incompletes was warranted: 39 percent of students in grades 6–11 ended the 2014–2015 school year with at least one incomplete.

As previously noted, such end-of-year outcomes function as lagging indicators within a system of improvement measures.[5] But knowing the results after the year is over does little to inform improvement efforts while school is in session. For this, more timely and immediate data—leading indicators—are needed. Fortunately, Summit's commitment to building an online learning platform made the development of such indicators a relatively easy task. The data already existed, but needed to be harvested out of the platform and made easily accessible. So the Summit analytic team began to prepare weekly data reports on incompletes for each student at each school. Suddenly, variation in performance—over the course of the year, by different school sites, and for different subgroups of students—became much easier to see. Where previously Summit leaders had some hunches about the dimensions of the problem they needed to address, now they had data to inform and guide their efforts.

Along the way, Summit also took advantage of improvement review processes offered by the Carnegie Foundation to SAIC members. Summit staff already knew about driver diagrams—a tool that organizes an interconnected set of hypotheses about the primary targets for improvement, key mechanisms for moving this improvement, and specific changes that might be tested and refined over time. The improvement reviews, however, pushed their thinking about how to develop and use one effectively. The conversations in these reviews deepened their understandings of a driver diagram as a tool designed to assist in explicating one's causal thinking—a working theory of improvement—as to how the changes they were introducing would ultimately culminate in the improved outcomes they wanted to achieve. Reviewers literally asked the question, "How do you think that the change ideas you are currently pursuing will actually culminate in the improved outcomes you seek?"

Like many groups starting an improvement journey, the Summit team had readily identified the basis for a measureable aim (i.e., reducing the numbers of students with incompletes on their records during the next school year) and they had also brainstormed some possible change ideas. However, the causal connections between these two sides of their driver diagram—how to get from change ideas to aims—remained ambiguous, a kind of "grey space" (see figure 3.1, panel A). This is a common hurdle when teams initially use a driver diagram. Making principle 3—*seeing the system*—come alive is central to developing a strong driver diagram, but thinking about improvement efforts in this disciplined fashion can be challenging at first.

Many educational change ideas do not directly affect the intended outcomes; rather, they work through some linkage of intermediate processes. Panel B of figure 3.1 provides a simple heuristic example. Suppose an instructional coach proposes a change idea to offer a professional development unit for teachers on lesson planning to improve students' access to academic language. The implied intent is to move a secondary driver (better teacher-developed lesson plans) which is hypothesized to link to a primary driver (improved classroom instruction). This primary driver may in turn reasonably be viewed as instrumental for improving student outcomes. Each arrow in Panel B expresses the logic of an if/then hypothesis. For example, *if* teachers develop better lesson plans, *then* classroom instruction will improve. Driver diagrams typically involve an interrelated set of such if/then propositions.

In general, improvement efforts can break down at any place along the path of a causal chain like this. The change idea might indeed have merit, but the team may still fail to achieve its aim because a key intermediate process had been ignored (i.e., not represented in the driver diagram) or because one or more intermediate processes present in the hypothesized chain still need further attention. For example, perhaps not enough time was provided for teachers to actually implement the new lesson planning protocol (a breakdown in the secondary driver). Or, perhaps issues arose not in the lesson planning per se, but rather in their in-the-moment enactments in classrooms (a breakdown at the primary driver level).

FIGURE 3.1   A heuristic example of developing a driver diagram

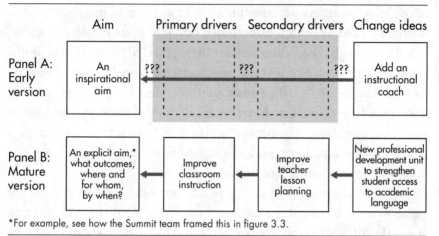

*For example, see how the Summit team framed this in figure 3.3.

With a deepening understanding of pitfalls like these, the Summit team began to interrogate the causal thinking embedded in their initial driver diagram. Exactly what would need to happen for any of their proposed change ideas to manifest in improved student outcomes? This involved filling in that "grey space" between the proposed change ideas and the outcomes they were after. Then, as they started to attend to these causal chains, new questions arose: How would they know whether these newly explicated linkages were actually happening? To find out, they would have to expand the evidence they looked at to probe their causal logic in action.

Summit leaders acknowledge that their initial efforts to identify change ideas were relatively unsophisticated. It was their first year at organization-wide improvement activity, and the hub team was anxious to get started. Largely relying on personal observations and anecdotal accounts, they undertook a very rudimentary form of a positive deviant study.[6] Teachers who had joined as part of the improvement teamed asked, "Who do we think is doing good stuff on incompletes, and what are they doing?" Since the data analytic team were now producing detailed reports on each student's progress over the course of the academic year, the improvement team was able to review these data as a way to cross-check their hunches about which teachers were minimizing the number of incompletes their students received. Team members then talked to these teachers to understand what might be working well for them. This led the team to an initial set of change ideas. As a first test, they recruited a small group of teachers in other classrooms to adapt and iteratively refine the practices they had identified. Over the course of the remainder of the academic year, opportunities were created for other teachers to learn from this work and engage in their own testing, refining, and adaptation of these change ideas across more diverse Summit school contexts.

Signs of progress emerged. Figure 3.2 shows the trajectory of incompletes over the course of two academic years for all students in the Summit network: 2015–2016 as their first small scale change efforts were beginning and 2016–2017 as these improvement efforts spread across their system of schools. As the team expected, the temporal pattern of student incompletes remained similar. The rate of incompletes rose rapidly early in the school year, leveled off, and then fell as it got closer to June. The data showed that the overall level of incompletes was down 5–10 percentage points throughout the 2016–2017 school year as compared with 2015–2016. These results

FIGURE 3.2   Reduction in the percentage of "incomplete" student grades

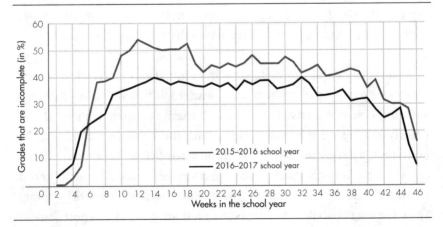

encouraged Summit leaders to think that there was value in working in these new ways, and this built support for broader take-up of improvement science efforts in the year ahead.

In tandem with this good news, however, a troubling pattern also emerged. Summit's new data resources meant that it was now much easier to see variation in performance for different subgroups of students, and a key finding stood out: incompletes for English learners were substantially higher than the rate for the rest of the student population. At the end of the school year, 29 percent of English learners' grades were incomplete, compared with just 10 percent for students who were native English speakers. And a closer look at other data, also now easily accessible, showed lower performance for English learners overall. These findings led Summit to the next leg of its improvement journey—one that would lead them to build an even stronger improvement capacity overall.

FOCUSING ON ENGLISH LEARNERS

Summit was able to identify the problem with English learners' performance because, by virtue of their improvement work, they had developed a data system that enabled them to track each student's progress week by week and day by day. The existence of these new data resources also made possible analyses that enabled them to develop detailed progress benchmarks for students on the road to college readiness. According to Adam Carter, "For the first time, we had a system that would give us leading indicators of success. We could ask, 'Who is, and who is not, on track toward college readiness?'"

These new data reports also made it easier for Summit's leaders to check on the progress of students in different racial and ethnic groups, students with disabilities, language learners, and others. These reports brought into even sharper relief the finding mentioned above: every subgroup was largely on track toward college readiness—except English learners. English learners lagged behind their peers on standardized test outcomes from the Measures of Academic Progress (MAP) test and on the Smarter Balanced

Assessment; they had higher rate of incompletes on performance tasks; they had a greater number of "attempts per pass" on the multiple-choice assessments; and they had a lower pass rate overall.

The gap in performance for English learners was a blow to Summit leaders, who had prided themselves on serving all students well. "That was hardest of all for me to see," Carter said. He quickly realized that this problem needed to be understood and owned by Summit educators if there was to be any solution. Absent this buy-in, Carter said, "There's no path towards better serving our English learners."

Carter brought together a group of teachers and leaders from eleven schools in the Summit network. They were joined by analytics staff and Kyle Moyer, who had led the 2016–2017 initiative to reduce student incompletes. Together, this group pored over the data, and they had the same reaction that Carter did: "It was like I punched them in the gut. We were not succeeding with English learners and although they hated to hear it, it sounded true." As the meeting concluded, participants were asked to indicate the importance and urgency of focusing on improving English learners' performance: It was unanimous—this would become the sharpened focus for Summit's improvement efforts moving forward.

From its inception, Summit Schools had embraced a strong equity aim. All staff who worked there cared deeply about this mission and did their best to advance it—and believed they were doing so. Operating here was a classic case of what psychologists refer to as *confirmation bias*.[7] When we deeply hold to certain ideas or concepts, we tend to believe that they are true, and this inures us to evidence that might cause us to question these beliefs. Educators see the effort being expended by all involved to advance learning for all of their students, but this actually makes it harder to see where they may not be succeeding. This is why improvers engage in disciplined inquiries anchored in data. The results from such inquiries push back at us, and in so doing, help us see what still needs to be challenged going forward.[8] This is also one of the ways in which improvement science is truly a science—it embraces the skeptical orientation that characterizes scientific practices more generally.[9] Beliefs about the importance of the work coexist alongside a nagging question *Have we really got it right?* In this regard, improvement science truly entails a different way of thinking and acting in educational practice.

Looking to Research Evidence

The Summit team had assembled a wealth of data on their English learners. As Adam Carter noted, these data documented the problem, but said little about what should be tried to solve it. For that guidance, they would need to look elsewhere.

Summit leaders began to review recent research findings that were directing attention to a broad range of student competencies that Summit educators came to call *habits of success*. These habits spanned five categories:

- **Executive skills:** Including stress management, self-regulation
- **School readiness:** Such as self-awareness, social awareness and relationship skills
- **Positive mindsets about self and school:** Such as growth mindset, self-efficacy, sense of belonging, relevance of school
- **Perseverance:** Including resilience, agency, academic tenacity
- **Independence and sustainability:** Such as self-direction and curiosity

Studies suggested that such factors are important predictors for student success.[10]

To explore the specific relevance of these factors in contributing to the lagging performance of English learners at Summit, the improvement hub administered two different student surveys, each of which tapped different aspects from the list above. Results from the first survey, developed by an organization called Youth Truth and previously used in Summit schools, indicated that English learners already had some healthy habits of success; they felt safer in school than non–English learners, for example. However, a second and different survey revealed their English learners suffered in two regards: they were less likely than their peers to express a growth mindset and they reported a lower sense of belonging in school.[11]

The concept of a growth mindset is anchored in a research finding that intelligence is malleable rather than fixed. Students who hold a growth mindset believe that with effort they can learn to master new and challenging material. These students tend to keep working even when they initially encounter frustration and failure. In contrast, students who hold a fixed mindset believe that no amount of hard work can help them to succeed. Once they experience struggle, these students see little reason to persist, which leads to a self-defeating spiral of failure. The lower levels of growth mindsets among Summit's English learners suggested one plausible root cause for their lower success rates. However, Summit leaders remained optimistic, since research had also demonstrated that it was possible to move students from a fixed to a growth mindset through direct student interventions and more supportive classroom environments.[12]

The relatively low sense of belonging reported by English learners on the survey suggested another possible root cause for their higher levels of incompletes. Belonging uncertainty is a common psychological phenomenon that people experience as they move into new and unfamiliar surroundings. When individuals feel uncertain about belonging, they tend to hold back effort, which undermines their chances to succeed. Summit improvers reasoned that differences between English learners' home experiences and the culture and ambitious instructional norms of Summit schools, could possibly be provoking this sense of unease. Based on these findings, the Summit team would revise their working theory of improvement to incorporate both of these social-psychological mechanisms into their improvement drivers.

Expanding Organizational Capacity

Buoyed by their initial success using improvement tools and methods, Summit's improvement hub felt ready to take on the challenges confronting their English learners. Their understanding of driver diagrams and how to use them had deepened, and they were now able to further articulate their working theory of improvement. They also were in a better position to develop practical measures to inform the work, and they had built a base of experiences in the design, coaching, and conduct of PDSA cycles.

Complementing this, by 2016–2017 Summit was well into a process of expanding staff capabilities to advance improvement efforts across its schools. As a result of other changes occurring at Summit, a number of teachers had a 25 percent reduced teaching load and were designated as "teachers on special assignment" (TOSAs) for the year ahead. The Summit team invited the TOSAs to participant in the English learner improvement project, and several individuals from different sites volunteered to do so. A summer workshop offered at the Carnegie Foundation through SAIC helped launch this new work, and additional coaching support followed during the academic year. The TOSAs, in essence, took on the role of school-site improvement facilitators. They helped in the design of PDSA cycles, conducted them in their own classrooms and supported other teachers at their schools to participate, and consolidated their school-based learning to share with the larger network. Additionally, a supportive set of school conditions facilitated the TOSAs' efforts. Summit's general strategy included extensive ongoing professional learning opportunities for staff at all school sites. Structured meeting times for teacher teams already existed, and some of this time was easily appropriated for work on the English learners' incompletes project.

Meanwhile, the hub continued to scan the research for ideas that might suggest other promising change hypotheses. The hub team was also regularly reviewing the PDSA cycles occurring in different schools, looking for especially promising ones that might be of value to other participants.

Taken together, capacity for continuous improvement was expanding from the Summit analytic staff and the initial improvement team into the work of the TOSAs and, through them, to the work of a broader group of school-based educators. An organized improvement capacity was forming, spanning from the classroom all the way up through the work of senior Summit staff and key leaders. Consistent with Tavenner's initial vision of a continuously learning organization, improvement science was being integrated into the overall work life of Summit schools.

The Improvement Process

As the Summit team paused to take took stock of their initial effort, they had sharpened their improvement aim from "All Summit students are on a trajectory toward college readiness by June 2017" to "The performance gap between Summit English learners and non–English learners is halved between June 2016 and June 2017, without any lowered performance of non-English learners." Embedded here is another lesson that improvement teams learn as their practice deepens. Initial aim statements often take the form of broad aspirational claims, as seen in Summit's first improvement aim: *all* students on a trajectory to success. Clearly, statements of this sort express important and broadly held social values, but such goals are not likely to be attainable. (Recall that federal leaders promised "No Child Left Behind" by 2014, and the nation is still waiting.) And when such statements don't appear creditable, this can undermine the sustained commitments needed to advance genuine improvement. Embracing aspirational statements as if they were realistic goals also tends over the longer term to reinforce a broad public pessimism about the possibility of making real progress. Instead messages abound that "We are still failing." In contrast, improvement science guides teams toward specific measureable goals. To be sure, these aims should be ambitious "reach" goals, but there also should be reason to believe the aims are attainable. As Carter put it about his own improvement learning, "If it is too big, we won't solve anything."

As noted above, the Summit improvement team had been diligent about keeping up with external research and examining what their own evidence suggested about priorities going forward.[13] Coupled with learnings from the PDSA cycles completed the previous year, the team set out to further refine their driver diagram, aiming to be more causally explicit and specific as to the issues confronting English learners. As part of this effort, the improvement team also conducted a second and more detailed positive deviant study. This time, the focus was on using data to identify teachers whose students were most on track for college readiness and for whom the gap between English language learners and non–English learners was narrowest. The team then observed and interviewed those teachers to identify specific practices that might expand the list of change ideas to try.

The revised driver diagram that resulted included four primary drivers and a number of secondary drivers for each (see figure 3.3). The first, second, and fourth of the primary drivers focused directly on how teachers

FIGURE 3.3   Summit's English Learner driver diagram*

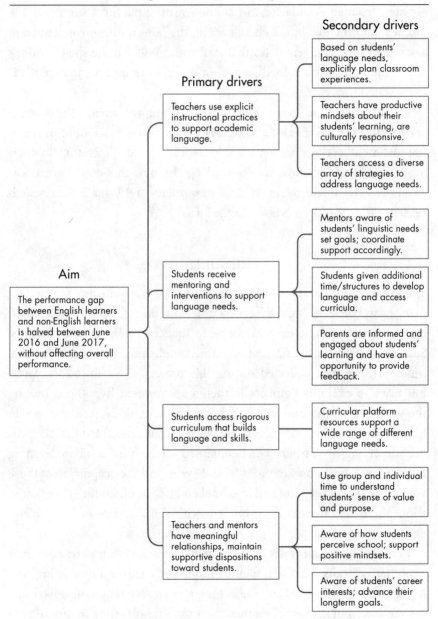

Secondary drivers

Primary drivers

Aim

The performance gap between English learners and non-English learners is halved between June 2016 and June 2017, without affecting overall performance.

Teachers use explicit instructional practices to support academic language.

Based on students' language needs, explicitly plan classroom experiences.

Teachers have productive mindsets about their students' learning, are culturally responsive.

Teachers access a diverse array of strategies to address language needs.

Students receive mentoring and interventions to support language needs.

Mentors aware of students' linguistic needs set goals; coordinate support accordingly.

Students given additional time/structures to develop language and access curricula.

Parents are informed and engaged about students' learning and have an opportunity to provide feedback.

Students access rigorous curriculum that builds language and skills.

Curricular platform resources support a wide range of different language needs.

Teachers and mentors have meaningful relationships, maintain supportive dispositions toward students.

Use group and individual time to understand students' sense of value and purpose.

Aware of how students perceive school; support positive mindsets.

Aware of students' career interests; advance their longterm goals.

*This figure represents an abridged version of Summit's more detailed driver diagram.

and mentors might better engage with students. The third, in contrast, set out a change agenda for the online learning platform team. For the teacher- and mentor-based change ideas, the Summit improvement team assembled two-page templates that staff could pull "off the shelf" and try out in their classrooms. In all, nineteen different change ideas were iteratively tested that year.

In sum, the team had woven into their improvement efforts guidance from external research, findings from their own data and previous improvement cycles, along with good ideas already operating in their own schools and classrooms. Resonating through this entire process is Tavenner's vision and voice: "What does our data say? What is the research evidence for these drivers and change ideas?"

RESULTS

The initial results of the incompletes efforts were impressive. The performance gap between English learners and non–English learners decreased by 50 percent, with no decrease in performance of non–English learners. Summit was well on its way toward accomplishing its immediate aim. Moreover, the data collected during this project also allowed the Summit team to examine empirically their improvement hypothesis linking the growth mindset and sense of belonging among English learners to improved student outcomes. Student survey results indicated that the proportion of English learners who maintained a fixed mindset about learning declined over the course of the 2016–2017 year, and the proportion of those who agreed that they belonged in school and that adults at the school cared about them also increased. In tandem with this, the rate of incompletes declined.

In other words, Summit's improvement data was giving warrant to their hypothesized causal chain. Implementing change efforts aimed at improving student growth mindsets and belonging had resulted in improved survey reports from students, and these improved reports were in turn, linked to more desirable student outcomes. Summit now had evidence to support this particular aspect of their working theory.

Digging Still Deeper

Staff at Summit were encouraged by this progress, but it was still only a part of the full aim they sought to achieve. The average incomplete rate had declined, but substantial variability in student performance remained, and more subtle aspects of this variability now captured their attention. Some English learners were still stuck, and a fair number of non–English learners were struggling too. So the hub team turned back to the core investigative question: "What is really going on here? What is the actual problem we have to solve?"

As the team dug into further analyses of data—in particular, focusing on the predictors of students progress over time—they came to see their problem in a new light. What originally was framed in ascriptive categorical terms—a gap in performance for English learners—became more nuanced. The team was no longer convinced that the issue was primarily one of language learning and cultural background. Rather, the data were showing that students who entered Summit schools with weaker reading and mathematics skills were more likely to struggle in the system. "The picture was clear: we don't have [so much] an English learner problem, we have a problem with students with low levels of reading and math skills," said Adam Carter. "It manifests in data on the progress of English learners because they are disproportionately represented in this group."

Based on these new findings, in 2017–2018, the Summit team began to focus on improving the performance of students who entered Summit schools in the lowest quintile in reading and mathematics achievement. This led to further revisions of their driver diagram. Much of what they had learned the previous year was still of value, especially the improvement efforts around belonging uncertainty and growth mindsets. Likewise, enhancing academic language development still mattered, but now they also recognized that they had both literacy and mathematics instructional issues to address. In addition, even with general improvements in instruction, more targeted supports were likely to be needed to accelerate the progress of students who entered with weaker backgrounds.

Summit leaders also drew on organizational experiences from the previous year to continue to build their capacity to get better at getting better. The analytic team, now fully integrated into a comprehensive Research and Development Team across Summit Public Schools, built new data tools that would enable teachers and school leaders to more easily identify students who were at risk and monitor their progress. Additionally, the improvement hub identified teachers who had been diligent about carrying out PDSA cycles, and provided opportunities for them to share their work with teachers new to the process. The improvement projects in 2016–2017 had benefited from the TOSAs having 25 percent of their time available to spend on this work. Although this allocation was ending, both Adam Carter and Kyle Moyer were convinced of the merits of having dedicated school site staff to support school improvement efforts. To increase this capacity going forward, they created three full-time facilitator roles to coordinate and support expanded improvement testing. Rather than relying solely on individual teachers and schools to figure out solutions largely on their own, the facilitators would take on active roles as co-developers with teachers of PDSA cycles, catalyzers for social learning across school sites, as well as supporting the conduct of PDSA cycles within schools. By doing this, Summit was taking one more step in exploiting the power of structured networks to accelerate improvements.[14]

Even with all of this capacity and support, Summit's results during this phase of work were not as fast or dramatic as in prior years, in large part because the problems they were now tackling had grown considerably in scope. Weaknesses in students' academic backgrounds developed long before students entered Summit and were unlikely to be remediated in just one year. Nevertheless, Carter felt that Summit's infrastructure to support improvement was much stronger than before, and the commitment to keep improving was strong too. "The work is not done here," he said. "We still have a long way to go."

CONCLUDING COMMENTS

Many different lessons can be drawn from this case. Four stand out, but in no particular order of priority. First, Summit leaders focused on building a hub improvement capacity. This included:

- **Investing in a central analytics team:** They recognized that they could not expect each school to do this kind of data crunching work on their own.
- **Developing mechanisms for the natural capture of data:** In this regard, the introduction of the Summit Learning Platform proved to be a key resource for informing their continuous efforts at improvement.
- **Creating capacity to manage improvement:** This involved both basic work in supporting school improvement teams in setting agendas, securing meeting times, facilitating good conversations, and tracking progress on PDSAs. At a more expert level, it meant infusing relevant research knowledge and curating opportunities for social learning across the improvement enterprise.
- **Orchestrating a seamless process for setting improvement priorities over time:** Summit's improvement team was conscious of potential conflicts arising between locally developed improvement priorities percolating up from schools and different centrally developed priorities mandated from above. They recognized the need for a coherent improvement system; not different silos of work, each advancing different agendas.

Second, Summit's experiences show the varied ways that imagining improvements can emerge. Their efforts illumine an important question in the practice of improvement, *Where do good change ideas come from?* Through positive deviant studies, Summit leaders advanced some of their efforts by drawing on expert knowledge resident in their own practitioners who were already doing a good job on minimizing incompletes. They also drew on external research findings and connected to relevant research expertise, especially on growth mindset and belonging uncertainty. These knowledge resources shaped both their understanding of the problems that needed to be addressed and provided a source of evidence-based change ideas to try out. Summit leaders also continuously analyzed their own data on students' progress, looking for places where students might be stumbling and seeking to understand why. In this last regard, Summit moved along a path similar to improvement efforts at Fresno and New Visions.

Third, Summit's story again illuminates the power of closely tracking, in real time, students' progress toward graduation and postsecondary success. It is important to recognize that this use of data to keep students on track is not limited to high school attainment; rather, it is of broad value across educational organizations. For example, it is now informing efforts to create learning pathways and related efforts that advance student progress to completion in community colleges and other postsecondary institutions.[15] It also relevant in tracking student learning—and accelerating progress where needed—in efforts like RTI programs.[16]

As noted earlier, end-of-year accountability data often provide the measures used in association with aim statements in driver diagrams. Even so, some caution remains warranted as the ways these data are reported can sometimes distract our attention from the issues that actually need attention. The Summit case is illustrative on this account as well. Like most end-of-year accountability reports, Summit improvers broke down results by various subcategories of students such as race, ethnicity, and language background. Looking at such data naturally led Summit staff to think about their problem as one peculiar to English learners. It was only as they shifted to looking at their data in a different way that other important issues about students' preparation and basic academic skills really came into focus.

Fourth and finally, this case illumines the sometimes paradoxical demands involved in leading improvement inside an educational organization. Improvement requires believing strongly in what you are trying to accomplish and building a community that advances agency for these changes. But simultaneous with that, improvement also entails challenging what you are doing and questioning where you may be coming up short. These two normative stances—the affirming and the critical—often do not coexist easily, especially in work as deeply personal, social and political as education. And yet maintaining both of these views is essential to leading improvement. The key actors in the Summit story—Diane Tavenner, Adam Carter, and Kyle Moyer—live this tension daily: they believe in the importance of what they are trying to accomplish, yet constantly question whether they are doing the right work in the right ways to advance their aims. So in a larger sense, this case is also a narrative about living the improvement paradigm and truly being a learning to improve organization.

4

Infusing Improvement into
a Charter Network

High Tech High

LIKE MANY PROGRESSIVE EDUCATORS, the founders of High Tech High (HTH), a network of charter schools in the San Diego area, had long been skeptical of "data." For them, data was synonymous with an overreliance on standardized test scores, and they felt strongly that this focus distracted from the broader educational goals truly necessary for students' success in life. Data was not viewed as a resource for improvement but rather as a problem to avoid.

High Tech High founders also placed a high value on empowering individual teachers to organize and carry out instruction as they might think best. Affirming teacher autonomy, accompanied by a deep suspicion of centralized initiatives, were founding norms at HTH. These educators had seen repeatedly how top-down initiatives erode the conditions necessary to advance the more compelling educational experiences they wanted for their students.

Given this origin story, HTH's evolution into an organization that depends on data, and where networked improvement communities (NICs) have now become integral to how the organization works, is unexpected. It is a story of how HTH's recognition that it was coming up short on its goal of college success for all of its students propelled leaders to explore new ways of trying to get better. Progress through some modest initial improvement projects catalyzed HTH educators' interest in learning more about the principles, tools, and methods of improvement science and generated momentum for expanding their use.

Today, High Tech High operates multiple networked improvement communities that work in parallel on problems such as improving math performance, science instruction, and college access for underrepresented students. It has developed a strong cadre of teacher leaders who ably organize and support these improvement efforts, and it has woven this work into a graduate school of education. HTH's professional preparation programs aim to ensure that the next generation of educators will have had both an initial exposure to improvement principles, tools, and methods and also experience working within an improvement-oriented environment as part of their socialization into teaching and leading. The goal is simple but also profound—to make this approach normative in the profession.

HIGH TECH HIGH CONTEXT

High Tech High was started in the late 1990s by a group of San Diego business and community leaders. They were concerned about the shortage of high school graduates prepared to go into STEM fields, and particularly the dearth of students of color and from low-income backgrounds. HTH founders envisioned a STEM-focused preparatory high school that would serve students from across the region. It would focus on project-based learning and provide numerous opportunities for students to learn in the community through internships, community service, and "real life" experiences.

Larry Rosenstock was recruited to serve as the school's founding principal. He had been principal of Cambridge Rindge and Latin High School in Cambridge, Massachusetts, an academically strong school with a well-regarded career and technical education program. The first High Tech High campus opened its doors in the 2000–2001 school year.

High Tech High founders were committed to equity and diversity. They enrolled students through a lottery based on zip codes, so that the student body would reflect the city's underrepresented communities. High Tech High has steadily expanded over the years and now includes sixteen schools—five elementary schools, five middle schools, and six high schools. The HTH network has received many accolades in its two decades of existence, and it is a highly sought-after destination for San Diego-area students. It also was the subject of a recent documentary film, *Most Likely to Succeed*, in which it was described as the future of American education.

EMBARKING ON A TRANSFORMATIVE JOURNEY: "OH THE PLACES YOU'LL GO"

Like many accounts of organizational change, HTH's journey starts with a leader who initially cultivated a small group of colleagues to work together, and over time this group grew their efforts into something quite special.[1] Ben Daley was one of the school's original faculty members. (He is now the president of the High Tech High Graduate School of Education). His interest in improvement came about in an unusual way. He had come across Atul Gawande's essay about hand washing and how attending to this simple process had dramatically reduced the number of deadly, hospital-induced infections.[2] Learning to get better at hand washing was literally saving people's lives. Daley was particularly intrigued by the fact that Gawande's account wasn't a story about introducing a new drug or technology, but rather about bringing the right kind of data to bear in a timely fashion to inform improvements on a very specific process.

Gawande's article startled Daley on multiple levels. First, it provided a new perspective on improvement. As Daley knew, educators tend to focus on adding more programs, presuming that if they can just find the right one, their problems will be solved. And the bigger and more innovative the new initiative, presumably the better. Gawande, in contrast, described identifying a very specific process as the crux of the problem and then systematically trying to make this process work better. The hand-washing story was about how attention to a seemingly small improvement can yield big results.

Second, the article offered a vision of data as a valuable resource for improvement rather than something that undermines the core work of professionals. The story seemed eminently sensible on this account, but it was also different from the way that many educators thought about data at the time. Third, health-care providers, like educators, share deep-seated norms about individual autonomy in the conduct of their practice. Yet the essay depicted professionals engaged in organized collective action to advance improvement together. Daley wondered whether these insights could have any bearing on efforts at HTH. Could working in these ways help their schools improve outcomes for students? Daley knew that a focus on data and working together through common practices might be a hard sell in the HTH context. But he was also both persistent and persuasive and trusted that he might be able to corral at least a few others to join him in launching a journey of learning to improve.

A Compelling Problem Comes into View

Beginning with its first senior class, in 2003, High Tech High reported annually on the success of its students in graduating high school, going on to college, and persisting in their formal education. These data typically indicated that around 80 percent of HTH's graduates intended to enroll in a four-year college. School officials annually shared those results with their school board and the larger public. The quality of data on which these reports were based, however, had never been deeply scrutinized.

The initial improvement group recruited by Daley began to look more closely at the data. They pored through paper files and contacted former college counselors. A year and a half later, they had more accurate numbers—and they were distressing: in fact, only 66 percent of graduates actually enrolled in a four-year college. Although this was a relatively high number against a national benchmark, it was far lower than the one they had previously thought to be the case. "We were shocked," said Daley. "We weren't happy."

HTH now had an improvement aim: increase the number of students, and especially underrepresented students, enrolling and succeeding in four-year colleges. The team also committed to using data to actively monitor progress toward that goal. A grant from the William and Flora Hewlett Foundation made it possible to hire a full-time staff person to collect and analyze data going forward. And because Daley had become familiar with efforts at the Carnegie Foundation for the Advancement of Teaching to bring improvement into education, HTH sent a ten-person team to the Foundation's inaugural Improvement Summit in the spring of 2014 to learn more about improvement science and networked improvement communities, and how they might apply this approach to improving college-going for their students.

Once HTH set this improvement goal, it began work on a leaky pipeline problem, much like the efforts of the Fresno Public Schools (chapter 1). Between high school entry and college success, many hurdles confront students that can slow their progress and, in worst cases, derail them. One leak had been obvious to HTH leaders when they opened the doors of their first school: many students all across the state were ineligible to enter the University of California or California State University systems simply because they had not enrolled in the right high school courses. To plug this potential leak, HTH made a commitment right from the start that every student, regardless of prior academic background, would take the A–G sequence of courses required by the state system. (Both Fresno and New Visions tackled a similar problem.) This was an important step—preemptively plugging one big hole—but pipelines can leak in many different places.

Improving Support for the College Application Process

As Daley and his group continued their examination of the problem, another leak became evident. Students did not necessarily know about all of the steps needed to apply to and matriculate into a college. They were acquiring the necessary academic credentials for being accepted into a four-year institution, but somewhere along the application and enrollment processes, they were falling out. This was an important concern. Solving it also seemed like a manageable goal, which was important, as this would be the group's first venture into using improvement science to solve a problem. But what might actually work here?

As part of their early exploration of this issue, they learned that one of their schools—High Tech High North County—had already begun to dig into students' experiences with the college application process. With assistance from a nascent improvement hub that was forming at HTH, the North County team surveyed students to find out what they considered especially challenging about the process. Based on these student reports, this team, together with their HTH hub colleagues, developed an initial working theory of improvement focused on four interrelated process changes: (1) HTH agreed to pay their students' college application fees; (2) the team created a checklist for advisers to ensure that students took all the steps they needed to apply; (3) advisers would be available to help students fill out and submit their applications during a staff day; and (4) English teachers in junior-year classes made writing a college application essay a part of the curriculum.

These changes, when packaged together, resulted in an immediate improvement. The enrollment rate for students in a four-year institution had hovered around 65.6 (± 0.6) percent for the graduating classes of 2011 through 2015.[3] This was HTH's baseline. One year into the improvement efforts, the enrollment rate jumped to 72.6 percent (see figure 4.1). The gap in enrollments between high- and low-income students also narrowed substantially; in 2015, only 58 percent of low-income students enrolled in college, compared with 70 percent of their more advantaged classmates—a gap of 12 percent. In 2016, this gap was cut in half, to 6 percentage points, even as the enrollment rates for both advantaged and less advantaged students, increased. The HTH team felt that they were headed in the right direction.

The type of statistical reasoning illustrated above—of comparing an observed outcome after introducing a change idea (i.e., 72.6 percent college enrollment) to results from a baseline period from several prior years (i.e., 65.6 percent, ± 0.6)—is commonly used in improvement science. Formally speaking, the baseline data represent the control condition against which post-intervention results are evaluated. The basic idea is to compare the

FIGURE 4.1   Evidence of improvement in four-year college enrollments

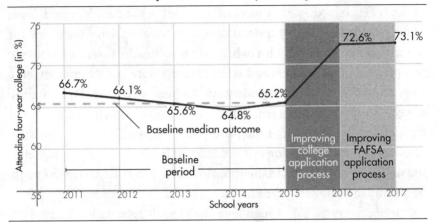

size of the observed change—in this instance, 7 percent—to the year-to-year deviations around the baseline median of approximately ± 0.6 percent.[4] HTH had witnessed an improvement by a factor of more than 10 over the random variation previously experienced. By this criterion, leaders judged the observed change to be substantively meaningful. They had accomplished something they valued.

Working on FAFSA Completion

Excited by these encouraging results, HTH leaders were ready for their next improvement challenge. Recently published research focused attention on a key barrier to college-going among low-income students: the application process for applying for federal student aid (Free Application for Federal Student Aid, or FAFSA) was difficult.[5] Failure to file this form was especially important in California, since FAFSA also was used to qualify students for a Cal Grant, through which low- and moderate-income students could receive up to an additional $50,000 for college tuition. Absent tuition support, many students could not afford to go to college. Yet research documented that many eligible students did not fill out the FAFSA and so lost out on a critical source of student aid.[6]

Daley's team wanted to understand if the FAFSA was an impediment in the HTH context, so they took a closer look at their student data. Their inquiry made it clear that a significant number of students were "leaving money on the table" and that, while college counselors were attending to this process, other teachers and school leaders were mostly unaware of it. Importantly, the California Student Aid Commission (CSAC) maintained a web-accessible database on active FAFSA applications, including the student's name, birthdate, and grade point average. This was a valuable resource, yet the improvement team learned that some college counselors did not know how to utilize this information to target students who might be lagging in completing the FAFSA.

The improvement hub at High Tech High took it upon itself to address this problem. Relying on school-based educators to regularly go out and cull this information from a state-level data resource was not a high-reliability process—one likely to get executed well regularly by different people working in varied contexts—in a place where the improvement team felt they really needed one. Going forward, High Tech High hub staff would now take responsibility for extracting the relevant information from the CSAC website. They then sent up-to-date individual student FAFSA completion reports to all school directors and college counselors at the end of each month in the fall, and biweekly in February, leading up to the March 3 application deadline. Armed with this timely information, school directors and college counselors could now more easily identify students who had yet to complete the form and then actively encourage and help them do so.

This test of change produced immediate results. The proportion of HTH graduates completing the FAFSA rose from 61.8 percent in 2016 to 78.4 percent in 2017.[7] Correspondingly, the proportion of all students earning a Cal Grant rose from 35 percent to 46 percent that year, and the proportion of low-income students earning a Cal Grant rose from 61 percent to 70 percent (see figure 4.2). But before they popped the champagne, there was one alternative explanation that HTH needed to examine. The team knew that, simultaneous with their change effort in 2016, the federal government had also eased the procedure for filling out the FAFSA. So the question arose: Was the good news the result of the government's change

FIGURE 4.2   Evidence of improvement in Cal grant awards

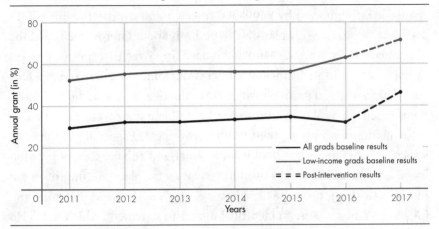

or their own? To check on this alternative explanation, they compared the improvements in FAFSA completion at HTH with those recorded for California as a whole. HTH's increase was 16.6 percentage points, while the increase statewide was only 6.9 percentage points. This was a big enough difference to convince them that their interventions were continuing on the right track.

Clearly, increased FAFSA completion was an important goal in its own right, as more of HTH's students were now securing college financial aid. However, in terms of HTH's explicit improvement aim—more students applying to and enrolling in college—the FAFSA project did not add much, if any, value. The proportion of HTH students enrolling in a four-year college rose slightly, from 72.6 percent in 2016 to 73.1 percent in 2017 (see figure 4.1), but the gap between high- and low-income students actually widened a bit, to 10 percentage points. While it is possible that a small improvement had occurred here, it is also possible that HTH leaders were just looking at random year-to-year effects. Recall that in the five years of data used as baseline for their college-going improvement efforts, ordinary year-to-year variation was about ± 0.6 percent. So the observed change in 2017 was well within that range.

To sum up, working on improving FAFSA completion was a warranted change idea, supported by published research and consistent with HTH's own data. It was a highly plausible hypothesis about improvement that the hub tested locally. And the team had indeed improved that specific process as documented in its immediate process outcome measures (i.e., FAFSA completion rate and grant awards). This initiative, however, did not move them much—if at all—in terms of their ultimate improvement aim. This is the nature of a *working* theory of improvement. Especially in the early stages, these theories are highly provisional and subject to modification based on learn-as-you-go experience. Not every plausible improvement idea actually turns out to be the right one—*right* in the sense that it is moving the specific measure(s) identified in an aim statement, which in HTH's case was the enrollment rate in four-year colleges.

Taking a Hard Look at Chronic Absenteeism

Remember the leaky pipeline? The projects described above focused on problems toward the end of the pipeline—breakdowns in processes around college and financial aid applications by high school seniors. But HTH leaders also knew that some students, especially those who were chronically absent, were at risk for falling out much earlier in their high school careers. Similar to the leaders at New Visions, HTH's hub drew on insights from recent research that had reframed educators' understanding of the causes and consequences of absenteeism.

As noted in chapter 2, while virtually every school in America records the attendance of each student every day, the traditional measure reported by school districts to the state and in school report cards is *average* daily attendance across all students and across all of the days that comprise a full school year. For example, the national average daily attendance rate for secondary students in 2012 year was 91.7 percent, meaning that, on average, more than nine in ten high school students were typically in school on any given day.[8]

More recently, the concept of *chronic absenteeism* has gained attention. It turns out that when a student misses a few days of school here or there, it rarely matters. A significant number of students, however, miss 10 percent or more of their school days, and these students perform much more poorly than those who attend regularly.[9] Research has shown that chronic absenteeism is associated with a wide range of negative student outcomes, that it can start as early as preschool and kindergarten, and that it can serve as an early warning sign of subsequent school problems, including dropping out of high school.[10] Chronic absenteeism is especially serious in high schools, where the long-term consequences for students can be most severe.[11]

Prior to reading this research, HTH leaders, like their counterparts in many schools, had not recognized chronic absenteeism as an issue needing attention. The average daily attendance rate across all of the HTH schools was about 95 percent, which they considered a vindication of their instructional approach. "We never looked at it," said Daley. "We had 95 percent [average daily] attendance and were of the mind that, if you do engaging projects with kids, they'll come to school." Their 95 percent rate seemed to affirm these beliefs.

Starting in One School

When one of the HTH schools began to examine its own data, however, the extent of the chronic absenteeism problem began to be revealed. Daley had noticed that the average daily attendance rate at North County high school was slightly lower (94 percent) than for other high schools in the system, and he had mentioned it to the incoming school director. "Unbeknownst to me, the dean and the site manager already had their eye on this problem. [In fact,] they had become consumed with the issue of attendance," said Daley. The school leaders had learned that more than 15 percent of their students were chronically absent. This finding stunned Daley and prompted the HTH hub to take a look at this issue across the system more generally. Daley recalled, "We had schools in which nearly a fifth of the students missed eighteen days of school or more . . . That's terrible!"

To address the problem, the HTH North County team—led by the site director, Isaac Jones; the site manager, Sheila Van Metre; and a teacher, Ryan Gallagher—developed and tested a change package that they came to call "Notice and Act."[12] Like the improvement efforts catalyzed by New Visions, a key driver in HTH's change package consisted of generating more timely and accurate student-level data for school faculty and staff. Specifically, the HTH improvement team began producing a weekly report on the list of students chronically absent for the North County school director, site manager, and dean. This was the *notice* aspect of the change package. In tandem, they also piloted a set of actions in response to the observed absenteeism. One of their acts was to develop an outreach initiative to engage parents seeking their help in solving this problem. As soon as a student had five absences, the school sent a letter, signed by the principal, to the student's parents. It noted the number of absences and explained the importance of regular school attendance. Then, if a student was absent ten days, the intervention escalated with a follow-up letter that reminded parents about the importance of regular school attendance, and requested a meeting between the student, a parent or guardian, and the dean. The site manager phoned the student's home to ensure that the meeting was scheduled at a convenient time.

These meetings were part of the school's effort to engage parents and students as co-problem-solvers with school staff. Refining a protocol for these conversations was another element in the change package. In engaging parents, school officials sought to reemphasize the importance of school attendance, establish a positive and constructive tone, identify the obstacles to more regular attendance, and find ways to remove those barriers. The meetings with parents surfaced a range of issues, and many of which were personally sensitive and called for individualized attention. In one instance, school staff learned that a student was too embarrassed to come to school because his clothes were not clean, so the school found a way for that student to routinely have clean clothes. Other students appeared to need a bit of "tough love," so staff developed an "attendance contract" informing them that they would lose course credit if they missed too many days.

The results were swift and dramatic. In 2013–2014, the first year of improvements, the chronic absenteeism rate at the North County school was cut in half, from 15.4 percent to 7.4 percent, and it continued to fall to 2.5 percent two years later. Here, too, another substantively meaningful improvement had occurred.

Moving from One to Three Schools

Word about the success of the Notice and Act intervention spread throughout the High Tech High network, and staff at two other schools were particularly interested in trying it out themselves. The idea of spreading a specific change package across the High Tech High network was novel for them—some might even say radical and controversial. As Ben Daley noted, one of High Tech High's core principles had been "teacher as designer." Both teachers and school leaders were skeptical of solutions imposed from outside or even for a solution developed in another HTH school. This would be HTH's first attempt to spread a specific change developed in one school to the others in the system using an improvement science framework. This move posed a potential challenge to the deeply situated norm of educator autonomy that was at the core of High Tech High from its founding.

Holding aside for a moment this normative challenge, Daley also knew from his own study of improvement science that the process of scaling improvement is itself iterative. Just because a change package works in one context does not mean it is ready to go everywhere. Inevitably, as it moves out to other places, new challenges arise and adaptations need to be tested in the new sites. So when the staff of two other network schools expressed interest in trying out the Notice and Act change package, Daley was encouraging. In the spirit of starting small and learning fast, moving out to a few more sites felt like the right next step.

The two schools that agreed to take up the improvement package in the 2015–2016 school year were High Tech North County Middle school, which was a partner to HTH North County high school, and High Tech High International. The leaders of High Tech Middle knew their high school counterparts well. They taught many of the same students, and often consulted with each other about strategy. The dean at HTH Middle, Kathy Tempco, was eager to focus attention on improving chronic absenteeism and testing the change package developed by colleagues at North County High. The site manager at High Tech High International, Karen Lowe thought that signing on would create an opportunity to spend some time at North County to learn firsthand from their experiences both about the change package and the process of conducting an improvement project more generally.

High Tech North County Middle school chose to implement the change package largely as it had been developed at the high school, but with one exception: staff members thought the letter sent to families after five absences was too harshly worded. As a first test of change, the dean decided to call parents prior to sending the letter. The dean felt that this extra step might create a softer landing and open up a context more amenable to joint problem-solving. It quickly became apparent, however, that these calls, added to everything else on the dean's plate, were too time-consuming to be sustainable. So the improvement team at North County Middle decided to revise the letter and make it more parent-friendly. In addition, they introduced another change idea to moderate the time demands involved in taking up this new process. Now, after a student had ten absences, the dean would try using a telephone conference call with families rather than an in-person meeting.

Staff at High Tech High International also tweaked the change package. Rather than mailing the parent letter, they sent it out as an email. Additionally, rather than reviewing data reports and sending out letters for any students who had crossed an attendance threshold in the past week, HTH International organized the analysis and outreach efforts around four key dates—December 15, March 2, April 20, and May 11. A cumulative record of student absenteeism at any of these time points would now trigger the outreach process.

So as the change package moved out from one to three schools, efforts to improve it continued. Notably, both North County Middle and HTH International showed substantial drops in chronic absenteeism (see figures 4.3 and 4.4). At International, the rate dropped from 11.1 percent to 3.6 percent in a single year. At North County Middle, the rate dropped from 7.2 percent to 0.9 percent. Moreover, although low-income students had been more likely to be chronically absent than their more affluent peers prior to the intervention, the gap between the two groups became insignificant once the changes were implemented. Also noteworthy was that prior to this improvement effort, both of these schools were among the

FIGURE 4.3   Evidence of reduction in chronic absenteeism at HTH high schools

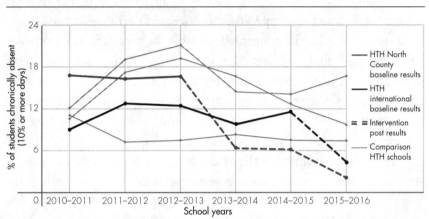

worst on chronic absenteeism rates in their respective divisions (middle schools and high schools). Now, these three schools—North County High, North County Middle, and HTH International—were the best-performing schools on this measure in the High Tech High network of thirteen schools.

FIGURE 4.4   Evidence of reduction in chronic absenteeism at HTH North County middle school

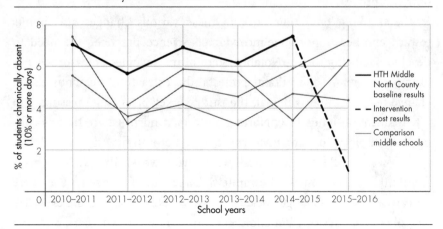

In addition to being an impressive chapter in HTH's improvement story, the effort to spread the absenteeism intervention from one to three schools offers insights about the improvement concept of starting small and learning as you go.[13] While these adaptations might be perceived as simply each site "making it their own," there was actually a deeper logic operating here. Specifically, the actual changes that occurred in the move from one to three schools reflect the workings of the triple aims of educational improvement—effectiveness, efficiency, and human-centeredness—as described in the introduction to Learning to Improve.[14] Meaningful and sustainable improvements exist at the intersection of these three aims. An overemphasis on just one may worsen results on one or both of the other two and ultimately undermine the effort. In focusing on the tone of the letter at HTH North County Middle School, for example, educators there were asking the question: "Could a more empathetic outreach be effected?" By making this tweak, they were seeking to advance a human-centered objective.

North County High had reduced chronic absenteeism, but it came at the price of increased time demands on the dean, and time is typically the most constrained resource in schools. So efficiency concerns prompted the question at HTH International, "Could we achieve similar improvements, but in a more efficient way?" That led its improvement team to test the use of emails, reduce the frequency of data reviews, and batch the parent outreach process.

The thinking operating through these various changes also points toward another important improvement science practice—the need to develop balancing measures in a system of improvement measures.[15] For example, in many educational projects, the extra time demands that a change puts on a staff will often constitute a key balancing measure. Too often education tends to operate under a tacit norm where time is concerned: "If I can just convince you that something new is worth doing, somehow you will find a way to absorb it in your work." This is a bit of magical thinking, as if time were infinitely elastic; but of course (at least here on earth) it is not. Change packages must be integrated into the everyday web of educators' work, and a critical consideration is whether or not the change is doable. This is why improvers gather evidence not just on what they hope to accomplish, as represented in measures of aims and various drivers, but also attend to other unintended changes that might be occurring. Increased time demands on an already overstretched work force will frequently be high on the list of unintended consequences.

A Stumble: Spreading It Systemwide

Based on the success of the change package in the first three schools, HTH leaders now felt ready to spread the change package to all thirteen schools. They had assembled good evidence of significant reductions in chronic absenteeism across three different contexts, so they knew that interventions along these lines could really work; and they had a reasonable, tested change package to support adaptive integration into the rest of their schools. Even so, they ran into new challenges. Staff at some schools were less welcoming and less concerned about chronic absenteeism than their counterparts in the first three sites. As a result, this tier of schools did not attack the problem with the same intensity, which meant that the take-up of the change package varied and progress slowed. HTH leaders were now confronting the prevailing norm of educator autonomy, mentioned earlier, that broadly characterizes the teaching profession and especially the teachers and directors across the HTH network of schools. As an organization, HTH had not yet internalized disciplined methods of improvement as normative, nor did the majority of their educators necessarily see themselves as members of a scientific improvement community.

It is instructive to look at this problem through the lens of innovation diffusion theory.[16] HTH leaders were still relatively early in the process of organizational transformation. First in North County High, and then in North County Middle and HTH International, they had found innovators and early adopters who were intrigued to work in these new ways, but the organization-wide normative shift still lay ahead. To be sure, the success of the first projects was noticed by others, but the value of disciplined, improvement science–based efforts and the confidence and know-how to carry them out was still at the periphery. Reflecting back on this episode, Daley observed, "It's definitely better than it was [referring to the chronic absenteeism rate], but we had more lessons still to learn about spread." He and other members of the hub reasoned that growing a professional community of practice around this new approach meant creating more opportunities for more people to engage these ideas and to work with others in these new ways.

DEVELOPING CAPABILITIES AND SUPPORTING EMERGENT LEADERS

Ben Daley and other hub members knew they needed to respect the organization's prevailing norms, even as they were trying to change them. They did not believe that they could mandate improvement, nor would they want to. Instead, and in response to the concerns percolating up from faculty and staff, they adopted a supportive communications strategy and coupled this with opportunities for interested staff to learn more about this new way of working.

As mentioned earlier, ten staff members attended the Carnegie Foundation's Improvement Summit in 2014. This group had returned to San Diego enthusiastic about people they had met and what they had heard. How to spread their enthusiasm was the question of the day.

Daley and other HTH leaders regularly talked to their community about the improvement projects in progress and shared results whenever they had new data. They also used their bully pulpit to express their hopes for HTH, the importance of its mission, and the opportunities they were creating to extend this kind of work. Basically, they aimed to motivate interest in improvement and then build on it wherever it emerged.

All of this was still quite new at HTH, and leaders were pretty much inventing the play book as they went along. To Daley's delight, "there was, in fact, a great deal of untapped interest." Over and over, they heard expressions along the lines of, "This is important work—work we should be doing." HTH leaders had set an original goal of engaging 20 percent of the staff in improvement projects by the following spring. According to Daley, they "blew through that goal" within a couple of months as more than a quarter of the faculty got involved in some way. Improvement efforts were spreading rapidly within the HTH community from a small group of early adopters to substantial faculty involvement. An early majority was forming.[17]

Stacey Caillier, a former HTH teacher who now directs the Center for Research on Equity and Innovation at the HTH Graduate School of Education, said that in retrospect they should not have been surprised by the breadth of faculty interest in improvement science. From her perspective, counterbalancing the norm of autonomy was another equally powerful belief. HTH teachers were all committed to reflecting on their practice and getting feedback from their students and peers. "Improvement science provided them with an opportunity to be more systematic and disciplined in these efforts," Caillier said. "They want to get better." Improvement science was a pathway to do that.[18]

Channeling Interest into Collective Action

Transforming the varied individual interests that had initially engaged staff around improvement into productive collective action posed the next organizational issue to tackle. Daley pondered how HTH could harness at least some of the newly emergent individual energies into collaborative work on shared problems. He saw this move as key to accelerating improvements at larger scale and on more complex problems. In essence, Daley was moving HTH to embrace the sixth improvement principle—*activating networked improvement communities*—within their own system of schools.

One of the first NICs that HTH launched focused on strengthening students' sense of mathematical agency. Like the educators at Summit schools, this NIC aimed to improve the growth mindsets and sense of belonging among traditionally marginalized students. As Curtis A. Taylor, a sixth-grade mathematics and science teacher at High Tech Middle North County, put it, the aim was "to abolish the phrase, 'I am not a math person.'"[19] HTH collaborated with Jobs for the Future, a Boston-based education organization, to do this.

The math agency NIC brought together about sixty teachers from fifteen high schools and middle schools in the San Diego area, including five HTH schools. They met virtually every week, and in person three times a year, to share change ideas and report on the successes and failures of their PDSA cycles. "Principals say that this is the best professional development teachers have ever been to," said Daley. "They are really seeing them change their practice."

In short order, High Tech High launched several other NICs to advance improvement aims around the Next Generation Science Standards, college access in STEM fields, language and literacy learning, and restorative justice initiatives.

HTH leaders had provided extensive direct support to colleagues involved with the college-going and attendance-improvement projects. Going forward, and to enable and encourage more teachers to get involved, HTH leaders decided to dedicate three of their five professional development days to support ongoing improvement projects. While this was not as intensive as the support for the small groups of teachers involved in the initial projects, it did create an opportunity for all teachers to be introduced to the ideas, with the hope that a subset would want to become more deeply involved.

Along the way, and to serve as a hub for the growing set of NICs, a Center for Research on Equity and Innovation had formed at the HTH Graduate School of Education. Today, the Center, which now has a staff of twelve, plays a major role in deepening and expanding improvement capabilities across the HTH network of schools. It convenes network members, manages improvement projects and activities, and facilitates both the virtual and in-person meetings. Caillier, the Center's director, said that one of its primary goals is to build teachers' capabilities so that they can eventually run their own improvement networks. To that end, Center staff coach and mentor emerging teacher leaders about the operations and functions of a NIC hub. "We definitely have gotten to a place where teachers are now running several [smaller] networks," she said. This was all part of an evolving HTH strategy to expand improvement capacity and support new leaders as they come forward.

The HTH graduate school has been on its own pioneering journey, evolving its mission and sense of purpose as to what a school of education aiming to advance the improvement of schooling might actually do. As part of this journey, it has become an increasingly important instrument in advancing ongoing improvement efforts at HTH more generally. Recently, the Center has also created a website that offers resources for improvement to the broader education community.[20] These include protocols for using basic improvement tools, such as fishbone diagrams, mapping "bright spots," and studying positive outliers. The web site also includes places for posting change ideas and associated PDSAs related to specific improvement problems.

Expanding the Majority: Developing the Next Generation of Teachers

In addition to investing in the professional development of existing High Tech High staff, HTH leaders have also made a long-term commitment to improvement science by integrating it as a core component in their own graduate school of education. In this regard, they are both building a proof of concept for the field and investing in their own future. An improvement research course is a core component in their graduate programs, and master's candidates are required to develop and implement an improvement project as a capstone for their degree. As part of new teacher induction support, these educators also participate in an ongoing HTH improvement network. Run by graduate school faculty working collaboratively with teacher and school leaders, these HTH NICs provide natural opportunities for graduate students to get involved directly in the work of improving schools. "This is not just some academic study of improvement," said Daley. "This is the real work of how we do things as teachers."

Through the combined efforts in HTH's system of schools and its graduate school of education, the core improvement questions set out in *Learning to Improve* now pulse through this organization: "What specifically are we trying to accomplish?" "What changes might we introduce and why?" and "How will we know if a change is actually an improvement?"[21] A strong core of HTH faculty now embraces improvement science, and by virtue of their GSE, a pipeline of new teachers, similarly oriented, will be joining them in the near future. Stable senior leadership continues to stay this course for the HTH system of schools and to develop new improvement leaders in their schools. Along the way, and not surprisingly, concerns still pop up from time to time about the role of test scores and preserving space for individual teacher initiative. And even when a promising new practice or change package demonstrates measurable improvements at a site or a few places, variable take-up across the network remains an improvement challenge.[22] However, despite these ups and downs, the path forward remains very clear. As Caillier concluded, "In the past, teachers were eager to innovate, but they often did not know where to start or whether their innovations were actually making a difference. Now, teachers know, in considering possible change ideas, to look at high-leverage practices that have research evidence of effectiveness. We were good at trying things," she said. "But how do you know it actually worked? That's been a transformation for folks. There are a lot of conversations about this now."

CONCLUDING COMMENTS

High Tech High embraced improvement science and in so doing eventually transformed the way that the organization carries out its work. To move this agenda forward, HTH leaders evolved an organic growth strategy. It began with an invitation to teachers and school-based leaders to work on a local issue that they personally cared about. Much like the improvement efforts in Fresno and Summit Public School, HTH's initial efforts aimed at problems that were modest in grain size. At the start, a small group of early adopters advanced efforts to improve specific processes such as FAFSA completion; advising students through college and financial aid application; getting timely data about chronic student absenteeism into educators' hands; and developing protocols for collaborating with parents and students to address the problems that the data identified. Many of these early adopters in turn became evangelizing leaders to spread this work across the organization. Supporting their efforts, HTH senior leadership created multiple opportunities for an increasing number of teachers and school-based leaders to learn about improvement science. They allocated both financial resources and staff time toward this end. And as improvement leaders emerged in schools, the hub recognized and cultivated these individuals to pluralize leadership for change beyond the initiating group.

High Tech High also built technical expertise in a hub at its Graduate School of Education, and this hub learned to support and manage an increasingly complex array of improvement efforts, including the initiation and facilitation of multiple networked improvement communities focused on different problems of practice. In short, the work started small and the initial changes were modest; as these early efforts were encouraged and supported by HTH leaders, they were also in essence seeding and cultivating an ambitious organizational transformation agenda.

Moreover, undergirding the changes at HTH was a compelling value proposition, central to the logic of improvement science, about the role of teachers as professionals. Improvement science places a premium on activating agency among frontline workers to identify pressing problems, to articulate possible change ideas while drawing on relevant research, and to deploy disciplined tests of change. Embedded within this activity are the core characteristics of a profession: its members know how to enact a body of work, and as a community, they are committed to and continuously engaged in getting better at doing this work. So the normative shift from a conception of teaching as a largely individual artisanal practice to an emphasis on collective action of members in a scientific-based improvement community was not as extreme as it might first appear.

Specifically, the embrace of improvement science at High Tech High built on the faculty's natural inclination to be reflective practitioners. This was coupled with a commitment to advance social justice by making meaningful, authentic educational opportunities accessible to marginalized students, who otherwise are too often left behind. Over time, improvement science just proved to be a better way to act on their beliefs and advance their aims.

The pressure to preserve teacher autonomy in public education has staying power because it pushes back against a long history of ill-conceived initiatives being imposed by policy makers from above or external audiences from the outside. Even when these reform ideas might have had merit, they were typically advanced in ways that failed to take into account the reality of educators' day-to-day work. In contrast, improvement science directly engages educators in the design and development of productive changes that they can actually achieve in their schools and classrooms.

Improvement science is now the way that HTH lives its work. As Ben Daley put it, "It is amazing. High Tech High went from a data-opposed organization to one that believed that data matters. It's been a major shift in the organization. I am totally surprised." This process of organizational change entailed both sustained personal reflections and extended conversations among all involved. It was not a forced replacement of one ideology with another by administrative fiat, but rather an assisted process of social learning. It followed an intrinsically pragmatic orientation, much like the work itself.

On balance, there remains much to respect in HTH's original organizing values, and its leaders will continue to navigate the boundaries between developing standard work practices that support quality outcomes more reliably while also respecting and celebrating individual initiative and innovation. Likewise, by embracing the use of data to improve, they remain mindful that most data are, at best, modest indicators of some larger educational values that educators hold. Maintaining a skepticism about data is in fact healthy, for the mechanical use of data can become a quick descent—especially when accountability pressures arise—that transforms some modest indicators that might inform efforts to improve into treating these measures as if they were the ends of education itself. Whenever this understanding about means and ends turns corrosive, it undermines the spirit of improvement, fails to effect the real changes being sought, and may even do harm.

So in closing this chapter, I return to the wisdom of Dr. Seuss and the advice he offered in concluding his book *Oh, the Places You'll Go!*: "All of life is one great balancing act."[23] This is the leadership dynamic at the heart of improvement work, and it is now the leadership stance that animates High Tech High.

5

Advancing Instructional Improvement

The National Writing Project

with Paul G. LeMahieu

THE PREVIOUS FOUR CHAPTERS have focused on improving how students progress through school. Each of the spotlighted organizations attended in different ways to keeping students on track toward postsecondary enrollment and success beyond. Chapter 1 described how the Fresno Public Schools attacked a leaky pipeline problem by identifying the many places across the four years of high school where a student might fall through the cracks and put their future at risk. At New Visions, discussed in chapter 2, improvement efforts focused on reducing chronic absenteeism, improving the accumulation of course credits, and a more planful approach to preparing and sitting for Regents exams. Chapter 3 recounts how Summit Public Schools aimed to solve an incompletes problem that threatened students' successful graduation from high school and how this project launched Summit on a transformative journey toward becoming a continuous improvement organization. Likewise, the improvement efforts at

High Tech High, discussed in chapter 4, also began with specific projects around improving college applications and reducing chronic absentee-ism—and evolved into a more expansive organizational change effort.

From these cases, and in the work of numerous other organizations and individual researchers cited in endnotes throughout these chapters, a great deal has now been learned about how schools can get better at advancing students' progress through school and minimizing the attainment hurdles that can easily trip them up. In contrast, advancing instructional outcomes, and specifically improving how schools can achieve more ambitious aca-demic goals, or deeper learning, poses a different and more complex set of problems.[1] Achieving better outcomes in this realm, reliably and at scale, represents the improvement frontier—the place where the field of educa-tion generally needs to learn how to do much better. For an exploration of how the improvement principles might be applied productively to this more challenging class of problems, we turn to an innovative effort under-taken by the National Writing Project.

When the Common Core State Standards were developed in 2009 and subsequently adopted by more than forty states, teachers of writing saw both an opportunity and a challenge. On one hand, the standards placed a strong emphasis on writing in all subject areas for the first time, which made writing more salient than ever before. On the other hand, they called for a new focus on writing as argument—a genre that had not been taught widely. In response to this challenge, NWP convened a subset of its writing project sites to prototype, test, refine, and scale new pedagogical practices and instructional resources. These developments were supported by pro-fessional know-how resident within the NWP community.[2]

NWP's story offers a glimpse into what an infrastructure supporting large-scale instructional improvement looks like. The account that follows shows how university-based researchers and school-based practitioners partnered to meld their diverse forms of knowledge and expertise to solve a shared problem. The chapter also elaborates on the multiple and diverse roles played by the hub of a networked improvement community (NIC) to organize and orchestrate a research and development effort occurring at a national scale. It describes how NWP drew on its well-established professional network of educators across the country and coupled that with the specialized academic, technical, and managerial expertise resident in NWP's national office in Berkeley, California, which functioned as the NIC's hub. In the course of carrying out its work, the NWP hub: managed improvement learning efforts across multiple sites; created a space for diverse voices to exercise agency in improvement; secured relevant research knowledge to inform the work; afforded critical technical expertise around evaluation, measurement, and analytics; organized processes for consolidating and facilitating the spread of emergent knowledge within the network; and ensured that the improvement principles continued to advance the overall enterprise. In taking on these new roles as the hub of a large-scale improvement network, the capacities of the NWP national organization evolved in significant ways as well.

THE NATIONAL WRITING PROJECT CONTEXT

NWP is predicated on a simple but profound premise: teachers are the best teachers of other teachers. In 1974, James Gray, a professor of practice in the Graduate School of Education at the University of California, Berkeley, started the Bay Area Writing Project (BAWP) by bringing together university professors and local classroom teachers to share their expertise and work with other teachers to improve how they taught writing. As Gray wrote, "For teachers, BAWP was a university-based program that recognized—even celebrated—teacher expertise. For academics and teachers alike, BAWP challenged the top-down, voice-from-Olympus model of so many university-based reform efforts."[3] Brought into the context of improvement science, Gray was channeling a core view about organizational change championed by W. Edwards Deming: those engaged in the work are central to its improvement.

As interest in BAWP spread, a number of affiliated sites began to spring up nationally and a small central office was created in Berkeley to serve as a base for this nascent professional community, and the National Writing Project (NWP) was born. From its inception, the heart of NWP has been the local writing projects co-led by classroom teachers and local university scholars. Currently, there are about two hundred such project sites throughout the country. Additionally, over three thousand teachers join the National Writing Project each year through an Invitational Institute.[4] At the Institute, they learn about current research relevant to the teaching of writing, have opportunities to refine their practices through demonstration lessons in front of colleagues, and begin to develop as instructional coaches who support colleagues at their local sites. Key in the formation of this intentional community is the personal writing and discussion of that writing that Institute participants engage in each day. This deliberate and signature experience binds teachers together in a community of shared memory.[5] Regardless of when and where a teacher might have participated in an NWP Institute, this common induction experience marks them as members of a professional community of writers committed to improving their students' writing. Many Institute participants go on to become "teacher consultants" within NWP. They are supported by both national and local site leaders to offer professional development programs in response to local needs in their own school and district contexts.

From its earliest days, and foreshadowing its eventual development into a networked improvement community, NWP would on occasion assemble special topic–focused networks in response to specific teaching and learning concerns arising in the field. Subsequently, these networks shared what they learned with the larger NWP community. This capacity to organize collective effort at a substantial scale on targeted problem-solving, combined with the strong human, intellectual, and social-organizational capacities that had been developing for decades across this community, uniquely positioned NWP to take up the challenges posed by the Common Core's increased emphasis on argument-based writing.

AN URGENT NEED FOR IMPROVEMENT: THE COMMON CORE STATE STANDARDS

In 2010, the National Governors Association and the Council of Chief State School Officers endorsed the Common Core State Standards (CCSS) to define "what students should know and be able to do." The standards were intended to raise expectations for student learning in English language arts and mathematics. On one hand, the CCSS English Language Arts standards were a boon to writing teachers because of the clear emphases set out for students' writing at every grade. However, as noted above, the standards were also a challenge because the "anchor" standards (standards applicable to all grades) placed new demands relative to argumentative writing that neither teachers nor their students were prepared to meet. The first anchor standard in writing, for example, calls for students to: "Write arguments to support claims in an analysis of substantive topics or texts, using valid reasoning and relevant and sufficient evidence." The ninth asks students to: "Draw evidence from literary and informational texts to support analysis, reflection, and research."[6]

Writing arguments of this sort had not traditionally been a major part of school curricula, and many elementary and high school teachers had little experience with or professional preparation to teach it. This created a serious disconnect for students as they moved from their K–12 education to postsecondary schooling. A study in San Diego, for example, found that many students who received an A or B in high school English classes failed English college placement tests. These tests expected students to be able to write a cogent argument using evidence to inform, describe, and critique a position or stance, whereas high school instruction had focused mainly on narrative writing and literature.[7]

Along related lines, K–12 writing instruction has tended to emphasize persuasion, which differs from argument in important ways. Persuasion often appeals to emotions, currently popular views, or historical traditions. In contrast, writers of arguments need to distinguish between reliable and unreliable sources and to marshal facts and organize them as a logical and coherent rationale to articulate a position, while both anticipating and refuting counterclaims. An essay based on the wishes of students to end or change school dress codes involves an exercise in persuasion. An essay calling for the abolition of the death penalty—with data, statistics, and logic supporting its claims—is an argument.

And NWP had come to acknowledge a weakness even within its own network when it came to argument writing. Prior to Common Core, "there just wasn't much emphasis on source-based arguments in professional development," said Linda Friedrich, NWP's research director. "And if it's not in professional development, teachers are not likely to be teaching it in classrooms." An important improvement problem had emerged for NWP leaders.

LAUNCHING A NETWORKED
IMPROVEMENT COMMUNITY

In response to this challenge, an initiation team formed at the NWP national office with the specific aim of improving how teachers taught students to write arguments. The team's first task was to develop a funding proposal for a networked improvement community around this problem, which they called the *College, Career, and Community Writing Project* (C3WP). The team eventually secured a 2012 grant from the US Department of Education's Investing in Innovation (i3) program to move forward. The team drew together a set of twelve NWP sites from high-poverty rural districts in ten states, including Alabama, Arizona, Arkansas, Louisiana, Mississippi, Missouri, New York, Oklahoma, South Carolina, and Tennessee. This network would prototype, test, and refine pedagogical practices and instructional materials that aimed to improve argument writing. The team also commissioned SRI, a leading independent research organization, to design a randomized control study to assess the overall effectiveness of these efforts. SRI randomly assigned forty-four districts associated with these NWP sites to either the (C3WP) treatment group, or to a control group that continued with the professional development that had preceded Common Core.[8] Along the way, the initiation team, which had gotten the C3WP project off the ground, became the hub that would support this emergent networked improvement community.

Making an Idealized Design Work

As NWP described C3WP in its i3 proposal, at least 70 percent of seventh- to tenth-grade teachers in each participating district were to receive ninety hours of professional development over two years (forty-five hours per year) focused on teaching source-based argument writing. The professional development would be delivered through local institutes offered by NWP teacher consultants, who, as noted above, were originally trained in NWP's Invitational Institutes and most had been practicing as teacher consultants for some time. The training would examine current research and professional literature, include classroom demonstrations, and give participants practice in the writing of source-based argument as well as a chance to study and try out effective practices in writing instruction. In addition, the C3WP hub committed to developing instructional "mini-units." These four- to six-day curricular units were designed to expose students to text sets consisting of collections of readings on some challenging content and representing diverse viewpoints on it. The units would be assembled by subject-matter experts and ask students to craft arguments drawing on ideas presented in the texts.

On paper, NWP's i3 proposal was well researched, organized, and clearly presented. Making it work, however, would necessitate extensive co-design and development efforts involving scholars and teacher consultants across the C3WP network. It played out as a story of failing fast, while learning fast and always pushing ahead.

Improvement efforts began when the first generation of mini-units was tested by a group of teacher consultants. The C3WP hub quickly learned that while they generally liked the text sets, these alone were insufficient to guide teachers' efforts at changing their practice.[9] The mini-units needed to be recast with teaching practice at the center and text-sets as a necessary supporting resource. Accomplishing this transformation required iterative testing of changes in the content, form, and structure of the mini-units, with practicing teachers asked to take a significant role in their improvement. The C3WP hub also learned early on that the teacher consultants needed more extensive support to scaffold their coaching, and so the resources accompanying the mini-units were also revised to provide more explicit guidance to the teacher consultants about how to support teachers' efforts to improve their practice.

As these improvement efforts proceeded, a fundamental challenge arose. There was a lack of agreement across the C3WP network as to what specifically they were trying to accomplish: *What truly constitutes a quality written argument?* It was NWP's long-standing practice to look at student work for evidence about whether the changes in teaching were leading to better student writing, but absent agreement as to what a "good" written argument is, advancing better-quality instruction would remain elusive. At this early juncture, C3WP was confronting the first and fourth improvement principles. With regard to principle 1, they needed a better answer to the question: *What specifically we are trying to improve?* And, relative to principle 4, they needed to *embrace practical measurement* to inform their efforts to get better. The C3WP hub, along with NWP leaders more generally, were stepping into new terrain. They were now pioneers, inventing new resources from scratch.

Centering on a Well-Specified Common Language to Guide Improvements

Through C3WP's early efforts to design professional development programs and instructional materials, it had become clear that teachers held different conceptions about what made for a good argument based on evidence. Robin Atwood, the co-director of the South Mississippi Writing Project, which was a C3WP site, explained, "We were separated by [not having] a common language. When people talk about argument writing, we might think we're all saying the same thing, but on further scrutiny, [we are not]. Everyone knew that to write an argument and to analyze an argument . . . [a student] needed a claim, and they needed to use sources to advance the claim. But that's where the understanding ended."

C3WP confronted what felt like an intractable problem. How could the community identify high-leverage instructional practices, develop coherent and appropriately supportive curriculum materials, and provide the coaching needed to improve instruction absent a shared perspective on argument writing to ground their work? Similarly, without this base of common understandings, teachers would not have a solid basis to determine whether they had implemented effective instruction or whether student performance was improving. "In conversations with Writing Project sites and teachers, there just wasn't a shared language to describe source-based argument," said Friedrich. "[And] there weren't criteria to describe whether kids were on a path learning to do this."

The lack of a common language to describe and identify ambitious instruction is endemic across the field of education.[10] Whether this activity is called "higher standards," "deeper learning," or "more ambitious instruction," at best these terms offer aspirational guidance; they point out a general direction toward which we should move, but the specific aims and how teachers might actually advance toward them typically remain underspecified.[11] NWP leaders had no alternative but to address this problem head on.

To begin the conversation, the C3WP hub introduced teachers to the research of Joseph Harris, an English professor at the University of Delaware and a leading expert on academic writing, including argument-based writing.[12] Because study groups in which participants read and discussed relevant research were already a core part of the C3WP's professional development strand, it created a natural way to bring Harris's work forward for discussion. Through these conversations, participants came to understand that argument writing is more than simply making a claim and citing evidence to back it up; rather, writers "do things" with evidence. One of these things is *forwarding*, in which writers use other texts or the authority of other authors to support a point. Another main strategy is *countering*, which is when writers challenge texts by pointing out their flaws or limitations, and they often do this by invoking the views of others or contradictory evidence.[13] Once teachers began to extract the moves that good argument writers make, ideas sprang up as to possible new instructional routines that they might try out in their classrooms. These insights led the C3WP hub to introduce a new strand of activity where teachers and researchers began working together to identify, prototype, and then iteratively refine instructional routines that might help students learn how to use the specific strategies of forwarding and countering.

By bringing Harris's work to the attention of network members, the C3WP team was serving in one of the critical roles played by the hub of a networked improvement community. A key responsibility is to broker practitioners' access to relevant research (and research expertise) that may help them better understand the problem they are attempting to solve and identify possible change ideas that they might try. In this way, a hub integrates scholarly and practical expertise around problem-solving. Interestingly, NWP leaders did not tell practitioners what to do; rather, the C3WP hub engaged them as co-learners in a thoughtfully designed and skillfully facilitated adult learning environment. The hub team infused that environment with relevant knowledge and guided conversations that created opportunities for a set of shared understandings to develop about what they should try to do next. In short, they gave life to the idea that improvement involves deliberately organized processes for social learning.

Navigating the Accountability Chasm

With these shared understandings beginning to form, teachers in C3WP were asked to examine samples of student work from their own classrooms. Some teachers were reluctant, however, because the request coincided with many states introducing new teacher evaluation systems that already had them on edge. These teachers did not want their new practice judged in what they perceived to be unfair ways. In response, the C3WP hub created a coding system to maintain individual teachers' anonymity as peers examined their students' work. "We were aware of teacher evaluation. It was a grave concern," Friedrich said. "So we made a conscious choice at this point not to create something that would have identifiable information."

Tensions like this are common in education, especially given the accountability climate of the past decade or so. Teachers have seen their practice and their school performance ranked poorly or judged failing based on measures they consider flawed. Hence, they were naturally reluctant to participate in an effort that held their students' work—and by implication their own work—up for critical judgment. Yet improvement requires sharing data so that educators can see the problems they aim to solve and open up conversations with colleagues who may be achieving greater success about what is working for them and how they might identify possible change ideas to produce better results all around.

Recognizing this tension, the C3WP hub went to some lengths to clarify that the reason for sharing this data was to produce information that might benefit all of them in improving their own teaching and their students' learning. This was information *for them*—to help them get better at something they cared deeply about. It was not to judge them or their schools. "The purpose of this is truly formative," said Friedrich. "It's truly to focus on how to better support our students." This meant creating a "safe space" to mitigate the ever-present concerns about evaluation so that the risk-taking associated with trying something new could occur.

In addressing this issue, C3WP had a powerful resource to draw on—the NWP community itself. Hub members had standing among the local site leaders and teacher consultants participating in C3WP. They were all part of a professional community of practice and a community of shared memory. Years of working together, anchored in a sense of common purpose and shared values, had formed a basis of trust between them. This reservoir of trust meant that the site leaders and teacher consultants could more easily foster positive C3PW connections with local classroom teachers, many of whom were their colleagues and neighbors. In short, the extant network of social ties developed and nurtured by NWP, some strong and others weak but still valuable, facilitated this effort's launch and cleared a pathway for the assessment development work that the improvement community was about to undertake.

Developing the Using Sources Tool to Inform Instruction

The early efforts to examine student work described above helped to advance understandings about the nature of good argument writing and, more specifically, to reach a clear and shared perspective on C3WP's student learning aims. Harris's scholarship had provided a starting point for the conversation. Looking at student work made the question of aims, and possible means to advance them, both concrete and practical.

As these discussions continued, a group of teacher leaders and university-based researchers from C3WP sites, along with hub staff, examined more student writing samples and began to form a set of criteria for examining a piece of student writing. The criteria included an evaluation of whether the writing presented a claim; whether the writing distinguished between a source's ideas and the student's; whether the writing used evidence from independent sources to support the claim; and whether the writing considered the credibility of the source material. The articulation of these criteria was, in essence, the first draft of a new assessment tool. The group also settled on a general format for a rubric. It would examine each piece of writing in terms of if, and how well, a student's essay demonstrated each of the criteria described above as either: "not present," "developing," "competently," or "effectively" represented.

During the process of drafting this tool, discussions emerged about its purposes and appropriate uses. Participants agreed that it should enable teachers to determine quickly whether a student's writing exhibited these key features of evidence-based argument, and if not, to target where a student might need more support.

Evidence from the tool should also help guide ongoing local professional development. If, for example, results indicated that some groups of students or classrooms were consistently struggling on a specific aspect, targeted additional coaching might be needed. Likewise, principals reviewing aggregate schoolwide data should be able to identify areas where the whole faculty might need additional support. In its most general use, the tool would afford school-based teams both a common language and a data resource to support their ongoing learning-to-improve argument writing.

The instrument, which eventually came to be called the *Using Sources Tool* (UST), continued to be developed through a series of tests of change, initially small and then increasing in size over time. To achieve this, the C3WP hub organized a sequence of activities where diverse participants across an expanding set of contexts would try out the tool and give feedback, each round catalyzing another round of revisions and further testing of changes. By working in this way, hub leaders sought to ensure that the changes they were making, based initially on a core set of research-based ideas, were actually moving tool development in the right direction. Failing fast in smaller initial tests created rich opportunities to learn; had they chosen instead to just roll out the early draft tool at full scale, they risked "failing big," which could have eviscerated their credibility and undermined the whole effort. In contrast, the process of iteratively testing and refining the tool, and building confidence in its use, helped to secure buy-in from the teachers. Those involved early on were actively engaged as co-developers of the tool. The knowledge they acquired, and the evangelizing spirit that they came to share, became significant resources in the subsequent spread of the UST across the network.

As a first field test of the tool, the C3WP hub asked teacher site leaders to take a close look at the initial draft. These teachers brought the tool to their midyear meetings and used it to analyze student work. This effort surfaced a number of concerns about the tool—ranging from a lack of clarity about its conceptual underpinnings to the basic nuts and bolts of using it efficiently. This quick feedback led the hub back to the drawing board.

Next, NWP enlisted C3WP sites in Louisiana, Mississippi, and Tennessee to serve as a more diverse and larger group of beta testers. These sites agreed to use the tool as part of professional development for their networks and to form inquiry groups to provide feedback about it. For this test, participants were given a draft of the Using Sources Tool that had been revised based on the first round of feedback. They used it to examine one thousand papers from students in grades 7–10.

Feedback from this second test indicated that further revisions were needed to make the tool both more explicit and efficient to use. The draft UST was still not able to guide teachers to consistent judgments as to whether a piece of student writing was truly effective or not. The teachers suggested that the UST needed to provide a more nuanced view of writing. In their view, the tool did not allow them, for example, to adequately characterize the quality of the claims that students made. That is, the tool asked whether or not a student had made a claim; it did not probe more deeply to determine if the claim was a statement that evidence could support or one that could be challenged on the basis of evidence. "Some claims are more sophisticated than others. The tool has to reveal that," said Robin Atwood.

The beta test also showed that some teachers still found the tool too time-consuming and difficult to use. According to Elyse Eidman-Aadahl, the executive director of the NWP, although the earliest versions of the tool made sense for the academic leaders in the national network, it did not work as well for teachers managing a myriad of classroom demands. Not surprisingly, NWP was confronting a problem that challenges virtually every effort to improve instruction: *It is all about time.* As has been noted in preceding chapters, time is typically the single biggest constraint confronting classroom teachers, and yet developers of instructional materials and tools often overlook it as a serious design issue. Improvers, in contrast, know that if a new resource is not practical, in the sense that it can be reasonably integrated into the day-to-day workflow of a classroom, it either will not be implemented at all or, if implemented, will not be sustained.

Like the leaders at New Visions (chapter 2), the C3WP hub wanted to be sure that the tool worked for classroom teachers, and that meant going back to the drawing board one more time. Their commitment to design-based, iterative development had prepared them for this kind of ongoing testing and refinement. "That's a hard moment that a lot of NICs face," said Elyse Eidman-Aadahl. "Some get there, and some do not. That's part of their formative moment as [leaders of] improvers." Eidman-Aadahl's comment speaks powerfully to everyone who is involved in design work. It is easy to fall in love with what you have designed and think dismissively, "It is perfect. Why can't they see that?" But again, this is where the first improvement principle—to be user-centered—comes to the fore: "If it is not working for *them*, *we* need to ask why not, and what do *we* need to do next to make it work better?" This framing demands humility in those who lead such work, which is what Elyse Eidman-Aadahl's comments speak to. It also means recognizing the limits of what you know, and in a deep and very personal way, living the improvement mantra, "Definitely incomplete and possibly wrong." In truth, this mantra is much easier to say than it is to embrace day in and day out while actually doing the work.

And so still another round of revisions occurred. C3WP leaders felt that by this point, they had learned a great deal, and that it was time to try the Using Sources Tool with a larger group of teachers at the next Invitational Institute. That test proved generally successful. The tool helped these teachers see variability in the quality of students' writing, and combined with the professional development they were now receiving, they could begin to envision what they had to do in their classrooms to address this. "It was an epiphany," said Friedrich. "Some of the writing they were seeing was not what they had hoped for. It was not the kind of source-based writing that they now knew they were working toward." The UST had helped to reveal this. "It was a powerful experience," she continued. "People began to see the power of using [a common] language in describing writing and a standard tool for looking at it."

Buoyed by this experience, the C3WP leaders held a webinar to introduce the UST to an even wider group of teachers and sites. They also held monthly check-ins with the sites to offer support. The check-ins gave them a window into how teachers were using the tool to analyze student writing, which in turn helped the hub learn how to better support teachers' decision making around instruction and student learning. The tool went through four more iterations, and each new test enabled more fine-grained improvements. Along the way, the tool itself was transformed. What had started as an expression of researchers' academic scholarship developed into a tool that maintained integrity with that scholarship, but could now be used effectively and efficiently across diverse practice contexts.

Figure 5.1 presents the current version of the UST. The earliest versions of the tool were considerably different. For example, the first question now specifically inquires about the nature of the claim (if any) presented in the argument. It asks if the claim is "nuanced, debatable and defensible." It also permits judgment about the sophistication of the claim. Moving from that early version to this final form required members of the C3WP community to articulate the essential attributes of an increasingly sophisticated claim, prototype alternative ways this might be represented in the UST, and then examine how reliably teachers could use this guidance in scoring samples of work. This same iterative process of development was applied to each of the other questions found in the UST as well.

So while the final tool looks simple—it is captured on one sheet of paper and consists of just eight items—the process of creating it was complex. The tool had to align with the best research evidence and maintain fidelity with what expert writing teachers see and do. And it had to be practical to use within the highly constrained time demands of daily life in classrooms. Additionally, it had to have good statistical properties, demonstrating validity for the set of uses described above. Achieving this meant bringing into the design process a broad array of expertise—academic, technical,

FIGURE 5.1 National Writing Project: Using Sources Tool

1.	**Does the writing present a claim?**

☐ The writing presents a claim that is nuanced, debatable, and defensible.
☐ The writing presents a claim that is debatable and defensible.
☐ The writing presents a summary statement about source material, but that statement is not debatable.
☐ The writing does not present a claim.

2. Does the writing distinguish between the student's own ideas and the source material, including the use of clearly indicated paraphrasing, quotation marks, or signal phrases?

☐ Not present ☐ Developing ☐ Competently ☐ Effectively

3. Does the writing select and use evidence from sources to support the claim?

☐ Not present ☐ Developing ☐ Competently ☐ Effectively

4. Does the writing comment on source material in ways that connect the source material to the claim?

☐ Not present ☐ Developing ☐ Competently ☐ Effectively

5. Does the writing characterize the credibility of the source material or author?

☐ Not present ☐ Developing ☐ Competently ☐ Effectively

6. Overall, how would you describe the writing's use of source material? Select the option that best describes the writing's overall use of source material.

☐ Skillfully integrates source material to fully support the paper's claim
☐ Uses source material to support the paper's claim
☐ Includes source material to somewhat support the paper's claim
☐ Summarizes source material, without connecting it to a claim
☐ Does not use source material
☐ Primarily or exclusively copies source material

7. Does the writing use source material for any of the following purposes? Check all that apply.

☐ Illustrating: I Use specific examples from the text to support the claim
☐ Authorizing: I Refer to an "expert" to support the claim
☐ Extending: I Put your own "spin" on terms and ideas you take from other texts
☐ Countering: I "Push back" against the text in some way (e.g., disagree with it, challenge something it says, or interpret it differently)
☐ None of the above

8. What do you see as next steps for this student?

and professional. Fortunately, all of this was already resident in the NWP national staff and the larger NWP community when the improvement effort started. Their ready access to these resources greatly accelerated the process of moving from an idea about a tool to one that worked robustly across diverse school and classroom settings.

In sum, the C3WP hub had recognized early on that they needed a practical tool that could inform improvement efforts across their community of teachers, teacher leaders, and their students. It needed to help teachers analyze student writing; catalyze and inform productive discussions among faculty about their teaching; and scaffold instructional interactions with students about their writing. In terms of the roles that measurement plays in improvement science, C3WP had created a leading indicator to inform its improvement work. The tool provides timely guidance to teachers, principals, and teacher consultants in their ongoing efforts to improve instruction and, as they would subsequently learn, generates evidence highly predictive of NWP's ultimate aim—students writing high-quality arguments.[14]

RESULTS

SRI's randomized control study found that C3WP produced substantial improvements in classroom instructional practices and students' writing proficiency. The study documented that teachers in both the treatment and the control groups spent a similar amount of time on writing generally; however, those in the treatment group spent considerably more time teaching argument writing. SRI found evidence of such teaching in 41 percent of the instructional days in treatment group classrooms, compared with only 13 percent for the control group. Teachers in C3WP districts were also more likely than those in the control group to spend time teaching skills specific to writing arguments, such as connecting evidence to a claim, selecting evidence from source material, developing a claim, and introducing or commenting on quoted texts and source material.[15]

Not surprisingly, student performance in argument writing was higher in the treatment districts. Based on the results of a standardized writing assessment independently administered by SRI and blind scored by NWP, the study found that students in C3WP districts outperformed those in control group districts in a number of areas (figure 5.2). These included:

- **Content:** The rigor, relevance, timeliness, and appropriateness of the evidence as well as related facts and substantive content used in argument
- **Structure:** The logical sequencing and organization of the elements of the argument so that it was readily understood and compelling
- **Stance:** The voice, tone, and style that signal the writer's relationship to the topic and content and that are appropriate for the purpose and audience of the writing
- **Conventions:** The age-appropriate control and use of grammar and mechanics (punctuation, spelling, verb agreement, and so on)

Overall, SRI researchers concluded that C3WP students "demonstrated greater proficiency in the quality of reasoning and the use of evidence in their writing."[16]

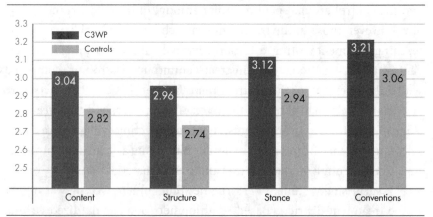

FIGURE 5.2   Students in C3WP schools out perform controls

CONCLUDING COMMENTS

NWP's efforts to improve argument writing offer a good example of what a well-designed and effectively led networked improvement community can accomplish. In just two years, the National Writing Project, through its C3WP initiative:

- Targeted an important instructional improvement problem
- Assembled an improvement network with the diverse practical, research, and content expertise needed to attack this problem
- Developed a working theory of improvement and launched multiple tests of change
- Achieved measurable improvements against an ambitious new instructional standard
- Set the stage for the extensive spread of the improvements realized.

C3WP has now expanded to include teachers in grades 4–6 in addition to the original emphasis on grades 7–10. It has also developed an additional instructional tool, deriving from the UST, that makes it possible for students to analyze their own written arguments. The initiative has spread nationwide to forty-seven states and over 125 Writing Project sites, and now serves nine thousand schools. It is a remarkable demonstration of how rapid progress on instructional improvement can be accomplished using networked improvement science when the right set of resources, conditions, and infrastructure exists to support such efforts.

To those familiar with past instructional improvement efforts, the account offered in this chapter may well sound familiar, but also innovative. Traditionally, efforts to improve instructional have typically done one of two things—buy a new curriculum or offer teachers more professional development. For example, NWP has historically been seen mainly as a professional development organization. With the C3WP initiative, however, NWP expanded its efforts to include the co-creation of instructional units with teachers, thereby bringing new curriculum into tighter alignment with supportive professional development. As the work progressed, they went one step further, integrating formative assessment capabilities through the UST into their instructional system. In so doing, they in essence "closed the circle" from what to teach (curricular content), to how to teach it (pedagogical practice), and to how to *know* what was actually being learned (formative measurement).

Organizing for Instructional Improvement

As noted in the introduction to this volume, organizational leaders and policy actors continue to press for better educational outcomes for students, and these are often expressed in aspirational terms such as deeper learning or more ambitious instruction. These are laudable goals, but to educators they pose a very big challenge that has eluded progressive reforms for close to a century. How exactly do we achieve these more ambitious learning goals reliably across the diverse contexts that comprise schooling in America? Several important lessons can be drawn from NWP's effort that could set us on a better course for the future.

First, NWP leaders came to terms with a critical orienting question: *What specifically were they trying to accomplish?* Addressing this question meant articulating an operational definition of quality writing based on how students select and use evidence to build an argument; how they distinguish between their own ideas and ideas learned from source materials; and how well they evaluate the quality and use of source materials. This operational definition created a common language within the improvement network that brought educators together and focused their individual and collective efforts. As they did this work, NWP was living the first improvement principle.

Second, NWP *embraced measurement* by developing the instructionally embedded Using Sources Tool. The information generated by this tool both informed instruction and provided ongoing evidence as to whether the new instructional activities that teachers were introducing into their classrooms were actually moving learning in the right direction. Importantly, the tool offered immediate and direct feedback about where students might be progressing and where they might need more support. Additionally, it helped to organize professional learning conversations between teachers as they looked at student work together, and offered formative feedback to teachers about their ongoing efforts to improve.

These two moves—specifying the problem and embracing measurement—joined together in C3WP like two sides of a coin. In *Learning to Improve*, my coauthors and I argued that you cannot achieve at scale what you cannot measure. And you cannot measure ambitious instructional outcomes unless you are very clear on what it is you are actually after. So these two considerations—specifying the aims and developing practical measures to guide progress toward those aims—are deeply intertwined.

Embedded here is a very general lesson. Developing practical measures for instructional improvement requires specificity and concreteness about observable qualities in instruction. It pushes educators to consider a core set of questions about what we should expect to see: in terms of the instructional tasks students are asked to undertake; in the social interactions occurring within classrooms around these tasks; and in the work that students produce. Advancing quality at scale entails agreement as to what this actually looks like so that a common standpoint operates: "This is good; this is better; this does not yet hit the mark." Without such specificity, achieving ambitious instructional aims reliably and at scale remains chimerical.

Third, running throughout NWP's efforts were multiple and varied *applications of disciplined inquiry*. NWP's team conducted iterative tests of change on both their mini instructional units and the Using Sources Tool. They also launched a randomized control trial to assess average program effects. Across iterative improvement cycles, they could readily see the variability in responses to their efforts operating in the network. In this regard, they were attending to the second improvement principle: *Variability in performance is the problem to solve*. This pushed them beyond just seeing instances where their efforts might be working well to also analyzing where they were not. And in the latter case, they constantly asked "Why isn't this working here, and what might we try differently in response?"

Complementing this, the randomized control trial provided useful validation evidence for external audiences. As is typically the case, the trial placed a premium on rigorously assessing average differences between the treated and untreated groups. Consequently, and by design, it did not offer much guidance to network participants about how actually to get better. In addition, because the primary focus of an RCT is on the *average differ-ence*, the design is not very informative about variability in performance. This matters enormously if the goal truly is that all children succeed. To advance on this equity aim, we need to be able to see the results for every child as they are emerging, and across all of the contexts in which students are being educated. NWP leaders understood these important differences between methodologies, and recognized that a mix of approaches could best enrich their work.

Fourth, and standing in sharp contrast to the way the educational prod-uct developers typically approach instructional improvement, NWP built a *system of changes* that could support the adaptive transformation of writ-ing instruction across diverse education contexts. This system included rich instructional units as the basis for students' argument writing; ongoing pro-fessional development on key pedagogical practices to enable teachers to use these materials well; and a practical formative assessment tool to examine students' writing that provides regular feedback to teachers, students, and the larger improvement community. And, as the SRI evaluation demonstrated, NWP also assured that more instructional time was actually spent on argu-ment writing. Each of these parts coherently connected one to another.

Fifth and lastly, NWP surrounded and infused its efforts to improve the technical core of instruction with a design-development orientation. C3WP operated as a continuous learning community that included NWP leaders, the C3WP hub, local site leaders, teacher consultants, and prac-ticing teachers as front line improvers. These teachers in turn regularly sought feedback from their students as well.

In sum, the efforts of the NWP hub were akin to conducting a sym-phony—multiple parts, each needing to work well on its own and all of it needing to be orchestrated well together. Achieving high-quality instruc-tional improvement at scale like this entails complex problem-solving. It takes research-based content knowledge about the subject matter tar-geted for improvement. It takes technical expertise in the organization to conduct various forms of disciplined inquiry. And it takes a large dose of practical expertise about the contexts in which participants work—the history, politics, and prevailing norms and practices where improvements must succeed.

Correspondingly, instructional improvement demands a network hub with multiple strings to its bow. The hub takes lead responsibility to initiate and sustain the engagement of network participants. It needs sophisticated project management capabilities to organize the work and keep it moving forward productively. It needs technical capacity to support execution of key activities including measurement and data analytics, problems study and systems analyses, as well as the iterative prototyping and testing of changes. And all of this, in turn, depends on maintaining trusting social connections between the individuals and institutions that join together to solve a problem. NWP's ability to advance improvements rapidly, such as occurred in C3WP, resided in the people who knew and trusted each other. This trust was anchored in a foundation of shared experiences at the Invitational Institutes; in the relationships initiated there and maintained over time through the local site research-practice partnerships; and in the constant nurturing of the community that began with James Gray and continues today through the efforts of NWP's national leaders. In broadest terms, NWP represents a lived commitment, not to a specific program or product, but quite simply to getting better at getting better.

One might think about this chapter as a story of an important instructional improvement *project*, but it is actually quite a bit more. The NWP story challenges us to take a step back and think differently about efforts aimed at improving curriculum and instruction. Reflecting on NWP's work invites us into a much larger conversation about what an *infrastructure for instructional improvement* actually might look like and how such an infrastructure can accelerate progress on closing the aspirational chasm described in the introduction to this volume.[17] I will return to this topic in chapter 7 as part of a commentary about future efforts to advance improvements more broadly across our nation's schools.

6

——

Transforming a
School District

——

Menomonee Falls, Wisconsin

with Ash Vasudeva

THIS CHAPTER DESCRIBES the evolution of a continuous improvement culture in the School District of Menomonee Falls, Wisconsin. The district's improvement journey began during a pivotal superintendent transition in 2011 and continues through its most recent superintendent transition in 2018. The journey was catalyzed by a new superintendent and supportive board and actualized by teachers, administrators, and students who incorporated continuous improvement practices into their daily routines. Several critical factors facilitated this seven-year transformation, including consistent board and district leadership support, the infusion of external expertise coupled with a deep commitment to developing internal capabilities, coherent messaging, and sustained systemwide attention.

Chapter 3 describes how improvement efforts at Summit Public Schools began around addressing a specific problem—high rates of course incompletes—and how this disciplined approach deepened and spread over time across the organization. Chapter 4 offers a similar account about seeding and cultivating improvement capacity in the High Tech High's system of schools. Here too, organization capacity building initiated in a project with a small group of teachers and grew into a network-wide enterprise.

Developments in Menomonee Falls, in contrast, carved a different path. Unlike Summit and High Tech High, where organizational transformation goals came into focus as their improvement projects evolved, district and board leaders at Menomonee Falls set out to transform their district. Their aim was to become a continuously improving enterprise from the classroom to the central office, from operations to instruction. Menomonee's story offers a view of deliberate leadership action to transform a system.

THE MENOMONEE FALLS CONTEXT

In 2011, the School District of Menomonee Falls, Wisconsin (SDMF) began searching for a new leader to replace its retiring superintendent. The district serves approximately four thousand student who live in an older Milwaukee suburb. It faced a host of challenges more typically associated with urban school systems such as high suspension rates, low participation in Advanced Placement, and significant achievement gaps between race, ethnicity, and income groups.[1] The district's high school had recently failed to meet its performance goals under NCLB. As a result, parents were notified that the school was "in need of improvement" and subject to a series of state-mandated corrective actions.[2] This situation was not lost on the local press; *Milwaukee Magazine* had ranked SDMF as one of the highest-spending, most underperforming school districts in Wisconsin.[3]

SDMF board president Faith VanderHorst recalls that, at the time, "student results weren't getting better or worse. We were just treading water." She added, "Our hearts were in the right place but there was no movement, no focus. We needed improvement but didn't know how to do it."

The district's performance challenges were compounded by a politically fraught and contentious environment for educators. A controversial new state-mandated evaluation system, which was largely based on students' standardized test scores, was being rolled out. At a time when unrest over this new evaluation system was growing, teachers faced an even broader state-level threat to their professional standing that came from the governor's office. Then-governor Scott Walker was rallying support for—and ultimately helped to pass—Act 10 legislation, whose sweeping changes to the state's collective bargaining laws severely curtailed the power of public-sector unions.

Reflecting on the emotional toll being taken on educators at the time, one school administrator reported, "You could feel the fear. Teachers felt like they were in the crosshairs." Veteran English Language Arts teacher Liz Sparks recalled the tensions that permeated the district's 2011 superintendent transition: "We had no [job] security and a new superintendent . . . we were all very uneasy." Sparks added that teachers were "afraid of being told what to do, of being 'standardized,' and threatening their remaining creative freedom."

This troublesome mix—listless academic performance, a controversial evaluation system, and an attack emanating from the state capital—was the context in which Menomonee Falls was attempting to hire a new superintendent.

A CONTINUOUS IMPROVEMENT PERSPECTIVE IN LEADING A DISTRICT

The board interviewed several candidates and knew that had found the right person for the job in Patricia Greco. Faith VanderHorst, who was on school board's hiring team, recognized the distinctive perspective that Greco would bring to the work: "I used to work at GE and was familiar with Lean Six-Sigma. When Pat came in and presented to the board, we knew we wanted her." And the feeling was mutual. According to Greco: "I knew I wanted to work with a board where implementing a continuous improvement approach would be valued." Greco signed her contract just prior to the start of the 2011–2012 school year.

During the 1980s, Greco had served as the principal of the district's largest elementary school, so she came into the superintendency with considerable knowledge about the district.[4] She had started her career as a special education teacher and had earned multiple certifications and advanced degrees in education commensurate with her teaching and administrative responsibilities. However, her interest in and knowledge about continuous improvement was self-taught; little in her formal academic preparation or prior work experiences had prepared her to lead in these ways. As she noted, "Most district leaders spend the bulk of their professional preparation on the academic side of the house [mainly teaching and learning inside of classrooms]. All of that is important but as a superintendent, you are also placed in a position of having to run the largest organization in most communities. I knew I wanted to pursue continuous improvement in a school district, but nothing in my graduate training prepared me to do the job that I wanted to do, even with two master's degrees and a PhD. How could that be?"[5]

As Pat read her way into this field, she was intrigued by W. Edwards Deming's groundbreaking work on the social organization of work in complex systems and his appreciation of the human factors involved in promoting change.[6] She also resonated with Deming's notion that the people closest to the work have the best view of how the system actually operates and therefore have important insights about how to improve it. Greco also knew that during periods of change, effective leaders need to have compassion for the challenges confronting staff and recognized that everyone at every level needs support to learn how their efforts could contribute to better system outcomes.

Greco was especially impressed by the improvement heuristic embedded in the Pareto principle (20 percent of processes are often responsible for 80 percent of results).[7] Greco asked herself, "How can I help my leadership team prioritize the right 20 percent to maximize the impact of our efforts to improve?" This perspective stood in sharp contrast to many of the improvement efforts at the time, which were "silver-bullet" solutions. New educational initiatives would be introduced with great hype but often without the practical support necessary to make them work consistently. Invariably, each new initiative would have an inspiring name and a catchy acronym. They accumulated over time to create an alphabet soup of individual programs that were isolated from one another and often layered on top of each other, with few if any of these consciously designed to coordinate well with what already existed. Disappointment at the lack of progress predictably followed, and then districts often moved on to the next new idea. Clearly, as noted throughout this book, collecting more new programs was not the answer to improving an educational system.

Instead, Greco wanted to introduce a strategic, systematic focus for making coordinated improvements at the district, school, classroom, and student levels. She knew that just as tactics need to be coordinated by strategy, strategy needs to be built on a *system for improvement* for an entire enterprise to move forward: "As leaders, we need to talk about the processes of change and the specific norms and improvement behaviors required of everyone working in the district."

As she began her tenure as Menomonee Falls' superintendent, Greco set out to engage everyone—students, board members, community leaders, and everyone in between—because improvement needed to be a shared endeavor. This input would then prepare the ground for the broad system-wide actions to follow. To activate staff, the district would draw in external partners to support their development in fostering new way of thinking about improvement; and Greco and her leadership team would attend personally to the human side of change. Each of these moves proved key in initiating a continuous improvement culture in the district.

LAUNCHING A CULTURAL TRANSFORMATION

A key concern for Greco as she entered Menomonee Falls' challenging political and academic context was the need for people to feel supported as they attempted new and different ways of learning. "We are fundamentally changing the expectation of educators' work [and thus] we needed to make them feel safe during the transformation and celebrate their successes [early wins]," Greco said. "We would have to be patient, invest in developing all of our people, and especially cultivate our internal improvement leaders for the work ahead."

Engaging Teachers and Their Union

The board set the stage for a smooth transition for Greco in the district. It demonstrated its goodwill and support for district staff by working with

the teachers' union to sign a new contract. While Wisconsin's Act 10 legislation had eliminated the need for collective bargaining, engaging the
union in this way signaled positive board intent and created an opportunity for a strong positive relationship to emerge between the union and
the new superintendent. As a routine going forward, Greco would meet
monthly for coffee at 6:00 a.m. with the union president to sustain their
personal connection.

Like many new superintendents, Greco also engaged in early listening
tours with staff. In the first ninety days of her tenure, she met with all personnel in all divisions, including support staff. In these meetings, she regularly asked a handful of questions: "What are you most proud of?" "Where
do you experience barriers when trying to do your work?" and "What should
the board and community know about the daily work of this school system
that may get overlooked by the media?" She encouraged school district
staff to write down and share their thoughts with her about these questions.
Based on this feedback, she then crafted messages that signaled direction
for the work ahead as she engaged in subsequent conversations with service clubs and other community groups, and in her communications with
families. Greco's sought both to highlight where the system was working
well and talk frankly about the challenges to working better. The balance
reflected in these messages was a key first step in articulating the district's
journey toward principled organizational excellence.

These "Chats with Pat" were not a one-time event; Greco continued to
meet with staff at each school and across all divisions three times a year.
These conversations gave her an opportunity to continue to learn directly
about the ongoing challenges staff confronted and to personally connect
with her school district colleagues and answer their questions. In between
these face-to-face meetings, Greco also wrote bi-monthly staff newsletters
in which she could tackle "old legends and misinformation."

A key message that resonated throughout SDMF's improvement efforts
was "We're all in this together." Drawing from Deming, Greco argued that
leaders need "to systematically drive out fear" of the many unknowns
accompanying the district's shift toward a culture of continuous improvement.[8] Whereas staff might have worried about data as something to be

used *against them* (e.g., how they experienced the state's new teacher evaluation system), inside Menomonee Falls, data became a resource *for them*, because it would now be used to inform their improvement efforts. Greco explained, "As a leader, I have to make sure the organization is as committed to helping the adults be successful as it is committed to helping children learn and succeed. Kids can't thrive where adults are miserable."

A Central Office Leading by Example

To reassure staff that they were indeed "all in this together," one of SDMF's first moves was to introduce continuous improvement into the work of everyone at the central office. Continuous improvement was a new way of working for all of the educators and operations support staff, not just another new program imposed by a central office on schools and the work of teachers. The central office also needed to get better at its core work of servicing and supporting schools.

More specifically, if the central office was truly about "servicing and supporting schools," then opening channels for leaders to actually ask for and listen to the concerns of school staff became an early priority. This improvement began with surveying school building leaders about how well central office services functioned and then asking for suggestions about how central office might better support students, their families, and school staff. Central office staff also met with school leaders, and continued this on a quarterly basis, to get direct feedback and strategize ways to improve. And they made public what they learned from these inquiries and identified specific targets for improvement. These efforts signaled the importance of transparency about data—in this instance, the survey results—and how data could be used constructively as a basis for improvement.[9] Indeed, by opening themselves up to performance feedback from schools, central office leaders were making themselves vulnerable. This was another important signal about the district's transformation into a culture of improvement.

Greco's aim was to deepen the community's ability to learn what really mattered most for student, staff, and system improvement. Being user-centered and systems-focused was a key mindset change for central office staff that required them to develop new skill sets along the way.

Early Wins

Complementing initiatives on improving direct support to schools were efforts to improve core district operations. After the state of Wisconsin had cut public K–12 school spending by more than half a billion dollars in fiscal year 2012, departments at Menomonee Falls needed to tighten their belts.[10] Leading the way, the facilities department used an improvement process called Define, Measure, Analyze, Improve, Control (DMAIC)—a close cousin of the PDSA cycle—aiming to reduce energy costs.[11] Their efforts ultimately saved tens of thousands of dollars a year; and every dollar saved was a dollar available for classrooms.

The facilities department began the project by asking each member of the team to brainstorm possible change ideas. A simple but also broad-based initiative emerged out of this—everyone working in the district would try to take some small steps toward saving energy. "Turning off a light or computer in one classroom doesn't seem like a lot, but when you add it up over a period of time and across multiple classrooms, it makes a difference," said Richard Fechter, the district director of facilities. The team kept testing more change ideas: switching to another vendor for natural gas; turning down the heat or air-conditioning a little earlier each day; and cleaning buildings one at a time as a team in the evening, so they no longer had the lights on in every school well into the night.

The facilities improvement team evaluated each change idea by survey-ing teachers and other school staff for feedback and by continuously moni-toring monthly energy costs. Sometimes, the results pointed to problems that needed tweaking, such as when faculty and staff said the schedule for lowering the heat and air-conditioning was too early for comfort. "We had to find that sweet spot," said Fechter. The success of these efforts in terms of cost savings, coupled with the positive feedback and recognition that they received about this new way of working, convinced everyone in operations that improvement work was worth taking the time to learn how to do well. "I see them really leaning into the process now," said Fechter. Subsequently, operations teams extended improvement efforts to numerous additional functions, including reducing health-care costs without sacrificing the quality of services, improving building safety protocols, and reducing employee work-related injuries.

As an entrée into using the principles, tools, and methods for improvement at the school level, a team came together at North Middle School to tackle student suspension rates, which were among the worst in the region during the 2010–2011 school year. Working together, the principal, counselors, improvement coach, and teacher leaders undertook a root cause analysis to better understand the sources of the suspensions problem. They conducted empathy interviews where they directly reached out to students to find out, from their perspectives, when and why discipline problems were most likely to happen. Students shared vignettes about escalating episodes in classrooms and hallways. Middle school staff met with eighth-grade student leaders to examine school behavior data together and to ask the students why they thought misbehavior occurred. Subsequently, the team convened focus groups with broader groups of students to give them a stake in the improvement work and to get their ideas for possible changes to the classroom learning context and the school environment more generally.

Based on these many coordinated strands of inquiry, the team worked together to identify possible changes to try out quickly, and then continuously refined the most promising among them. They drew on research about restorative justice to inform their efforts, and school teams were trained in these practices. The district then used periodic surveys of students, staff, and parents to find out whether these improvement cycles were having a constructive impact on the the learning culture in the district's schools. The results were impressive. By sustaining these efforts over time, North Middle School reduced its suspension rate by 127 percent from 2010–2011 to 2017–2018.[12]

Drawing on External Expertise

Accompanying these initial projects was a major investment in developing the district's internal capacity as an improvement organization. Everyone—central office administrators, operations staff, teachers, principals, and students—was supported and encouraged to engage in continuous improvement efforts relevant to his or her particular work. This collective orientation served to protect continuous improvement from getting pigeonholed or marginalized as work for some people and not others. It also created opportunities to build shared understandings districtwide about the methods, tools and processes of continuous improvement. And it demonstrated the district's commitment to developing everyone as improvers. Each person in their respective role had capacity to "help make this place a bit better."

For technical expertise to help her advance this system transformation, Greco brought in the education division of the Studer Group. Studer had developed a track record in turning around underperforming hospitals.[13] The Studer team had shared a body of organizational change literature with hospital leaders and developed a set of tools and professional learning experiences to help translate ideas and language from industry into health care. Greco was impressed by the group's ability to explain systems theory, adult learning theory, and change theory in ways that made the complexity of these ideas accessible and "doable."[14]

Studer's Janet Pilcher and Robin Largue worked directly with Greco to help district leaders to adapt the improvement-based terminology from healthcare and industry into language that made more sense to educators. (Pilcher and Largue subsequently formed Studer Education.) "Educators resisted referring to students as customers or defining learning as a product," explained Melissa Matarazzo, a lead coach for Studer Education; so "The phrase 'employee training' became 'professional development'; 'customer focus' shifted to 'student- and stakeholder-focused'; and 'business results' re-emerged as 'student learning results.'"

An Early Commitment to Internal Leadership Development

Studer Education staff helped Greco bring a strong organizational development perspective to the work in Menomonee Falls. They maintained that the first two years of comprehensive change in any organization requires a focus on capacity- and capability-building. During this period, it is critical that districts take time to develop a cadre of skilled, respected central office and school leaders, who model and lay the groundwork for change. As Studer Education lead coach Matarazzo put it:

It's important for leaders to practice what they preach. In a system where you're managing this level of change and improvement, leaders have to be at the top of their game in terms of how they're managing employees, how they're delivering service, and how they're achieving outcomes. In a system like Menomonee Falls, you can't afford low-performing or low-skilled leaders. Leaders need to go first. I don't think we can have effective system transformation without leaders who are fully engaged and capable.

To support this in Menomonee Falls, Studer designed a Leadership Development Institute, a program of professional learning for select district staff who met on six occasions over the course of the academic year. The Institute's objective was to create a strong base of Menomonee Falls educators who would be adept in improvement principles, tools, and methods—a foundational step toward assuring that these new ways of improvement thinking and acting became hardwired across the system. In addition to ongoing support from Studer Education, the district also turned to local improvement partners such as the Waukesha County Technical College Center for Business Performance Solutions. Technical College faculty trained key district personnel in improvement tools used in business and manufacturing industries, and helped staff adapt these for use in education. All school and district leaders (including instructional coaches and curriculum leaders) were trained in decision analysis, situation appraisal, opportunity analysis, project management, and additional improvement tools applicable to their specific work.[15]

In tandem with this broad-based commitment to leadership learning, SDMF leaders also sought to identify "early adopters"—the most improvement-oriented educators within each of their schools and departments. They were searching for people whom they viewed as strong, flexible, and willing to take initiative. They reasoned that these early adopters might eventually lead the continuous improvement transformation districtwide, so finding them and supporting their development and promotion within the district was a priority. As central office leadership positions opened, they also recruited like-minded educators from other Wisconsin school districts. Over time, this two-pronged human resources strategy allowed Menomonee Falls to develop leadership teams with expertise in continuous improvement in each school and in the district's central office.

Investing in Developing All Teachers

Another important change initiated by Greco was to overhaul the role of the district's curriculum coaches. The coaches were talented people but in their previous positions they had been unable to break through the performance doldrums that characterized Menomonee when Greco took over. Greco reframed their roles as "improvement support specialists," and they were among the first to enroll in Studer's Education Leadership Development Institute. They were being groomed to play a key role in moving continuous improvement into classrooms. Working together, they designed an adult learning framework that viewed classroom improvement as a professional practice that matures over time through sustained interactions with a coach or a more expert colleague. Subsequently, these specialists would use the framework to support teachers as they reflected on the classroom improvement cycles they would be carrying out. This group also worked as a districtwide team to pen a Classroom Continuous Improvement Handbook. Eventually they became the district's internal instructors with responsibility for all-staff improvement training including the onboarding of all new employees to the district. Externally, they shared Menomonee's story at many national conferences, including the Carnegie Foundation's Summit on Improvement in Education, and they became a key conduit for bringing insights about good work that was going on elsewhere around the country back into the district.

The Director of Teaching and Learning, the improvement support specialists, and school principals began working together to build improvement skills and capabilities among all teachers and other certified staff members. Their goal was for every teacher to learn how to plan and carry out tests of change, gather and analyze data from the tests to assess impact, and use those results to inform the next round of testing (i.e., PDSA cycles).[16] Greco maintained that introducing PDSA cycles into classrooms could foster both the emergence of a common language for teachers as they introduced instructional changes and encourage use of classroom data to constantly question whether the changes being tried were resulting in improvement. The PDSA orientation aligned well with Greco's training and early experience as a Reading Recovery teacher, as this literacy program emphasizes the use of ongoing student data to inform strategic teaching.

Principals met with the improvement support specialists to identify the first cohort of teachers in their respective schools to receive the introductory training. They intentionally selected colleagues who worked well with others and seemed most likely to be early adopters of these new ways of working. Initial training for these teachers consisted of two half-day workshops with about six weeks between the sessions. The first workshop focused on aligning the "classroom as a system." Elementary teachers focused on reading or math and upper-grade teachers were asked to identify one content area and grade level or course for their focus during the training. They were asked to identify standards and curriculum expectations for that content, post them in a student-friendly language, and consider how they could align immediate learning goals with short-cycle formative measures. In other words, they were asked to determine what evidence they would use to self-assess whether their instructional moves were actually an improvement.

Teachers next learned how to identify the students' work behaviors that aligned with these instructional goals and how to structure the classroom as a learning system that supported the enactment of these behaviors. Then teacher and students began PDSA cycles to learn together. Each cycle typically ran for about two to three weeks and concluded with a conversation where students gave feedback to their teachers as to what was working and what needed adjustment to better support their learning. Six weeks later, during the second workshop, teachers met with the improvement support specialists to analyze evidence from these improvement cycles.

Eventually, every teacher in the district moved through these same professional development workshops in waves of fifty to seventy-five teachers at a time, organized by content area and grade level. Once this systemwide basic training was accomplished, the improvement support specialists shifted their efforts to onboarding new staff. They also continued to coach individual teachers as needed, and met with grade-level teams during early-release Wednesdays. All of this was in place by the end of Greco's first two years as superintendent.

Multiple adult learning goals were simultaneously being advanced through these experiences. Participating teachers committed to trying to improve something in their classrooms that they personally cared about. At the same time, through teachers' individual PDSA cycles, their work with the improvement support specialists, and structured opportunities for social learning within school teams and across the district, they were deepening their capabilities to design and carry out improvement cycles. And along the way, district and school leaders were identifying specific instructional processes, such as the feedback and evaluation conversation between a teacher and student, where better protocols could be identified and tested more broadly across the system.

Liz Sparks, who has taught English Language Arts in Menomonee Falls since 1997 and is currently the district's curriculum co-chair, recalled her introduction to PDSAs: "It was hard to understand at first. I knew initiatives came and went, so I was skeptical." What helped Sparks and her colleagues embrace continuous improvement was the flexibility they had to apply these processes and principles to issues in their own classrooms. For example, the English department decided to focus its initial improvement efforts on students' use of grammar, which faculty felt would be a more manageable improvement task than writing. It took two years of improvement cycles, but during the second year, Sparks and her colleagues began to see growth on students' grammar scores. This encouraged them to tackle more ambitious instructional improvement objectives in the third year, including writing, and they eventually began to see improvements here as well. Liz's commitment to improvement was by then fully cemented: "It had become a natural and normal practice—and we saw the benefits clearly." Likewise, instructional coach Shelly Wolf, a member of the sixth-grade improvement team, reported that while it took some time, "Teachers now see the value [of continuous improvement], and that it's really making a difference."

Critical to supporting these developments was how district leaders nurtured and sustained a safe culture for teachers to take risks. As Sparks noted, "Pat [Greco] just remained calm and steady. She stuck with the same message and remained kind and encouraging. We went deeper with the process each year, but she maintained a constancy about the message." Through this process, staff came to understand professional learning as an extended process that needs to be supported by mentors or coaches, and they became more proficient in continuous improvement through sustained practice. Greco explained, "In their first six months, we expect new employees to be trained in continuous improvement, followed by a period of just trying it out in their classrooms with the support of coaches. By year three, we expect everyone's full engagement with continuous improvement as a regular part of their work." (Interestingly, Greco's three-year time frame coincides with the time it took Liz Sparks to fully embrace this discipline.)

Menomonee Falls was deeply committed to developing all of its people as improvers and expanding their roles as they demonstrated mastery. For example, Suzy Thomas, the district's Director of Quality and Analytics, came into this role after having been a high school mathematics teacher, an instructional coach, and an associate principal. This depth of experience helped her integrate the data and analytics that discipline the work of improvement with the practical needs and constraints of educators working in schools and classrooms.

Lastly, Greco was also realistic recognizing that, even after ample opportunities to learn and engage, some staff would be unable to get on board and needed to be counseled out. She explained, "When we've made it clear what the expectation is—we've provided training and coaching, we've provided regular check-ins with feedback, and we've made continuous improvement visible through model classrooms within the district—and still an employee is resisting change, then we know that the person is not a good organizational fit. Our leadership responsibility then is to manage them out of the system." Fortunately this proved a rare problem to address.

As she reflected on all of this, Greco commented, "I don't think you can improve a system if the leaders can't lead and sustain the shift into improvement. The steps needed to align a system [around continuous improvement] are not technically hard to understand. Rather, it is shifting the collective mindset of people and their daily work behaviors that are the hardest leadership demands necessary to sustain over time."

Engaging the Students Too

Continuous improvement processes did not stop with teachers and other district staff. Among the benefits Sparks and her colleagues saw was how their continuous improvement efforts created opportunities for students to become active agents in improving their own learning. A visitor to Menomonee Falls is now likely to see students engaged in conversations not only about *what* they're learning, but also about *how* they learn. Students have become comfortable talking about their learning goals, progress, and challenges, and they also have strategies for bringing their teachers and parents into these conversations. Menomonee Falls students routinely use a Plus Delta protocol to provide feedback to their teachers on techniques and lessons that help them to understand new academic content (Plus), and also suggest changes where existing practices are not helping them to learn (Delta).[17]

With guidance from teachers, even children in the primary grades are able to set their own weekly academic goals, articulate the learning strategies that work best for them, and track their progress in data binders. Having students monitor their own progress "makes a difference in student ownership," according to Liz Sparks. "They track their results and when it moves it has personal significance. They see value in it."

Embedded here is an important improvement lesson salient to both adults and students. The immediacy of feedback—having timely evidence directly related to the actual work people are doing—is a powerful resource for getting better at getting better. Ambitious teaching and learning is challenging and often involves considerable struggles for both teachers and students. Real-time feedback, in the form of "Yes, there is evidence that we are actually progressing" or "Maybe we need to try something different," both informs improvement and also motivates improvers to keep moving forward. In contrast, end-of-year test score reports typically provide little of either. To inform and sustain ongoing improvement efforts, other forms of evidence, which are more immediate and closer to the actual day-to-day work, are needed. This kind of evidence was generated through the PDSA cycles conducted by teachers in Menomonee Falls.

Interestingly, the same focus on immediate evidence coming out of the day-to-day classroom work was also central to the instructional improvement efforts of the National Writing Project (chapter 5). There, the development of the Using Sources Tool played this role.

Embracing a Common Language Anchored in Standard Work Routines

Menomonee Falls' orientation was that organizational performance largely depends on how well people work together rather than on the solitary efforts of individuals acting alone. Once the initial broad-based staff development was completed and momentum had begun to build as a result of successful improvement cycles, the next move was to focus on improving core work processes to be more productive for both adults and students. Greco explained, "We have employees that have worked in our organizations for decades. [In the past] we gave them a job responsibility, a set of keys, a job title, and then left them largely on their own. We needed to improve our core work processes so that people of good intent can do good work." These core work processes were classified as "always actions" and "check-ins."

Always actions seek to integrate evidence-based practices into the standard routines used by staff throughout the district; for example, one always action for teachers is to have classrooms with well-defined rules and procedures that are clearly communicated to students.[18] Commonality across classrooms in these basic routines creates a more coherent environment for students, and where behavioral expectations are clear, problems become less frequent. An always action for school leaders in providing formative feedback to teachers is to identify both strengths observed and areas targeted for improvement. Collectively these actions function as a set of shared practices that anchor the district's improvement efforts around teaching and leading. Over time, the district's leadership team, working with Studer, formalized these practices as districtwide standards of service excellence and incorporated them into employee performance standards.

The *check-in* processes are simple, intentionally designed conversation protocols between supervisors and employees. Greco and Jo-Ann Sternke, superintendent of the Pewaukee (Wisconsin) School District, modeled one of these processes at the Carnegie Foundation's 2017 Summit on Improvement on Education. Greco began with some personal conversation, asking Sternke about her family and weekend plans. Then she segued into questions about what specific improvement aim she was targeting, what was working [change ideas being tried and evidence examined] and what was not, and then asked questions about how could she help. Greco concluded the check-in by asking, "Who on your team has really made a difference that I might say thank you to?"

The core of the check-in is essentially a soft form of an internal accountability protocol for improvement. The flow of the conversation aligns closely with the core improvement questions set out in *Learning to Improve*: *What specifically are you trying to accomplish? What change might be introduced and why?* and *How will you know if the change is actually an improvement?*[19] An important marker of the transformation into a continuous improvement enterprise occurs when these questions become normative in an organization's day-to-day conversations and actions. Embedding the improvement questions in a simple and fast routine like this check-in becomes a powerful driver for organizational change. It reinforces individuals' identity as members in an improvement community that works in common ways.

The last question as part of the check-in processes—"Who should I thank?"—also reinforces agency by creating regular opportunities to recognize and celebrate staff efforts as improvers of the work. Carlene Hansen, a fourth-grade teacher in Menomonee Falls, reflected, "I think it's one of the strongest pieces in our continuous improvement system. It makes each of us feel valued that our work and our thoughts are being acknowledged."

LEADING UP: ENGAGING THE BOARD AND THE COMMUNITY IN THE WORK OF IMPROVEMENT

The transformation of a whole school district into a culture of continuous improvement is not a quick fix. Even in a relatively small district like Menomonee Falls, it took sustained leadership attention spanning seven years. While the board was strongly supportive of the basic approach, Greco nonetheless still experienced some pressure to rapidly translate it into academic outcomes for students. She needed to convince board members to stay the course and "let the discipline of improvement kick in, rather than focusing on the emotion of the metrics."

Importantly, continuous improvement also needed to become central to the board's work if it was ever to be truly institutionalized in the district. Greco sought out opportunities for board members to engage as learners alongside school and district staff. She extended invitations to board members; for example, to professional development sessions offered by external partners such as the Studer Group and Waukesha College. The board chair even accompanied her to a Carnegie Foundation expert convening. Creating opportunities for board members to be participants in the process both deepened their understanding about district improvement and helped to sustain their support over the seven years it took.

Public communications was another important element in SDMF's strategy. "If you think about the culture piece in working with a board, it is important to celebrate quick wins with them as well," Greco noted. The district's leadership team presentations to the board and more general news releases were designed to publicly celebrate each improvement success, big and small, and to personally acknowledge the people who made these successes happen. District leaders kept the board's attention focused on how personnel were embracing continuous improvement across the school system. For example at one board meeting, Greco thanked her high school improvement team for being innovators and taking risks to implement and adapt a new reader workshop practice across their classes. In another case, school custodians were acknowledged after they took it upon themselves to dig cars out of the parking lot after a heavy snowfall hit during a high school basketball game. Such accounts helped the community "experience the difference between an improvement project and an improving organization."

To ensure that the board saw how continuous improvement acted as the thread that wove together diverse efforts, the district's leadership team developed a (macro) scorecard to establish baseline measures for their efforts to enhance their functioning as a service organization to schools. Likewise, every department in the school system had its own specific (micro) scorecard to monitor progress aligned to targeted improvement priorities. Jeff Nenning, the district's director of technology and assessment, focused on the technical design of the scorecards and validity of the underlying data, allowing leaders to leverage systems change by homing in on specific high-leverage challenges that cut across multiple schools. Once these priorities were identified, improvement teams were formed to address them. These teams were charged with using improvement processes (beginning with root cause analysis, for example) to make progress on these problems. Every forty-five days, they presented to the board on the status of their work and received feedback on next steps. These "forty-five-day reports" became regular agenda items at board meetings. That meant that conversations about continuous improvement were now ingrained in how Menomonee's board of education did its work as well.

Greco knew that broad-based community support would have to be built to sustain improvement. So SDMF's achievements were widely aired in both the local press and at national conferences: "If you can get a feature article in, say, the state school board journal, that can be a big help. Being invited to offer a session at a national meeting like the Carnegie Summit on Improvement in Education—board members take notice. You've got to find these wins wherever you can. This is all part of managing up in the interim until those lagging measures really start moving."

INSTITUTIONALIZING CONTINUOUS IMPROVEMENT IN POLICY

On April 23, 2014, the Menomonee Falls School District passed a seminal resolution. It recognized how continuous improvement had been embraced all across the district, and it formally committed the district to transform and sustain a model of continuous quality improvement into the future. The resolution called on district leaders to develop "systemic, systematic, and sustainable continuous improvement efforts to ensure that all district students receive the highest possible standard of learning that prepares each graduate for a successful workplace or post-high school learning experience." For its part, the board pledged its support for the mission by providing "staff with access to appropriate quality training and development that ensures staff will sustain and enhance their skills and competencies."[20]

According to Faith VanderHorst, the board resolution has been instrumental to institutionalizing continuous improvement: "While three or four of us have been on the board through [Greco's] tenure, the whole board will eventually turn over. If they [a future board] want to do away with continuous improvement, they will have to actively go ahead and repeal it. [By putting continuous improvement] in policy we made sure that the financial commitment to doing this work keeps going."

In addition to affirming continuous improvement in policy, the board also subsequently made a key personnel commitment to ensure that the district stays the course on continuous improvement. On March 5, 2018, it chose Corey Golla to become the new superintendent upon Greco's retirement. Golla had been serving as the director of curriculum and learning since 2016, and prior to that he had been the principal of Menomonee Falls High School.[21] Over the years, he had become Greco's right hand in supporting and guiding the transformation efforts across the district. The board's decision helped ensure that the district's culture of continuous improvement would continue under new leadership. As Golla noted, "The culture of improvement is so deeply embedded throughout the organization [that we're not going to] heave a big sigh of relief and then just go back to the way it was. This is really the way we do our work now."[22]

RESULTS

Between 2011 and 2018, the School District of Menomonee Falls transformed from one that was focused on NCLB compliance and "chasing programs that looked like improvements" to one that systemically embraces continuous improvement across its instructional, administrative, and operations systems. And the Menomonee Falls way of doing things was returning impressive results. SDMF now performs in the top 13 percent of Wisconsin school districts, based on the Wisconsin Department of Public Instruction's State Report Card. In addition to the operations improvements and reduction in student suspensions it had achieved, Menomonee Falls High School earned the Silver Award from the College Board, and was one of seventeen schools recognized with the Pacesetter Award from the Wisconsin Advanced Placement Advisory Council (WAPAC) for substantially improving AP performance and participation.[23]

In addition to being named one of the best places to work by the *Milwaukee Journal Sentinel* for three years in a row, the Menomonee Falls district has become a learning laboratory for other improvement-minded school systems. It now offers a two-day workshop twice a year to an audience of 250-plus aspiring improvers who come from around the country to learn more about continuous improvement the Menomonee Falls way.[24]

CONCLUDING COMMENTS

Building a culture of continuous improvement in Menomonee Falls involved multiple complementary strategies that developed over time. In *launching* continuous improvement, district leaders focused on creating a supportive environments for change. By actively assuaging staff fears that improvement data would be used against them, district leaders created new ground for the use of evidence as a key resource in their shared efforts at getting better. This was just one part of a larger strategy to create safe spaces for staff to engage in new ways of thinking and acting around change. By encouraging exploration and experimentation with continuous improvement processes simultaneously at all levels of the system, improvers also avoided programmatic isolation where the efforts might be taken up by some people but not others. All were key steps in laying the foundation for school system transformation.

Sustaining and deepening efforts drew on complementary strategies for developing individuals' improvement capabilities and vitalizing new ways for people to work together. Supported by external partners such as Studer Education and Waukesha Community College, the district leveraged a diverse array of technical expertise to build its internal capacity for improvement. Evidence-based practices became the system's backbone for improvement, as reflected in core work processes of always actions and check-ins. These practices, in turn, created a common language for doing improvement work and provided the basis for more productive organizational collaboration.

Finally, *institutionalizing* continuous improvement required ongoing board engagement to secure a long-term commitment to this problem-solving approach. Proactively engaging board members in learning opportunities (such as working with Studer or participating in Carnegie Foundation events), centering board conversations around improvement updates on forty-five-day cycles, and frequently communicating successes and setbacks helped to invite board members to be full partners in the work and fellow travelers in the district's improvement journey. This is truly a story of weaving together over time a complex set of elements into a rich and distinctive tapestry of organizational change.

7

Charting Paths Forward

IN *LEARNING TO IMPROVE*, my coauthors and I articulated a set of principles to guide the work of improvement, and we introduced some tools and processes that have proved helpful in conducting such work. This companion volume presents dynamic portraits of how six organizations put these ideas and methods to use and made real progress on important educational problems. The aim in sharing their stories is to provide a window into the day-to-day activities of those involved in the work and into the ideas that guided their actions. Our narratives about them explore the *what, how,* and *why* that shaped each organization's journey toward quality in continuous improvement. While each story is distinct, I hope that the collection offers deep, practical insights to guide readers' own efforts to "do improvement."

This closing chapter draws together observations from the six stories with additional reflections from other efforts to support and teach improvement that we have been directly involved in at the Carnegie Foundation for the Advancement of Teaching. In a few places, I also reach back to some of my earlier experiences with school improvement in Chicago. Synthesizing across these multiple sources, the chapter offers an account of key actions in organizing continuous improvement in systems of schools and how institutional leaders act to advance this agenda. Along the way, I also address a select set of larger questions now salient in educational research and practice. As more and more educators have begun to explore the principles of improvement science and initiate improvement networks, these questions and the discourse around them represent an important context for current and future efforts to help schools and the systems in which they operate get better at getting better.

The stories recounted in this book about the Fresno and Menomonee Falls school districts and the High Tech High and Summit charter management organizations offer an encouraging account about the kinds of improvements that individual school systems (both traditional school districts and charter management organizations) can achieve through building their internal capacities for continuous improvement. Complementing these developments are our accounts of the distinctive value added contributed by two intermediary improvement organizations—New Visions for Public Schools and the National Writing Project. Many of the aims that the public now hold for public education and the problems that educators now need to solve are too big and multi-faceted for individual schools to tackle by going it alone. The accomplishments of these specialized intermediaries working with networks of schools and districts offer guidance for how educators might join with one another to advance better progress on the larger and more complex problems they share.

Weaving these developments together offers a perspective as to what a more robust infrastructure for educational improvement in America might look like. I suggest below that two core investments are needed: (1) developing capacities inside every school system to engage in high-quality continuous improvement on smaller and more localized problems; and (2) combining this with sustained support for intermediary improvement organizations that assemble and maintain the diverse forms of expertise and relationships of trust needed to support collective action on solving the larger and more complex problems shared among our nation's schools. This combination, I believe, is essential in addressing the question with which this book began: *How can we close the growing aspirational chasm to provide quality education for every child?*

ORGANIZING FOR IMPROVEMENT

As noted throughout this book, continuous improvement is not the next "new program" to be embraced by school systems alongside other initiatives such as introducing a new curriculum, a technology, or some additional new services. All of these may be thought of as the *what* of schooling— ideas about what schools should do or the resources they should use. In contrast, continuous improvement focuses on *how* schools can both make current programs work better and take best advantage of whatever new initiatives they might introduce to secure quality outcomes reliably in their local contexts. In the course of their efforts, each of the organizations profiled in this volume recognized that disciplined, systematic improvement action was truly a new and different way of working. This moved them to make key investments in developing their capacities not only to solve an immediate problem, but more generally to reframe how they get better going forward.

Building Staff Capabilities

Disciplined improvement efforts of the type recounted here are different from standard operating processes found in most educational organizations. Consequently, developing and supporting educators to become improvers represents the first core investment. At Menomonee Falls, for example, broad-based staff development in improvement was at the heart of the district's efforts from the very beginning. Similar investments grew over time at both Summit and High Tech High. In all three instances, embracing continuous improvement took on the character of an aspiration for organizational transformation. Rather than being the new professional development theme for the year, continuous improvement became a commitment to a sustained, ongoing practice. All three organizations invested in developing current school and central office staff to "do" improvement, and new staff were trained in these practices when they came on board. Being oriented toward improvement became a key consideration in recruiting personnel as well.

The organizations also invested in developing capabilities for coaching improvement at various levels, ranging from school-based teacher leaders, to instructional coaches, to principals, to senior school system personnel. Early on, each relied on external organizations to develop these coaching capabilities; their longer-term goal was to deepen the bench internally. These actions, along with others described below, recognized continuous improvement as a formal and permanent element in the organization of school systems.

Investing in the Capacities of an Improvement Hub

Supporting improvement also makes new system-level demands on educational organizations, and responding to these demands represents a second core investment. As noted in the introduction, although each of the organizations profiled used somewhat different names for the resources and structures they put in place, for simplicity, all of these developments are described in these pages as the work of an *improvement hub*.

In general, the hubs took on a broad range of responsibilities. These included:

- **Vitalizing an improvement network** that brings participants together to accomplish some valued aim. Hubs encourage and support network members' sense of agency as they identify and begin to address an improvement problem. They orchestrate a set of processes that deepens participants' understandings about the problem and that lead to the network's initial working theory of improvement, typically visualized in a driver diagram. When impediments arise, the hub also helps to clear the path so that the work can progress and participants' agency is reaffirmed.

- **Developing an analytic capacity** both to inform efforts at understanding problems, and to generate and organize timely data in response to the question: *How will we know whether the changes we are introducing are actually an improvement?* Recognizing the difference between accountability data and measures for informing improvement was an "Aha!" moment experienced by several of the organizations described in this volume. Because this difference posed new challenges to each of them, and because a similar phenomenon has surfaced in Carnegie's direct work with other groups as well, I attend to this topic at greater length below.

- **Integrating research knowledge, consolidating learning, and spreading improvement.** Designing and sustaining an environment for social learning about educational problem-solving represents the third core responsibility of an improvement hub. Toward this end, the hub ensures that relevant research evidence and access to research expertise infuses the network's ongoing efforts. The hub systematically surfaces the best of what is being learned by different network teams and quickly shares promising developments across the network. Others are encouraged to build on these efforts, adapt them as necessary, then test them in their own context, and share their learning. The hub also guides the processes of periodic revisions to the driver diagram based on what is being learned over time. The orchestration of this social learning is what transforms seemingly random individual efforts at trying to get better into systemic improvements that encompass a network.

I discuss each of these responsibilities and their import in more detail below.

Vitalizing an Improvement Network

Improvement depends on people working together. The processes of iteratively testing change ideas, refining them, and then spreading and adapting the most efficacious ones involves numerous social interactions carried out across a network and over time. The hub of an improvement network is constantly tending to these relationships. It celebrates successes, identifies the relevant learning from failures, intervenes whenever the wheels start to grind, and supports everyone to keep on keeping on.

Developing evidence of efficacy, as most notably seen in the stories of New Visions and the National Writing Project, is an important resource for spreading the tools and practices developed by a network. But improvements do not typically spread just because such evidence exists. They are also heavily dependent on the expertise and social connectivity of the educators who have developed these new tools and practices and on their evangelizing spirit to spread them. Quite simply, network participants are more likely to try something new if comes to them through someone they know, trust, and respect, and who invites them to join in.

Undergirding this activity are the core elements that form networked improvement communities. These include a commitment to achieving a measurable aim for a shared problem; a common language for attacking the problem and advancing progress toward the aim; attention to relevant research that bears on their concern; sharing results of the multiple improvement cycles occurring across the community (both those that failed and those that succeeded); and a norm of building on the best of what others have learned in order to make progress toward their aim at scale. These elements form the core operations of a scientific community focused on the improvement of practice. The work of the hub, then, is to develop these inquiry practices, advance these scientific norms, and vitalize the social interactions of network participants to initiate and sustain all of this.

Improvement efforts also require project management capabilities, and the bigger the network and the more complex the problem it takes on, the more extensive these capabilities need to be. For example, the stories of the National Writing Project, New Visions, and Fresno Unified School District, recount how numerous face-to-face meetings had to be scheduled and organized. Much of the work of improvement has a spontaneous character and this can create extra demands on project management staff, so agility is greatly valued. In between face-to-face events, the hub needs to support the ongoing testing of changes. As the network grows in size and especially if it is geographically dispersed, virtual asynchronous information sharing and communications systems are also needed.

Even though these operational issues surface only occasionally in the chapters, this work was constantly occurring in the background within each organization. Typically, it is only when these processes break down that they become the focus of attention. But for every breakdown that might occur, there may be hundreds of processes that simply happen as they need to. While these supports may appear behind the scenes, they are not less important.

Developing an Analytic Capacity

Early on in Carnegie Foundation's efforts to support other organizations' improvement activities, we routinely query about extant data relevant to their targeted problem. We often are shown beautiful, color-coded displays of end-of-year assessment results and other annual statistics such as attendance, disciplinary infractions, dropout rates, and similar types of data. These data are regularly reported back to each school. Where interim assessments exist, such as common end-of-unit tasks or universal progress-monitoring results, these too are routinely provided. Typically, results are broken down by racial/ethnic groups and other subgroups of special interest, including English learners and special education students. We have found that the staff in assessment and accountability offices are generally eager to hear about other ways that they might present this information to make it more user-friendly and useful to schools.

In an improvement context, such data often form the outcome measures attached to an aim statement.[1] However, they are typically of limited value in understanding the root causes of problems. To inform improvement efforts, data that is more proximal to the ongoing work of educators and their students is needed. In the New Visions case, for example, much of that hub's early activity involved assembling diverse sources of extant data to better understand the issues needing address. Unfortunately, the data were not easily accessible nor organized in ways that were informative for the work at hand. One of the early and unexpected tasks that they had to take on involved sorting through the district's forty thousand different high school course codes. The hub had to discern how various course titles aligned with state graduation requirements, because this was one of the places where students were falling through the cracks—students were taking courses and accumulating credits, but in some instances not the right ones. To make progress, the information on individual students' course-taking had to be assembled, cleaned, and standardized. Initial analyses of these data generated key insights about the problems that had to be addressed. They also afforded some guidance as New Visions staff began to engage with school-level leaders in designing new data visualization tools and what eventually emerged as the Strategic Data Check-in Process.

Similarly, reaching back to my earlier work in Chicago, when a concern about student mobility surfaced, my colleagues and I at the Consortium on Chicago School Research had to wade into the school district's administrative history file, where each students' current home address and school placement sat at the top of a historically organized stack of records about that student. Out of these historical administrative records, we created a set of indicators that allowed us to track students' movement across schools as they unfolded over time.[2] These new measures were based on information that was already in hand, but again quite different from that typically found in end-of-year school reports on annual student mobility rates.[3] Here too, in an effort to better understand a problem, we were led to different ways of working with these data than was standard practice.

Taken together, these examples illustrate an important point. Beyond just organizing and integrating separate sources of data, improvement work also involves displaying these data in new ways that make students' pathways to success over time visible. This is at the heart of investigating pipeline problems, as discussed in the Fresno story (chapter 1), and such problems occur frequently in education. As a general rule, concerns about leaky pipelines will often lead to examining patterns of student progress over time to identify places where the system is breaking down. More specifically, informing improvement typically depends on visualizations that help us see the *flows of individual students over time through the system*. The stock and flow visualization developed at New Visions, and other more detailed data tools that they subsequently developed, provide an illustration of this.

Another example draws again on work that I collaborated on in Chicago, which focused on students dropping out of high school. Rather than attending solely to annual high school dropout rates, year by year and school by school, researchers at the Consortium on Chicago School Research began to examine more fine-grained information on individual students' experiences in the transition from middle school to high school and during their first semester in ninth grade.[4] They learned that the new measures they had constructed strongly predicted the likelihood of students dropping out of high school, typically a year or more later. It was out of these longitudinal analyses of individual student-level data that the first on-track indicator was born. These data about students on track for progressing through high school subsequently informed dramatic improvement in graduation rates in Chicago, rates that had been stubbornly resistant to change for decades.[5]

These examples are just two among many different ways of analyzing and representing data that might usefully inform efforts at solving some problem. It is important to note that responsive analyses of the type mentioned above were tailored around the particular concern that each of these improvement teams was investigating. They are not cookbook recipes for how to look at data for improvement. Thoughtful data investigations require a deep understanding of the work that educators and their students are engaged in, identification of critical questions embedded in their work, and the creative invention of specific analyses and visualizations that may illuminate possible system breakdowns. Doing this well requires the collaboration of practitioners and analytic staff to discern what kind of data, organized in what kind of way, might be most insightful. In the course of these investigations, some analyses will prove to be dead-ends, but others may yield genuine insights. You need to keep looking and wondering and inquiring, "What is really going on here?"

Moving on from understanding the problem to testing changes related to specific primary and secondary drivers, improvers often will need to develop new practical measures to inform these efforts. The Using Sources Tool (UST) developed by the National Writing Project's hub is a good example. It was designed to generate evidence as instruction was occurring that could inform its improvement.[6] Development of this tool proved to be a key change idea in NWP's overall working theory of improvement. Recall that one of NWP's key drivers was intensive teacher professional development aimed at improved writing instruction. Individual students' essays and accompanying UST reports provided evidence for conversations during teachers' professional development sessions about possible changes that they might introduce into their writing instruction. The UST also generated timely feedback data as to whether subsequent instructional changes were actually moving students' writing in a better direction. This same evidence also functioned as a leading indicator for NWP's ultimate aim: improved scores on end-of-year writing assessments.

Drilling down to the most detailed level of improvement activity, the testing of change ideas often requires development of new measures as well. In the early stages, when a change idea is being tried out in one or a small number of contexts, qualitative narrative accounts from the participants may often suffice to inform modifications and elaborations on a change idea and may create sufficient warrant for further trials in additional sites. As a change idea spreads to more contexts, however, new issues will almost inevitably arise. Adaptations will occur and variability in effects will manifest. The change may work well in some places but less so in others. As these adaptations occur; a few may turn out to be a further improvement, but others may be maladaptations. To see this natural variability as it is unfolding and to learn from it, improvers need targeted process-level measures. Fortunately, the qualitative accounts generated early on often provide useful insights to guide the development of process-level measures to inform learning about change ideas as they spread out to more contexts.

To illustrate this, I return to an example introduced in *Learning to Improve*. As part of the Community College Math Pathways initiative, a change package was created to address a secondary driver called Starting Strong.[7] The improvement team had noticed that many students in remedial math classes were often disconnecting from instruction early on and just giving up. The team wondered how to break this pattern. One specific change they considered involved an intervention to encourage students toward a growth mindset during the first week of class. An initial try-out in one classroom proved promising—the students engaged in the activity and found it interesting, and the teacher could envision doing this regularly with her students. So the intervention passed a very basic feasibility test. Another small-scale test followed, and positive effects were noticed in students' subsequent classwork. As this change was introduced in a larger number of classrooms, a set of process-level questions arose. First, was the intervention actually occurring in the first week, and for which students and classrooms? Answering this was relatively easy, since the intervention occurred online and "click data" was readily available. Second, was the intervention being used as originally designed or had individual faculty made some adaptations, and if so, what adaptations and why? This required a short implementation report from each faculty member. And third, were the predicted outcomes from the introduction of this process reliably occurring?[8] To answer this, data was collected through students' responses to a handful of survey questions about their mindsets toward learning math.[9]

While the practical measures used to inform improvement may look simple, developing good ones is often a complex task that makes manifold demands on an improvement hub. It often requires bringing together an array of expertise—academic, technical, and professional—to invent, fine-tune, and validate the utility of these measures. The measures need to align with the best research evidence relevant to the specific problem. They must maintain clinical validity in the context of educators' work, signaling where improvement attention should focus. They must be practical—usable within the highly constrained time demands of day-to-day life in schools. Additionally, they have to have good statistical properties relative to their use within a working theory of improvement. In this last regard, the measure needs to be sensitive in detecting meaningful changes that have occurred. For example, in the NWP context, if the professional development initiatives were working, improved results should be seen in data from the Using Sources Tool. Likewise, the data generated by this practical measure should function as leading indicators, predicting the next stage targeted for improvement. Stronger UST reports in the NWP network, for example, should indicate that better end-of-the-year student writing outcomes are forthcoming.

In summing up, then, the analytic activities supporting improvement are numerous and varied, starting with investigating the problem to solve, developing evidence to inform early-stage testing of change ideas, and—as promising practices move out to larger-scale implementation—addressing questions about adaptations and variability in effects that will typically loom large. The driver diagram represents a web of hypothesized connections and the system of measures eventually developed are akin to its "vital signs." Is the system of changes working as expected? More specifically, are positive results emerging stage by stage, as predicted in the driver diagram, from change ideas to secondary and primary drivers and ultimately to the specified improvement effort's aims?[10] This is the analytic work of informing improvement.

Integrating Research Knowledge, Consolidating Learning, and Spreading Improvements

Part of the hub's role in cultivating practitioners' agency for change involves encouraging ideas to bubble up and be tested through individual initiative. If a network stops there, however, networkwide improvements remain unlikely. As noted in the introduction, this is what typically happens in the sharing activities that characterize many professional learning communities.[11] In contrast, orchestrating a more disciplined form of connectivity is essential for broader-based improvements to occur. Consequently, designing and maintaining a deliberately structured social learning environment represents another key responsibility of a network hub.

Part of this hub function, as noted earlier, is ensuring that the best research-based knowledge and access to relevant expertise infuses the work of the network, as the National Writing Project hub did when they drew on Joseph Harris's scholarship about crafting written arguments. Similarly, at several junctures, Summit Public Schools improvers turned to outside research expertise for guidance about the learning outcomes they sought. Likewise, New Visions engaged numerous research partners over the years. In Fresno, Jorge Aguilar directly played this conduit role when the district moved to address its undermatching problem.

The hub is also responsible for building processes for consolidating the learning that is developing in local sites, spreading this consolidated learning, and then encouraging further adaptive testing. The phrase *flare and focus* captures much of the dynamic of these social learning processes. As a hub cultivates broad agency for change across a network, it encourages diverse ideas to surface and changes to be attempted. Inevitably, some will be very promising and others not. This is the *flaring* aspect of the work—getting people involved in doing PDSA cycles, sharing what happened, and hearing from others.

Building off of this flaring activity is ongoing attention to identifying where the most promising changes are emerging, ensuring that they are visible to others, and structuring conversations that encourage network participants to consider how they might build on them. This is the *focusing* aspect as hub leaders aims to guide collective work in productive directions.

This focusing activity entails a constant surveillance of the landscape of improvement as closely related efforts may initiate independently in different places. Connecting these sites so that each can draw on the learning of the other is another important part of maintaining forward momentum. And since improvement work often takes place within the formal organization of school systems, the hub also has responsibility for ensuring that appropriate data flows and communication routines are in place up and down in the organization. This is a core practice in implementation science and central to vital improvement networks.[12]

Ideally some of these social interactions will be face-to face, but it is likely that many will need to be carried through virtual, web-based connectivity as well. Designing these online learning environments poses some distinctive demands as networked learning neither perfectly matches the vertically organized reporting structures found in bureaucracies, nor does it align exactly with the web-based friends' networks that are increasingly popular. This simply reflects the fact that a networked improvement community is a deliberately designed set of social arrangements organized to accomplish a shared specific aim. Consequently, virtual platforms facilitating this social learning need to be designed with these distinctive characteristics in mind.

Finally, a bit of clarification about the term *hub* itself. I have been describing a set of central functions that need to be developed and maintained to support a vital, networked improvement community, so it is appropriate to describe these functions as the formal responsibilities of a hub of a distributed network. But it is also important to clarify what is *not* intended by this term. The dynamics of social learning in an improvement network involve a dense web of multidirectional social connections. This means that the hub of a networked improvement community differs from the more familiar hub-and-spokes arrangements typically operated by professional services providers. In these organizations, improvement learning takes place within the hub, and then the hub pushes out new implementation guidance to separate sites (i.e., the individual spokes). Little cross-site learning may occur in such arrangements. In contrast, in a networked improvement community, learning is occurring simultaneously in separate sites, across the sites, and within the hub itself. It is the hub's responsibility to facilitate this social learning and to continuously focus it so that coherent efforts toward problem-solving are sustained.

In this regard, a better image for an improvement community is that of a *learning web*.[13] A key role of the hub is to cultivate a web of interconnectivity, support good communications, and maintain healthy social relationships. Like the managerial tasks described earlier, these processes largely take place behind the scenes, but they are far from trivial, and the hub must be resourced and have the necessary authority to execute on them. That said, it is important to underscore once more that a hub's use of its resources and authority is to advance improvement learning across the whole network. The hub is not the sole or the most important learner. Rather, it seeks to breathe life into the dynamic underlying the expression "all teach, all learn."

The Grain Size of the Problem and the Capacity Required of a Hub

The stories depicted in these pages offer two different routes to developing a hub. Both Summit and High Tech High started small with regard to their improvement aims and projects. As the work progressed, they realized the power of working in these new ways and recognized that new resources would be needed to support the changes. So they invested in developing their hub improvement capacity. New Visions and the National Writing Project, in contrast, already had sophisticated hubs when their work began. New Visions was especially impressive in terms of its analytic capability, and the National Writing Project was equally sophisticated in operating as a networked social learning organization. These base capacities gave both organizations the ability to take on complex and large-scale problems right from the start.

There is good news here, but also an important caveat. Engaging in disciplined improvement is possible across a range of educational settings, although the pace, complexity, and scope of the initial activity clearly depends on an organization's starting capacities. In the case of the attack on chronic absenteeism at High Tech High or the incompletes problem at Summit Public Schools, the problems initially addressed were modest in grain size, and the hub capacities needed when these efforts began were also modest. Where the presenting problem is larger in scope and the intended reach greater, good-sized hubs with the character of specialized professional teams are needed. This was true at both New Visions and the National Writing Project, given the ambitiousness of their aims and the intrinsic complexity of their work.

A further example is the Carnegie Foundation's effort to attack the high failure rates in developmental math courses in community colleges. Over a period of eight years, the Foundation supported a specialized internal staff focused on this problem. This staff in turn was guided by a distinguished group of external consultants, including math faculty from community colleges and academic researchers whose expertise aligned to the primary drivers in our working theory of improvement. This hub was responsible for initiating and supporting improvement activities spanning new curriculum development, faculty development efforts, initiatives to better support students' persistence to completion, responses to particular concerns around the literacy and language needs of English learners, and the development and use of formative assessments and other data feedback mechanisms to support continuous improvement. Moreover, the hub was doing all of this while also nurturing the emergence of a faculty improvement community that was in the process of expanding to over one hundred participating colleges. Clearly, it takes a multiperson hub with diverse sources of expertise to orchestrate a major instructional improvement effort of this sort.

To the point, as the grain size of problems becomes large, as in the efforts just illustrated, individual schools, and many districts and some states, will typically lack the capacity to make rapid progress going it alone. (This is especially true in rural contexts, where school districts tend to be small and geographically dispersed.) These are places where capitalizing on the power of working in improvement networks that span across schools, districts, and states is paramount. So, investing in targeted educational problem-solving networks is an essential companion to developing improvement capacities in individual schools and districts. Together, they form the constitutive elements in a national infrastructure for educational improvement.

I have focused up to this point on how the six improvement stories illuminate the task of building capacity for continuous improvement. In the next section, I look at the same stories, but now from the perspective of organizational leaders and how their efforts advanced these changes.

THE ROLE OF EXECUTIVE LEADERSHIP IN TRANSFORMING EDUCATIONAL ORGANIZATIONS TOWARD CONTINUOUS IMPROVEMENT

As noted in the introduction, the narratives shared in this book can be read as stories about organizational leaders bringing continuous improvement into their respective contexts.[14] Over the last several years, I have had numerous opportunities to talk with each of the individuals who lead these organizations and spend time with them on their home turf. Many of our conversations focused on specific challenges they confronted as they tried to move their organizations in this new direction. Below I share some observations about their work and the distinctive demands of leading improvement.

I begin by simply positing that executive leadership for improvement is essential.[15] One person alone cannot transform an organization—indeed, if nothing else, this book has shown that improvement entails cooperative collaborative efforts among many different individuals. But in conjunction with this observation, I also assert that the orchestrated systems of action that need to be initiated and sustained over time for changes to culminate in genuine improvement will not happen without the directive guidance of the organization's executive leader. Ample evidence of this can be found in all six stories recounted here.

Three big ideas join together in forming the topic for this section: leaders, transformation, and continuous improvement. I have already written extensively about the third element—the multiple and varied ways of engaging continuous improvement in educational organizations. The discussion below focuses on the first two concepts: the notion of transformation and the roles of executive leaders in bringing it about. By the term *executive leader*, I mean anyone with role authority to substantially direct the work of the entire organization. This includes superintendents of school districts and the chief executives in charter management organizations. Although executive leaders of the intermediate organizations New Visions and the National Writing Project also sought to advance transformative agendas, they did not command the same formal authority within their partnering organizations; therefore, in this discussion, I draw mostly on the leadership efforts in Fresno, Summit, High Tech High, and Menomonee Falls. For simplicity, I refer to these various individuals as *leaders* and the work they do as *leadership*.

Transformations

The idea of transformation connotes a journey. It implies that there is something that an organization is trying to move away from and something it is trying to move toward. Multiple transformations were at work in the stories told herein.

At the most general level, each account describes a departure from the long-standing practice of implementing new "silver bullet" programs toward advancing sustained, systematic and disciplined efforts to solve specific problems. Mike Hanson and Jorge Aguilar at Fresno, for example, tackled multiple leaks in the pipeline from high school entry to college enrollment that contributed to their undermatching problem. Pat Greco at Menomonee Falls and Diane Tavenner at Summit Public Schools both challenged their systems to become learning organizations, relentlessly seeking to get better at what they do.

This transformation meant revisiting accepted norms around autonomy in educators' practice and blending it with network mechanisms where educators work together to make progress on shared problems. This was highly visible in the efforts of Ben Daley and others at High Tech High and in the rapid progress that came about through the leadership efforts of the NWP hub. Both instances were based in a fundamental shift in educators' identity from an artisanal perspective—where every situation is unique and everyone must figure out what to do on their own—to membership in a professional scientific community focused on shared problem-solving. Embedded here is a highly significant shift from *I* to *we*—a shift notable in how people talked about their improvement efforts from, for example, "I am interested in ...." to "We are working on ...". As I describe below, leaders cultivated this shift both through how they allocated resources and through their day-to-day walk and talk.

In some ways, the biggest and most obvious transformation common to all six organizations was around the types and uses of data. As already noted above, improvement teams learned to look at extant data in new ways; they also invented new practical measures and processes for using data, such as the Strategic Data Check-Ins pioneered at New Visions and the CCILC tool for college advising in Fresno. This shift—from seeing data as driving accountabilities to seeing it as informing improvement efforts—was huge. For educators, it represented a normative change from "data being *about* us" to hold us accountable to "data being *for* us" to help us improve what we do. In this informing improvement spirit, leaders such as Mark Dunetz at New Visions and Jorge Aguilar at Fresno aimed to get the right data into educators' hands at the right time so that they could improve outcomes for students. This was not business as usual.

Executive Leadership in Thought and Action

The leaders in these six stories also used their role authority to advance a transformative agenda in their organizations. For each, leading improvement played out in distinctive aspects of what they said and what they did daily and in the habits of mind that guided them along the way.

Uses of Formal Authority

The most obvious way that these leaders moved change was through the strategic use of the authority vested in their roles. Discretionary resources are always scarce; how leaders allocated them both directly fueled improvement efforts and simultaneously sent strong signals throughout their organizations about their priorities. Several specific moves stand out with regard to advancing an improvement agenda.

First and foremost, as mentioned earlier, these leaders committed to building human resource capabilities for continuous improvement up and down their organizations. They invested broadly in the professional development of staff around improvement principles, methods, and tools. Moreover, they saw this not as one-time training but rather as a form of professional capability development that needed ongoing support. This was central to the improvement stories at Menomonee Falls, High Tech High, and Summit Public Schools. Likewise, leaders in all six organizations took special notice of those demonstrating expertise and passion for the new ways of working. These early adopters became prime candidates for further development and promotion through the system over time.

Second, leaders formally recognized improvement as a regular part of the work that people do and allocated staff time for it to happen. Summit Public Schools, for example, created a new analytics unit and funded full-time positions to support their internal improvement networks. In Menomonee Falls, improvement responsibilities were integrated into revised roles for instructional coaches. At High Tech High, roles for faculty in the new graduate school of education were designed so that they could be directly involved in improvement efforts in HTH schools. Leaders also allocated professional development days to sustain teacher engagement in improvement projects, and appropriated extant meeting times within schools as contexts for reviewing progress on improvement cycles and refining the next of round of changes. In short, these leaders confronted head-on the reality that improvement takes staff time.

Third, leaders invested in developing an analytic infrastructure to inform improvement, as detailed extensively throughout this book. Of the six organizations, New Visions was perhaps the only one with such capacity prior to the improvement effort. The shift from data for account-ability to data for improvement meant bringing diverse forms of expertise normally not resident in schools into close collaborative work with local educators. Leaders reached out for technical support on topics such as information systems, practical measurement, statistics and data analysis, and collaborative technology platforms. They also accessed research-based content-knowledge expertise and melded this with the professional prac-tice acumen held by teachers, principals, and other school system staff. This collective expertise made it possible to develop useable evidence directly tied to targeted improvements, and to devise good routines for productive conversation among educators around such evidence.

Finally, accompanying these strategic investments was the powerful sig-naling of the leaders' personal presence in this work. They remained proxi-mate to the improvement activity from the outset and then throughout. Responding to the failures that inevitably occur in improvement cycles represents a critical leadership test. This is another key area where a sig-nificant normative transformation is required in supporting educators through the risk-taking that is characteristic of innovation and deep learn-ing about practice. The leaders in these stories were deliberate about build-ing a culture of trust so that learning together could occur, getting better together would occur, and students would be better served. The leaders marked out contexts for their improvement conversations as safe places for discussion about both successes and challenges.

The Walk and Talk of Daily Work

The last observation highlights how in many small ways leaders vital-ized the transformation to continuous improvement through the conduct of their day-to-day work. The improvement orientation resonates in the micro-scripts that they relied on in their everyday conversations. Pat Gre-co's interactions with staff were guided by the core improvement questions: "What is the specific problem you are trying to solve? What changes might you try?" "Why these particular changes?" and, "How will you know if the changes are an improvement?" We heard the same inquiring force in the reflections of Diane Tavenner at Summit and Ben Daley at High Tech High. These leaders coupled a supportive orientation with an empirical bent and a healthy dose of skepticism. As they mulled over possible change ideas with colleagues, they probed: "Why do we think this problem is happening?" "What is the research evidence?" "What does our data suggest about changes we might consider?"

And then there are the stories that leaders tell in more public contexts about the progress made and the challenges still ahead. Pat Greco regularly celebrated what individual staff were accomplishing while also publicly recognizing that "we still have miles to go." And the most powerful among these stories were then retold by others; for example, when the janitors in Menomonee Falls saw a problem—snowbound cars at an evening basketball game—and then just took it upon themselves to shovel them out. That story reflects the sense of individual agency to act that staff developed, accompanying the embrace of continuous improvement throughout the district. As organizational strategists Chip and Dan Heath describe it, such accounts signal powerful moments well beyond the immediacy of the particular action. Their recounting becomes part of a larger mythmaking about organizational identify and transformation.[16]

Through the combination of their day-to-day actions and the strategic allocation of resources, executive leaders in these six organizations demonstrated over and over again what they valued. Although their actions vary in specific details, their nurturing of a followership for improvement followed a general pattern. These leaders recruited an initial small group of improvement innovators; they actively supported the professional development of an enlarging set of early adopters; and they continued to encourage expanding participation of others over time until a majority of staff were engaged in some fashion. Eventually, these new ways of working became sufficiently widespread that they took on normative force: "This is how we do our work here now."

The Think and Feel of Guiding Improvement

Leaders do a lot of the work of improvement in the conversations that they have with themselves. The idea of a strategic plan has become so commonplace in education that not a lot of attention is paid to what creating such a plan actually entails. Basically, to develop and operationalize a strategic plan, leaders need to know explicitly both what they aim to achieve and be able to detail at the outset the key steps necessary to get there. They are expected to have ready answers to questions such as "What is your end game?" and "What is your three-to-five-year plan to accomplish it?" But the lived reality rarely feels like that.

In contrast to strategic planning, improvement efforts tend to have an evolutionary character. Leaders may hold a strong sense of improvement aspirations as they begin, but exactly how to achieve them remains unclear. Considerable ambiguity characterizes the process. Leaders may have a good sense about first steps, but the overall sequence of steps toward a measurable aim largely evolves through a process of learning by doing.

Consequently, improvement leaders have to live with uncertainty, remain open to what is being learned as people join together in problem-solving, and be able to entertain plausible alternative ideas about future action, even when those ideas may sometimes appear to be in tension with one another. For example, staff at Summit Public Schools, who were deeply committed to advancing social justice, had specifically targeted improved outcomes for English learners and were investigating a host of change ideas aimed at this particular group. As their initial work proceeded, however, evidence began to accumulate that they were facing a different and more general problem to solve, which wasn't peculiar to English learners. Navigating between the emerging evidence and the deeply held personal commitments of Summit teachers created a leadership challenge. Another example can be seen in the work of Carnegie's Community College Math Pathways. Individual hub members had a strong personal commitment to improving students' growth mindsets about mathematics. The end-of-first-year data, however, indicated that students' belonging uncertainty was the strongest individual predictor of failure to complete the course of study. Growth mindset clearly remained important and had internal champions; in contrast, no one "owned" belonging uncertainty. This created a leadership challenge: "How can I focus more staff attention on the latter while not undermining the good work and personal commitments individuals held to pursuing the former?"

These examples illustrate some of the life of the mind of an improvement leader. These individuals live on the boundary between belief about the importance of the aims they seek to achieve and skepticism about their current courses of action: "Do we really have this right?" "What else might be going on here that is important, but we are not really thinking about?" This capacity to simultaneously engage belief and doubt is central to leading improvement work.

In a closely related vein, the evolutionary aspect of improvement work requires leaders to maintain a sense of humility as to what they really know and can do. This is a departure from the aura of invincibility that some leaders try to project, and it coincides with a recognition about improvement knowledge more generally: the guidance afforded by a working theory of improvement is provisional and always subject to change as new learnings surface. This is captured in the mantra accompanying these working theories: "Definitely incomplete and possibly wrong."

This view about the nature of improvement efforts shapes how leaders approach their work with others as well. The advice to "fail fast" and "learn from failure" has become commonplace, but no one really likes to fail, regardless of the speed. Improvements can involve considerable struggle and demand grit and persistence, and improvement learning often does not come easily. Sorting through alternative routes to problem-solving can be uncomfortable, and especially so for educators who are new to working in improvement teams. Leaders need to be aware that these emotions will arise in others and have compassion for the psychological stresses that change creates. This was part of why Pat Greco, for example, remained so attentive to calling out improvement wins, both large and small, and thanking all involved. Such celebrations acknowledge the difficulty of the work and the importance of keeping staff upbeat by recognizing the progress made, and also reinforce their efforts to keep moving forward. In various ways, leaders across all six sites were attentive to the psychodynamic struggles that staff were confronting.

In sum, the work of leading organizational transformation toward continuous improvement challenges the ways leaders *think*. It requires a metaphorical shift from thinking about themselves as "decision makers" to "leaders as learners" and to "leaders as builders of learning organizations." Those who took on these roles in the six sites discussed in these pages were avid individual learners, and they sought to nurture improvement learning in everyone they touched. Equally important to this way of thinking is what might be called a *feeling* mindset—a spirit of improvement mindfulness—to have patience with everything unresolved in the work and to learn to love the questions themselves as leaders challenge themselves to think harder and more deeply.

A Key Contextual Resource: Stable Governance to Stay the Course

In closing this discussion of executive leadership, I note one key resource that supported each leader as they advanced improvements in their respective contexts. Improvement efforts typically involve long-term commitments. Five of the six organizations whose stories are told in this book stayed the course for seven or more years. While NWP efforts were accomplished in half that time, that was possible only because for decades prior, they had been building and sustaining an instructional improvement infrastructure that allowed them to accelerate their pace on a new problem.

The two charter management organizations, High Tech High and Summit, benefited from a governance structure where stable and supportive relations existed between school founders and their governing boards. In the two school district stories, superintendents Mike Hanson of Fresno and Pat Greco of Menomonee Falls skillfully and deliberately engaged their boards and unions in supporting and advocating for the work. In a different vein, leadership at New Visions closely attended to its relationship with the larger New York City Board of Education, because significant funding flowed from NYCDOE and shifts in district policy could either advance or impede New Visions' efforts.

In these various ways, stable and sustained external governance arrangements made it possible for these improvement leaders to advance the work.

While *continuous improvement* means different things to different people, an important part of the definition is continuously staying the course, remaining focused on solving targeted problems, and buffering the activity from the entropy in the external environment that can easily derail meaningful change. The frequent churn in governance arrangements that many school districts experience can easily undermine the very best of improvement skills and intentions.

ADDRESSING SOME QUESTIONS
EMERGING IN THE FIELD

Before closing, I want to address a few issues that have emerged since the publication of *Learning to Improve*. As interest about improvement science and improvement networks has expanded rapidly, questions have arisen about how improvement science carried out in a network relates to some other "big ideas" current in the field. Sometimes these discussions are framed in oppositional terms, as if such ideas must be mutually exclusive. I take up three of these topics below, seeking to articulate ways that these various ideas can be construed as productive interconnections and complementarities rather than conflicts.

Isn't This Just Another Model?

The education landscape is rich in models—program models, evaluation models, change theory models, professional development models, accountability models, school turnaround models, and on and on. Is improvement science just another model? The stories shared in this volume show that it is not.

We see across all six accounts a diverse set of methods being used to help improvers better understand the problems they want to solve and to generate timely data about the changes being attempted, the markers of progress, and the drivers still needing more attention. Empathy interviews and participant surveys were common as all six organizations sought to better understand their problems. These enabled improvers to bring the voices and insights of those engaged in the work—educators and students—into the conversations about the actual problems needing to be addressed. Other tools, such as journey maps of individual students' progress through schooling, and the statistical analogues to these tools, such as the stock and flow analyses conducted at New Visions, help illuminate where students might be falling off track.[17] As teams zero in on specific processes to improve, mapping how these processes currently worked can offer additional insights to inform action.

In addition, as improvers shifted from trying to understand a problem better to identifying plausible change ideas, several teams conducted positive deviant studies in their own locale, seeking to identify plausible change hypotheses that they might test. Improvement teams also scanned for extant research knowledge relevant to the problem at hand. Although residing in the background of these stories and not explicitly detailed in the chapters, several of the improvement teams adapted for this purpose a form of the ninety-day cycle process frequently used in improvement science.[18]

The testing of change ideas also took multiple forms. At High Tech High, improvers compared baseline performance to results after a change was introduced. The National Writing Project used a traditional randomized control group design to assess average effects, combining this with an ongoing examination of changes in students' written products as professional development efforts proceeded. The iterative testing of select processes using PDSA cycles appear in the narratives for both Summit and High Tech High.

In short, there is no single best way to organize and conduct an improvement project. How a team proceeds depends on the nature of the specific problem at hand; what is most important to learn at any given point in the process; and what is feasible in terms of time, resource demands, and local practicalities. In this regard, improvement science is pragmatic and opportunistic. An incredible toolbox exists to assist this work, and when carefully chosen, different tools can be valuable resources in the service of some greater good. But it is important to remember that all of these instruments are just tools to help us achieve an improvement aim. They are a means to an end, not the aims sought.

More generally, although the term *model for improvement* does appear in the literature, my coauthors and I explicitly did not use it in *Learning to Improve*, nor do I use it here.[19] Within the pluralist context of education practice, research, and policy, calling anything "the model" is hubris. But there is actually a deeper epistemological reason to avoid the term. The concept of a model suggests a list of parts, a set of directions as to how they go together, and a standard sequence to follow. Think of the detailed instructions and parts of plastic airplane model kits or the step-by-step recipes in cookbooks. In essence, a model says "This is how you do it"; more generally, it implies that there is one right way to achieve the aim. In contrast, the six stories told here illustrate how improvement efforts can proceed in varied ways. Participants used different tools to investigate their system and understand their problem. They used different forms of evidence to test changes, and these ran the gamut from anecdotal notes, to qualitative study, to surveys, to process run charts, to observational studies and experimental designs. Likewise, leaders drew on extant social connections and nurtured participants' agency in deeply localized ways.

Tying all of this together, then, is not the concept of a "model," but rather a different way of thinking and acting in the interest of advancing improvement. In this sense, the six improvement principles outlined in the introduction are best thought about as a *paradigm*—a coherent, integrated world view that guides how organizations can get better at getting better. One way to test the functionality of this paradigm is to ask, "Do any of these principles seem non-essential—meaning we don't really need to think about or act in accord with one or more of them?" One might ask, for example,

- Is it important to focus on understanding the actual problems to be solved versus just jumping on some common or currently popular solution?
- Is it critical to understand the perspectives of those involved in the work when we endeavor to improve on it?
- Is it necessary to consider variation in performance—among students and across contexts—and how our educational systems

operate to create and sustain these different, and typically inequitable, outcomes?

- As teams actually try to improve, is it possible to envision meaningful changes occurring reliably at scale without data to inform these efforts?
- Are better outcomes achievable absent basic processes of disciplined inquiry where change ideas are tested against evidence?
- As the problems to address grow larger and more complex in scope, could progress be better advanced without exploiting the power of networks to accelerate improvement learning?

I suggest that the stories presented in this volume offer testimony about the power of these six improvement principles in action and how they work together as a set to guide a different form of human activity around practical problem solving.

Don't We Want Disruptive Innovations Instead?

Current reform thinking often calls for *disruptive innovation*. This concept draws off of the pathbreaking work of Clayton Christensen and colleagues, who coined the term in the early 1990s.[20] In Christensen's formal definition, disruptive innovation is a process by which a product or service initially takes root in some simple applications at the bottom of a market. The innovation typically enters by being less expensive and more accessible. Then relentlessly, through processes of continuous improvement, it moves upmarket and eventually displaces established competitors. The term has become virtually synonymous with Silicon Valley, where disruptive change is the technologists' creed.

As this concept has gained salience, it has taken on a broader set of meanings well beyond Christensen's detailed theory. It has now become part of an organizing rhetoric calling for fundamental political changes in how our society operates. Calls to "disrupt the system" have grown as frustrations mount about continued inequities in educational outcomes and access to educational opportunities. Through this lens, the small incremental changes that are the seeming focus of continuous improvement are questioned as running contrary to advancing more fundamental societal aspirations. Interestingly, this broader political use of the term does share with Christensen's theory a common aspiration—securing better social services and products that are more equitably available.

In truth, there is no "instead" as posed in the question that opens this section. Embedded in Christensen's theory is actually an answer. Disruptive innovations and continuous improvement are not opposing forces. They are complementary and can and should work hand in hand.

In the context of education, many early advocates for charter schools saw them as potential engines of innovation in public education. This volume has highlighted the work of two of the most innovative charter management organizations operating in the United States. Both High Tech High and Summit Public Schools are challenging the traditional ways of organizing teaching and learning, in ways that closely aligned with a vision of disrupting the conventional routines of schooling as detailed by Christensen and colleagues in their 2008 book, *Disrupting Class*.[21] But importantly, educators at both Summit and High Tech High learned early on that moving from their ambitious aspirations to reliable performance meant building their internal capacities to get better, bit by bit. In short, continuous improvement is the mechanism that can transform a disruptive idea into something that actually works. It is not an either/or choice.

How Does Continuous Improvement Address Inequities in Educational Outcomes?

As interest in continuous improvement has grown, challenges have also bubbled up about how this activity relates to advancing a social justice agenda. More specifically, how does continuous improvement help educators make real progress on the inequities that seem impervious to changes in our context?

Inequity is a powerful concept, but it holds different meanings for different people. This book has focused on how specific processes of schooling contribute to persistent inequitable outcomes. These unsatisfactory and disparate outcomes are predictable, often based on a child's family background or the community in which that child lives. In America's highly stratified society, these disparities tend to follow strongly along lines associated with race and poverty. But for the purposes of this book inequity means more generally any place where our educational institutions systematically foreclose opportunities to some children, and where predictable failures occur year after year after year.

In absolute terms, of course, there is no assured relationship between continuous improvement and eliminating disparities in educational outcomes. Improvement science consists of a diverse set of tools and methods that can be pointed at all kinds of problems. For example, Menomonee Falls used improvement methods to save money on utility bills and other operational costs. These accomplishments were highly meaningful in that every dollar saved in operations was a dollar preserved for direct work with students in schools and classrooms, but there was no explicit equity target in these efforts. In contrast, Menomonee's effort to reduce middle school suspensions, where previous outcomes had aligned along traditional race and class lines, had an explicit equity focus.

Noting this, I want to emphasize that the improvement paradigm does afford distinct resources for attacking long-standing disparities in educational outcomes if efforts are directed toward such aims. Three of these resources have been illustrated throughout the six narratives in this volume.

First Resource: Targeting Disparities in Outcomes as the Problem to Solve

The first improvement principle guides improvers to be specific about the problems they want to solve. Given persistent inequities in educational outcomes, this principle directs us to place the sources creating these disparities in outcomes at the center of the work. Strong examples include the efforts to close the attainment gap between English learners at Summit Public Schools and the efforts to open up better postsecondary opportunities for low-income students and students of color in Fresno Unified School District and High Tech High. In each setting, a specific disparity in outcomes was targeted, and the improvement team then iterated continuously until better results were achieved.

Now this guidance may seem relatively obvious, but the work described in this volume is actually quite different from the way most school districts go about trying to improve outcomes. As noted throughout, districts have tended to reach for the new idea and to add new programs, hoping that something might eventually make a difference with regard to longstanding inequities. The traditional logic directs the primary focus of educational leaders to implementing the new thing, ideally fast and wide. In contrast, leaders in this book's six stories placed primacy on developing a better understanding of the actual sources sustaining the inequities they sought to address, then specifically testing a set of changes, based on what they were learning, in efforts to reduce it. Attacking the disparity remained in the first position.

Second Resource: Bring New Voices into the Process

The first improvement principle also guides improvers to be user-centered. It directs them to bring in the voices of the people who are most directly impacted by the work—be they students, parents, faculty and staff, leaders, or custodians—into the conversation. It exhorts them to sense the dynamics of disparities through others' eyes, emotions, and understandings. Attending to students' voices, for example, played a central in understanding the causes of the high rate of student suspensions in Menomonee Falls and offered insight for where productive changes might focus. Similarly, the voices of parents, students, and guidance counselors played a key role in crafting change ideas in Fresno's attack on its undermatching problem. And principals' voices were crucial in the iterative design processes that created broadly useable data tools at New Visions.

In her book about reading the Declaration of Independence as a defense of equality, Danielle Allen tells us that respect for other voices is the most basic expression of the concept of equality.[22] In a related vein, when I was new to Chicago, I attended a number of board of education meetings to learn more about the school system. Back then, any member of the public had the right to request two minutes to speak at a designated time during the proceedings. More often than not, however, most of the board members either left the meeting or were otherwise occupied during this time (this would be the 1990s version of looking down to check their cell phones). So everyone in Chicago had the right to speak—but not necessarily to be heard.

Attacking inequities in outcomes means truly listening. Listening doesn't necessarily mean endorsing every idea voiced, but it does mean acknowledging others and taking their experiences into account. Listening is at the core of improvement because it opens possibilities to reach beyond what improvers think they already know. It can challenge deficit thinking and the accepted ways that victims are blamed for a dysfunction that is actually in the education system. Listening can also attune improvers to previously ignored resources for change—like the change ideas that often arise from users—but only if those users are invited into the conversation about improvement. Their voices are a resource waiting to be summoned up and built on.

Third Resource: Scrutinize Variation in Performance

The improvement principles also direct our attention to the mechanisms that produce observed disparities in outcomes. The guidance to study the sources of this variation pushes us to think about the actual causes at work in the predictable failures that we see time and again in our educational systems. As noted in the introductory chapter, educational research, policy, and practice typically focuses on "averages." Yet, as earlier discussions have emphasized, an average obscures information about which kinds of students a program or intervention works for (and not), and in what contexts. In attacking disparities, however the central question really is: Who benefits and who gets left behind? When a program fails, where does it fail? In what kinds of schools and for what kinds of students?

Importantly, improvement science brings the core question about the sources of inequitable outcomes from the periphery to the center of the inquiry. If you want to solve a problem, you have to really see it. Improvers in the six stories made these sources of disparities in student outcomes visible and then attacked them one by one.

INVESTING IN A NATIONAL IMPROVEMENT INFRASTRUCTURE TO ACCELERATE EDUCATIONAL IMPROVEMENTS

As argued in *Learning to Improve*, the general research on networks shows that they can function as an extraordinarily powerful arrangement for developing and quickly spreading new knowledge. Consequently, forming improvement networks offers real potential for closing the growing aspirations gap mentioned at the start of this book. It will take, however, both organization and commitment to accomplish this. More equitable outcomes are not an easy by-product of some invisible economic hand, the magic of a silver bullet program, a democratized internet, or any other "fixes" that sound almost effortless. They demand a fieldwide investment in the design, support, and maintenance of an improvement infrastructure for public education.

Unfortunately, this kind of improvement-centered activity is not yet central to either private philanthropy or the work of major federal agencies such as the Institute of Education Sciences and the National Science Foundation. From time to time, these public institutions do announce new funding priorities linked to pressing educational concerns. They support research programs on a vast array of topics such as the Developing Child, Adolescent Literacy and Comprehension, Educational Achievement of English Language Learners, Rural Education, and STEM education. Research centers are created, grant competitions initiated, and fleets of studies follow. Meetings are held for researchers and others, papers are published, and effect sizes reported. The products of these inquiries are judged against standards set out in the corresponding academic fields and are reinforced through peer-reviewed journals. Positive findings eventually find their way into various evidence-based websites. The developments within this class of educational research activity over the last several decades, both in terms of the conceptual frameworks deployed and the sophistication of the methods used, is quite impressive. The best of these efforts, as judged against the standards associated with the line of work, is truly extraordinary. Adopting an improvement perspective, however, leads to a different set of questions to ask about the work: Have any of these research centers actually changed student outcomes reliably, at scale, anywhere? Is there evidence that many more students are now, for example, reaching kindergarten ready to learn or exiting middle schools better prepared for a rigorous high school experience? Are fewer English learners languishing year after year in school systems? Positive answers to these kinds of questions are harder to find within this applied research paradigm, as this paradigm is not specifically designed to answer them.

As noted in the introduction, the evidence-based paradigm places primacy on developing strong causal inferences that a program *can* work. In contrast, learning *how to make it work* in diverse hands, operating in different environments, and with varied groups of adults and students simply is not its goal. Advancing these outcomes demands different forms of inquiry and a distinct and different form of social organization.

The efforts of improvement networks such as New Visions and the National Writing Project exemplify this new direction. Both attacked pressing educational problems. Both demonstrated efficacy at considerable scale, and both continued to scrutinize evidence so that they could continue to learn how to adapt their practices so as to embed them effectively in even more places. Their stories highlight what improvement organizations, designed and supported as a form of a standing improvement infrastructure, can accomplish with regard to educational problem solving. Both organizations deliberately built and advanced their capabilities within specific targeted problem domains. Because of these standing organizational capacities, they were able to act nimbly to:

- Identify root causes for a specific set of on-the-ground improvement problems
- Assemble an improvement network with all of the practical, research, and content expertise needed to attack their focal problem
- Develop a working theory of improvement and launch tests of change
- Achieve measurable improvements (at some considerable scale) against aims of clear social value

Their stories offer remarkable demonstrations of how America's educational systems can progress more rapidly. I would submit that few, if any, individual districts, new educational organizations, or individual research projects, operating in more traditional ways, could accomplish anything like this on the time frame and scale that they have.

Now imagine a future where a *standing national infrastructure* like this existed. It would consist of multiple robust improvement organizations operating across diverse subject matters, educational problems, and the different contexts of schooling. Standing supportive relationships would exist between these organizations and teachers, schools, and districts. And because of their own internal improvement capacity building, the districts themselves would now have expanded capabilities to bring into these partnerships. In this future, disciplined inquiries are engaged in by practitioners and researchers collaborating together within problem-solving networks that aim to advance targeted student outcomes reliably at scale. Such an improvement infrastructure would enable the practical learning necessary to finally move the US education system from the rhetoric of every child succeeding to actually approaching that goal, whether it be getting all students to be productive readers by grade 3; all new teachers succeeding in their work; all students graduating from high school college and career ready; or all students progressing regularly through postsecondary education to attain their desired degrees. Today, absent this kind of large-scale practical improvement infrastructure, we muddle along without any realistic mechanism for achieving these societally valued aims.

So, embedded within the improvement stories shared here are also important lessons for philanthropists and policy leaders about the value of sustained investments in developing and supporting an improvement infrastructure of the type exemplified by the National Writing Project and New Visions. Just as these organizations were able to quickly appropriate the intellectual and social resources cultivated through past efforts to fuel initiatives on new targeted problems, so too could a national improvement infrastructure, consisting of an array of such organizations, both take on high-leverage problems of current concerns and function in a standing capacity to attack other issues as they emerge in the future.

Importantly, we need to recognize that the kinds of applied research and professional capacities that are now resident in organizations like New Visions and the National Writing Project took years to develop and require ongoing stewardship to maintain. The relationships that they have nurtured with districts, schools, and individual educators operate as a standing resource that allows them to move quickly to initiate new work. This is quite different from the more common practice where a researcher might come with some money in hand searching for a place to try out a new idea. In short, the success stories represented by New Visions and the National Writing Project are the product of deliberate infrastructure building, and much more investments of this sort are needed to accelerate effective improvements across the education field.

Both foundations and government need to look beyond their current programmatic strategies, which often may last for only five or six years before they move onto something new. Many of the problems we want most to solve are complex and, as illustrated in this book's stories, demand a sustained commitment over time. But even beyond time, there is the also the need for an explicit improvement infrastructure to address them. Put simply, we need more organizations that can actually help us solve important problems across a large number of places.

SUMMING IT UP

In closing, I return to an observation introduced in *Learning to Improve*. There is no shortage of reform ideas in education. How to make these ideas work, reliably and at some scale, however, is another matter. There is a big difference between knowing what we as educators think we should do, which basically involves having a set of change ideas, and knowing how to make these ideas actually work effectively in the hands of many different individuals across varied contexts. Developing such practice-based know-how is the objective of improvement research. This is true whether it is carried out within a single organization, such as an individual school or system of schools like Fresno, Menomonee Falls, High Tech High, and

Summit, or across a multisite improvement network like New Visions and the National Writing Project.

The organizations highlighted in these pages engaged the people involved in the work in improving how work gets done. Along with this practical expertise, they regularly drew on the best available research evidence, and in some cases, this meant bringing researchers directly into the work. Practitioners, however, were no longer just passive recipients of researchers' and policymakers' pronouncements. As improvers, they were active agents of change who operated within the analytic discipline that characterizes a professional scientific community aimed at practical problem-solving. In such a community of practice, educators draw on evidence from others working on the same problem. They enliven a norm of building on the good work of their predecessors.

These stories also show how improvement efforts have the character of a learning journey. These are not the conventional "annual improvement plans." The six organizations evolved working theories of improvement by deploying a variety of inquiry processes to guide them in understanding their problems and as they pursued iterative tests of change. They learned their way into robust solutions that actually worked on the ground.

While each organization began with an explicit improvement aim and a strong sense of direction, the expansiveness of the changes they needed to make emerged only though a process of learning by doing. On the more personal side, improvement meant living with ambiguity, because rarely is there a straightforward roadmap to follow. While some of the organizations began with a modest improvement project in mind, others were more ambitious from the start. Regardless, along the way, all experienced a mindset shift as they began living the improvement principles.

Finally, not only did these educators make headway on specific problems, their efforts also enlarged the capacities in their respective organizations to address new problems in the future. So embedded in these six stories is a North Star—one that brightens the path ahead for all of us and offers some next steps toward getting better at getting better.

Notes

INTRODUCTION

1. Stuart Luppescu et al., *Trends in Chicago's Schools Across Three Eras of Reform* (Chicago: University of Chicago Consortium on School Research, September 2011).

2. Elaine M. Allensworth et al., *High School Graduation Rates Through Two Decades of District Change* (Chicago: University of Chicago Consortium on School Research, June 2016).

3. Sean F. Reardon and Rebecca Hinze-Pifer, *Test Score Growth Among Chicago Public School Students* (Stanford, CA: Center for Education Policy Analysis, November 2017), https://cepa.stanford.edu/sites/default/files/chicago%20public%20school%20test%20scores%202009-2014.pdf.

4. National Center for Education Statistics, *The Condition of Education 2019*, NCES 2019-144 (Washington, DC: US Department of Education, National Center for Education Statistics, 2019).

5. V. Bandeira de Mello et al., *Mapping State Proficiency Standards onto the NAEP Scales: Results from the 2017 NAEP Reading and Mathematics Assessments*, NCES 2019-040 (Washington, DC: US Department of Education, Institute of Education Sciences, National Center for Education Statistics, 2019), https://nces.ed.gov/nationsreportcard/subject/publications/studies/pdf/2019040.pdf.

6. Anthony S. Bryk et al., *Learning to Improve: How America's Schools Can Get Better at Getting Better* (Cambridge, MA: Harvard Education Press, 2015).

7. On balance, it is important to recognize that these concerns about transforming promising ideas into widespread success are not peculiar to education. They appear in general organizational management literature; see, for example, Larry Bossidy and Ram Charan, *Execution: The Discipline of Getting Things Done* (New York: Crown Publishing Group, 2002) and Robert I. Sutton and Huggy Rao, *Scaling Up Excellence* (New York: Crown Publishing Group, 2014).

8. Quoted in National Education Service, *Shaping America's Future III: Proceedings of the National Forum on Transforming Our System of Educating Youth with W. Edwards Deming* (Bloomington, IN: National Education Service, 1992).

9. See the classic work by William Ryan, *Blaming the Victim* (New York: Vintage Books, 1976).

10. The four tiers of evidence can be found in https://ies.ed.gov/ncee/wwc/essa.

11. On this point, see Michael J. Weiss et al, "How Much Do the Effects of Education and Training Programs Vary Across Sites? Evidence from Past Multisite Randomized Trials," *Journal of Research on Education Effectiveness* 10, no. 4 (2017): 843–They report that variability in program effects is commonplace across a range of educational and social interventions.

12. See Elizabeth Tipton et al., "Implications of Small Samples for Generalization: Adjustments and Rules of Thumb," *Evaluation Review* 41, no. 5 (2017): 472–505.

13. See, for example, the results presented in chapter 6 of Anthony S. Bryk et al., *Organizing Schools for Improvement: Lessons from Chicago* (Chicago: University of Chicago Press, 2010) on the lack of progress in truly disadvantaged school contexts.

14. For a realistic appraisal of the limitations of this knowledge base, even given its scale see *Best Care at Lower Cost: The Path to Continuously Learning Health Care in America*, Institute of Medicine of the National Academies, (Washington, DC: National Academies Press, 2012).

15. For the seminal contribution on this point, see Dan C. Lortie, *Schoolteacher: A Sociological Study* (Chicago: University of Chicago Press, 1975).

16. On the importance of building a practical knowledge base for teaching, see James Hiebert, Ronald Gallimore, and James Stigler, "A Knowledge Base for the Teaching Profession: What Would It Look Like and How Can We Get One?" *Educational Researcher* 31, no. 5 (2002): 3–15.

17. This problem of variability in performance represents one of the core facets in Deming's theory of profound knowledge for improving organizational productivity. See W. Edwards Deming, *The New Economics for Industry, Government, Education* (Cambridge, MA: MIT Press, 1993). It shows up in many fields, including quality performance studies in healthcare. See, for example, Atul Gawande, "The Cost Conundrum," *The New Yorker*, June 1, 2009, https://www.newyorker.com/magazine/2009/06/01/the-cost-conundrum.

18. For a further discussion of the concept of practical measurement, see Bryk et al., *Learning to Improve*, chapter 4. Also, in the context of healthcare improvement, see Donald M. Berwick, Brent James, and Molly Joel Coye, "Connections Between Quality Measurement and Improvement," *Medical Care* 41, no. 1 (2003): 130–138.

19. David Tyack and Larry Cuban, *Tinkering Toward Utopia: A Century of Public School Reform* (Cambridge, MA: Harvard University Press, 1997).

20. For a further discussion see Donald J. Peurach, William R. Penuel, and Jennifer Lin Russell, "Beyond Ritualized Rationality: Organizational Dynamics of Instructionally-Focused Continuous Improvement" (forthcoming, in *Sage Handbook on School Organization*).

CHAPTER 1

1. "Educational Attainment, 2017" data for Fresno County, CA from the U.S. Census Bureau, 2013–2017 American Community Survey 5-Year Estimates, retrieved from the US Census Bureau, American Fact Finder on October 28, 2019, https://factfinder.census.gov/bkmk/table/1.0/en/ACS/17_5YR/S1501/0500000 US06019.

2. California Department of Education, retrieved from Ed-Data.org on October 14, 2019, http://www.ed-data.org/district/Fresno/Fresno-Unified.

3. California Department of Education, Ed-Data.org.

4. See Anthony P. Carnevale, Nicole Smith, and Jeff Strohl, *Recovery: Job Growth and Education Requirements Through 2020* (Washington, DC: Georgetown University, Center on Education and the Workforce, June 2013). The report estimated that 65 percent of all jobs in 2020 will require some postsecondary training, up from 28 percent in 1973. See also Anthony P. Carnevale, Steven J. Rose, and Ban Cheah, *The College Payoff: Education, Occupations, Lifetime Earnings* (Washington, DC: Georgetown University, Center on Education and the Workforce, 2011).

5. Quoted in Clarisse Haxton and Jennifer O'Day, *Improving Equity and Access in Fresno: Lessons from a K12–Higher Education Partnership* (Washington, DC: American Institutes for Research), October, 2015.

6. Haxton and O'Day, v.

7. Haxton and O'Day, 17.

8. Haxton and O'Day, 34.

9. Anthony P. Carnevale and Jeff Strohl, "How Increasing College Access Is Increasing Inequality, and What To Do About It," in *Rewarding Strivers: Helping Low-Income Students Succeed in College*, ed. Richard D. Kahlenberg (New York: Century Foundation Press, 2010), 71–190, p. 79.

10. For a further discussion of these topics, see Paul Tough, *The Years That Matter Most: How College Makes or Breaks Us* (Boston: Houghton Mifflin, 2019).

11. Tough, *The Years That Matter Most.*

12. The University of Chicago Consortium on Chicago School Research found that almost two-thirds of high school graduates in Chicago enrolled in colleges that were less selective than those they were actually qualified to attend. Among those who met the requirements for a "very selective college"—15 percent of the graduates—only 38 percent enrolled in those types of institutions.

Moreover, African American and Latino/Hispanic students were much more likely than their white and Asian peers to undermatch. See Melissa Roderick et al., *From High School to the Future: Potholes on the Road to College* (Chicago: University of Chicago, Consortium on Chicago School Research, March 2008).

13. For a national study reporting on this concern, see Jonathan I. Smith, Matea Pender, and Jessica S. Howell, "The Full Extent of Academic Undermatch," *Economics of Education Review* 32 (2013): 247–

14. Unless otherwise specifically noted, the quotes included in the case chapters come from interviews conducted by Bob Rothman and chapter authors, and from other personal conversations that I had with leaders in these organizations between 2017 and 2019.

15. Anthony S. Bryk et al., *Learning to Improve: How America's Schools Can Get Better at Getting Better* (Cambridge, MA: Harvard Education Press, 2016), 176–177.

16. The National Student Clearinghouse is a national source of linked individual student and institutional data on the enrollment and degree attainment of individual students as the flow through our nation's K–20 educational systems. For more information about their data services, see www.studentclearinghouse.org.

17. Vincent Harris (former executive officer for district accountability and improvement within the Equity and Access office at Fresno Unified School District), in discussion with the author, October 25, 2018.

18. Harris, October 25, 2018.

19. The resulting key drivers and change ideas forming a working theory of improvement are often visualized in a driver diagram, as seen in figure 1.2. For a further discussion of a working theory of improvement and driver diagrams, see chapter 3 in Bryk et al., *Learning to Improve.*

20. We use the terms *change concept* and *change idea* interchangeably in this volume. Within the formal literature of improvement science, however, there is a distinct difference; the term *change concept* represents a general mechanism (e.g., professional development, hire more staff, introduce a coordinator) that could be deployed in many different situations in response to some specific problem in a particular context. In the Fresno context, expanding access to information is a change concept. The "I Am Ready" packets mailed to students' homes, in contrast, is a change idea. For further discussion see Gerald L. Langley et al., *The Improvement Guide: A Practical Approach To Enhancing Organizational Performance* (San Francisco: Jossey-Bass, 2009), appendix A.

21. See Caroline Hoxby and Sarah Turner, "Expanding College Opportunities for

High-Achieving, Low-Income Students" (SIEPR Working Paper no. 12-014, March 2013). For a general audience discussion of this work and a specific discussion of the College Board's failed effort to try to scale it, see Tough, *The Years That Matter Most*.

22. Harris, October 25, 2018.

23. Harris, October 25, 2018.

24. A study in Chicago found that, of the twelfth-grade students who aspired to a four-year degree, 51 percent were accepted to a four-year college but only 41 percent actually enrolled in the fall; see Roderick et al., *From High School to the Future*. Another study, using national longitudinal data, estimated the rate of summer melt between 8 percent and 40 percent; and most disconcerting from an equity perspective, the data were clear that low-income students were much more likely than students from higher-income families not to enroll in colleges even when they had completed the whole application process and been formally accepted. See Benjamin L. Castleman and Lindsay C. Page, "A Trickle or a Torrent? Understanding the Extent of Summer 'Melt' Among College-Intending High-School Graduates," *Social Science Quarterly* 95, no. 1 (March 2014): 202–220.

25. This fusion of researcher and practitioner expertise is central to the improvement paradigm discussed in Bryk et al., *Learning to Improve*, chapter 7. See also Anthony S. Bryk, "Redressing Inequities: An Aspiration in Search of a Method" (speech presented at Fourth Annual Carnegie Foundation Summit on Improvement in Education, San Francisco, California, March 27, 2017). This orientation builds more generally on developments in research-practice partnerships that have evolved over the last two decades. For further discussion, see William R. Penuel and Daniel J. Gallagher, *Creating Research-Practice Partnerships in Education* (Cambridge, MA: Harvard Education Press, 2017).

CHAPTER 2

This chapter should be cited as Sharon Greenberg and Anthony Bryk, "Supporting Improvement Through an Analytic Hub," in Anthony Bryk, *Improvement in Action: Advancing Quality in America's Schools* (Cambridge, MA: Harvard Education Press, 2020), 47–75.

1. For an account of New Visions' small schools and school support work in the context of broader education reform efforts in New York City, see Maureen Kelleher, *New York City's Children First: Lessons in School Reform* (Washington, DC: Center for American Progress, 2014), https://cdn.americanprogress .org/wp-content/uploads/2014/03/NYCeducationReport.pdf. For additional information about the outcomes of small school reforms on graduation rates

and postsecondary achievement, see Rebecca Unterman and Zeest Haider, *New York City's Small Schools of Choice: A First Look at Effects on Postsecondary Persistence and Labor Market Outcomes* (New York: MDRC, 2019), https://www.mdrc.org/sites/default/files/SSC-First_Look%20Brief.pdf.

2. New Visions' definition of "college ready" is "not in need of remedial courses upon entry to post-secondary."

3. When this change was enacted, New Visions was one of the handful of private organizations asked to serve as a PSO, and it operated one of the largest PSO networks serving high schools in New York City during the time period described in this case. For additional detail, see Kelleher, *New York City's Children First*, 19–25.

4. When this case was written, New Visions was supporting seventy-one schools as an Affinity Network (the successor to the PSO structure). Formal authority for school management remains with the Department of Education.

5. Dunetz became New Visions' president in 2016.

6. The organization Attendance Works defines chronic absenteeism as 10 percent or more absences in a given school year. This definition has been taken up by many schools and districts. For more information, see Phyllis W. Jordan and Raegen Miller, *Who's In: Chronic Absenteeism Under the Every Child Succeeds Act* (Washington, DC: Georgetown University, FutureEd, September 2017).

7. Eighty-six percent of AMSII students qualified for free or reduced-price lunch, 14 percent were special need, 11 percent were English learners, and 94 percent were Latino/Hispanic or African American. See Susan Fairchild and Michelle Meredith, "The Relentless Nature of Improving Attendance," *Learning Deeply* (blog), edweek.org, February 23, 2016, https://blogs.edweek.org/edweek/learning_deeply/2016/02/the_relentless_nature_of_improving_daily_attendance.html.

8. "Chris Roberts" is a pseudonym.

9. Susan Fairchild and Steffon Isaac, "Strong Attendance Systems Are the Product of Ordinary Solutions," *Learning Deeply* (blog), edweek.org, May 9, 2016, https://blogs.edweek.org/edweek/learning_deeply/2016/05/strong_attendance_systems_are_the_product_of_ordinary_solutions_and_disciplined_practice.html.

10. In total, Fairchild spent four days observing at the school that academic year. See Fairchild and Meredith, "The Relentless Nature of Improving Attendance."

11. Fairchild and Isaac, "Strong Attendance Systems Are the Product of Ordinary Solutions."

12. See New Visions for Public Schools, *New Visions Improvement Science Report 2016* (unpublished report, April 10, 2016), available publically on Google Docs,

https://docs.google.com/document/d/1lYEmiTNHiqTYVsrEkArS_g-FyjeN0 lNyBae9mK24BVA/edit?ts=5cdede8e).

13. While qualitative inquiries at AMSII were field-based, with improvement staff working alongside practitioners, improvement analytics are typically the responsibility of an individual or an analytic team in the network hub.

14. For a further discussion of the use of the Pareto principle and associated references, see the Fresno case in chapter 1. For a further discussion of this idea of high-leverage practices, see Anthony S. Bryk et al, *Learning to Improve: How America's Schools Can Get Better at Getting Better* (Cambridge, MA: Harvard Education Press, 2015), 47.

15. It is for this reason that Attendance Works has urged states not to differentiate between excused and unexcused absences when they create policies around absenteeism. Excessive class-cutting and tardiness also factor into the absentee count in some states and districts. See Jordan and Miller, "Who's In."

16. See *New Visions Improvement Science Report*, 29.

17. For a detailed discussion of this working theory of improvement, see *New Visions Improvement Science Report*.

18. Part of the change effort was to figure out which adult should be on point to respond to different student behaviors; for example, the division or classroom teacher, the attendance coordinator, the dean, etc.

19. Along with the effort described above, the hub was beginning to build the first spreadsheet tools at the network level. While New Visions had past experience building static tools, the hub recognized the need to build more dynamic tools that would make it easier for schools to address the variability in daily decision making. For further discussion of New Visions' effort to develop tools, see Sharon Greenberg and Anthony S. Bryk, *New Visions Teaching Case* (unpublished case study, Stanford, CA: Carnegie Foundation for the Advancement of Teaching, 2019).

20. See Fairchild and Meredith, "The Relentless Nature of Improving Daily Attendance."

21. See Karl Weick and Kathleen Sutcliff, *Managing the Unexpected: Resilient Performance in an Age of Uncertainty* (San Francisco: Jossey-Bass, 2007). Although the language used in this section is different from theirs, we are deeply indebted to their conceptual framing of the core concept of a high-reliability organization.

22. This is another key idea embedded within the concept of high-reliability organizations. See Weick and Sutcliff, *Managing the Unexpected*.

23. Louis Gomez, Anthony S. Bryk, and Angel Bohannon, "Attend to Failure to Advance Equity" (working paper, Stanford, CA: Carnegie Foundation for the

Advancement of Teaching, 2019).

24. See, for example, Elaine Allensworth and John Q. Easton, *What Matters for Staying on Track and Graduating in Chicago Public Schools* (Chicago: UChicago Consortium on School Research, 2007); also see Ruth Curran Neild, Scott Stoner-Eby, and Frank F. Furstenberg, "Connecting Entrance and Departure: The Transition to Ninth Grade and High School Dropout," *Education and Urban Society* 40, no. 5 (July 2008): 543–569.

25. In fact, the hub's first attempt was to understand course-taking, but this immediately proved problematic. NYCDOE had exerted little oversight on course descriptions and titles for years. Spawned by their small schools movement, different course offerings and titles had proliferated such that when New Visions began this work, over forty thousand different high school course codes existed in NYCDOE. Thus, before New Visions could analyze course-taking in its network, the hub had to deploy staff to understand what different course titles actually meant, determine equivalencies and redundancies, and standardize descriptors. This activity proceeded as the hub began work on other performance measures, like credit gaps. And when New Visions' analysis of course offerings was eventually completed, the NYCDOE eventually adopted it as its own.

26. As explained in note 25, New Visions actually had to standardize the codes before the credit "clean-up" work was possible.

27. Since the writing of this case, New Visions has published the Strategic Data Check-In protocols that support interaction between its coaches and school staff as well as usage of the New Visions Data Portal. These protocols are the result of multiple iterations as the work with schools and the data tools have evolved. See https://sdc.newvisions.org/overview-of-sdcs.

28. See Susan Fairchild et al., *Student Progress to Graduation in New York City High Schools: Part II: Student Achievement as Stock and Flow: Reimagining Early Warning Systems for At-Risk Students* (New York: New Visions for Public Schools, 2012) for a discussion of this early work.

29. In essence, the stock and flow analysis is the quantitative compliment to the more qualitative journey map narratives used in the chartering efforts for the Tennessee Early Literacy Network. For a discussion see Sharon Greenberg and Anthony S. Bryk, *Tennessee Early Literacy Network Teaching Case* (unpublished case study, Stanford, CA: Carnegie Foundation for the Advancement of Teaching, 2019). Both aim to help improvers see the system from the lived experience of the students going through it. For a full color version of the stock and flow diagram and accompanying description, see https://www.carnegiefoundation.org/stockandflow.

30. This school, like AMSII, is a New Visions charter that serves a "typical" population of New York City students but achieves better-than-average results. Nevertheless, the educators at Telly were not satisfied with current outcomes and saw room for improvement.

31. In subsequent iterations of this work, New Visions encouraged high schools to partner with feeder middle schools to start a range of interventions for struggling students prior to high school. For further discussion of this effort, see the Greenberg and Bryk, *New Visions Teaching Case*.

32. The New Visions Data Portal design was developed through years of iteration of earlier generations of New Visions tools. During the 2018–2019 school year, the portal was being used in more than four hundred New York City public schools.

33. See Mike Rother, *Toyota Kata: Managing People for Improvement, Adaptiveness, and Superior Results* (New York: McGraw-Hill Education, 2009).

34. For further discussion of the concept of standard work and its centrality to improvement, see Bryk et al., *Learning to Improve*, chapter 2.

35. For a further elaboration on this point see Anthony S. Bryk, *Redressing Inequities: An Aspiration in Search of a Method* (Stanford, CA: Carnegie Foundation for the Advancement of Teaching, 2017), https://www.carnegiefoundation .org/wp-content/uploads/2017/04/Carnegie_Bryk_Summit_2017_Keynote.pdf.

CHAPTER 3

1. Eric Ries, *The Lean Startup* (New York: Crown Publishing Group, 2011).

2. Summit Public Schools, *The Science of Summit* (Redwood City, CA: Summit Public Schools, 2017), 10, https://summitps.org/wp-content/uploads/ 2018/09/The-Science-of-Summit-by-Summit-Public-Schools_08072017-1 .pdf.

3. The remaining 19 percent of students identify themselves as other (9 percent), two or more races (7 percent), and Filipino (3 percent). These figures were taken from *Continuous Improvement Case Studies: Summit* (a report prepared for the Gates Foundation, 2018).

4. The Student Agency Improvement Network was a networked improvement community dedicated to equip students to persist in the face of rigorous learning challenges. With support from the Raikes Foundation, it included six school networks, including Summit Public Schools, that educated nineteen thousand students. For further information, see https://www.carnegiefoundation .org/our-work/previous-improvement-work/saic/.

5. For a further discussion of systems of measures in improvement science, see Anthony S. Bryk et al., *Learning to Improve: How America's Schools Can Get*

Better at Getting Better (Cambridge, MA: Harvard Education Press, 2015), chapter 4.

6. See Bryk et al., *Learning to Improve*, chapter 2. We note that positive deviant studies bear a family resemblance to school effectiveness studies dating back to the pioneering work of Ron Edmonds (see Ronald Edmonds, "Effective Schools for the Urban Poor," *Educational Leadership* 37, no. 1 [1979]: 15–24). The latter offers what are essentially causal explanations for how some schools "beat the odds," encouraging others to follow along this same path. These effective school studies are often criticized, however, in that it is possible that other schools may well share the same "effective" characteristics but not achieve the same results, as causal claims or intimations of causality remain problematic. The first stage of a positive deviant study resembles an effective school study in that its aim is to identify plausible change hypotheses, with the key word here being *hypotheses*. These hypotheses are then to be tested, refined, and validated through repeated PDSA cycles in other sites. The evidence of effectiveness derives from the actual tests of change, rather than the initial list identified. Put differently, an effective school study is purely observational; a positive deviant study brings some experimental evidence to bear.

7. See Jerome E. Groopman, *How Doctors Think* (Boston: Houghton Mifflin, 2007); Daniel Kahneman, *Thinking, Fast and Slow* (New York: Farrar, Strauss, and Giroux, 2011); Eva Jones et al., "Confirmation Bias in Sequential Information Search After Preliminary Decisions: An Expansion of Dissonance Theoretical Research on Selective Exposure to Information," *Journal of Personality and Social Psychology* 80, no. 4 (2001): 557–Also see Bryk et al., *Learning to Improve*, chapter 7.

8. For a further discussion of the role of measurement and disciplined inquiry in improvement efforts, see Bryk et al., *Learning to Improve*, chapters 4 and 5.

9. See Atul Gawande, "The Mistrust of Science," *The New Yorker*, June 10, 2016, https://www.newyorker.com/news/news-desk/the-mistrust-of-science. Gawande talks about the need for this in medical practice. In brief, it is a commitment to a systematic way of thinking, an allegiance to a way of building knowledge and explaining the universe through testing and factual observation. According to Gawande, this isn't our normal way of thinking—it is unnatural and counterintuitive, and has to be learned. Scientific explanation stands in contrast to the wisdom of divinity and experience and common sense. Common sense once told us that the sun moves across the sky and that being out in the cold produced colds. But a scientific mind recognized that these intuitions were only hypotheses; they had to be tested.

10. See K. Brooke Stafford-Brizard, *Building Blocks for Learning: A Framework for*

Comprehensive Student Development (New York: Turnaround for Children, 2016); Camille A. Farrington et al., *Teaching Adolescents to Become Learners: The Role of Noncognitive Factors in Shaping School Performance: A Critical Literature Review* (Chicago: University of Chicago Consortium on Chicago School Research, 2012); American Institutes for Research, *The Science of Learning and Development: A Synthesis* (Washington, DC: AIR, 2017).

11. Kyle Moyer, "EL Improvement Project," Summit Public Schools, presentation to the Carnegie Foundaiton for the Advancement of Teaching, April 5, 2017.

12. See Carol S. Dweck, *Mindset: The New Psychology of Success* (New York: Random House, 2006). Aso see David S. Yeager, *The National Study of Learning Mindsets, 2015–2016* (Ann Arbor, MI: Inter-University Consortium for Political and Social Research, 2019), https://doi.org/10.3886/ICPSR37353.v This study documents that the effects of a growth mindset intervention tend to be amplified by subsequent experiences in classrooms where teachers hold these beliefs about their students and create reinforcing feedback loops.

13. Summit Public Schools, *The Science of Summit* (Redwood City, CA: Summit Public Schools, 2018).

14. Louis Gomez et al., "The Right Network for the Right Problem," *Phi Delta Kappan* 98, no. 3 (November 2016): 8–15. This article discusses the difference between sharing networks and more structured improvement networks of the type that was evolving at Summit Schools. Each serves different purposes. Analogous to developments in networked science, structured improvement networks are especially well suited for tackling complex problems that aim to advance productive solutions at some scale.

15. See the success in eliminating the minority gap in college graduation at Georgia State University described in David Kirp, *The College Dropout Scandal* (New York: Oxford University Press, 2019).

16. See *Getting on Track Early for School Success: An Assessment System to Support Effective Instruction*, Foundation for Child Development, www.fcd-us.org/assets/2016/04/Lit-Tech-Report.pdf.

CHAPTER 4

1. Acknowledgments to Dr. Seuss, *Oh, The Places You'll Go!* (New York: Random House Books for Young Readers, 1990) for this section's heading.

2. Atul Gawande, "On Washing Hands," *New England Journal of Medicine* 350, no. 13 (March 2004): 1283–1286.

3. This is based on a calculation of the median value across the five baseline years and the median absolute deviation around it.

4. What I have described here is the intuitive basis in parametric statistical

methods for making probabilistic statements comparing observed events against chance. Nonparametric statistics, often accompanying run charts, can be used as well. In general, less emphasis tends to be placed on achieving statistical significance in improvement projects. Rather, we are looking for substantively meaningful change. So even when formal hypothesis testing is used, it is at best a guide to action. In improvement, more important than making a precise probabilistic statement, relative to some null hypothesis, about what may have happened in one set of contexts at one point in time is the larger pattern of evidence that accumulates over time and places. That is, do these effects sustain over time, and can a change package that was initially developed in one sample of contexts be effectively adapted in other contexts? Rather than placing exclusive emphasis about what happened in one place or small set of places, a blending of learning objectives is at work: "Did we observe a meaningful change? Can it be sustained, and can it spread?" In short, *sustained replicable results* is the true gold standard.

5. See, for example, J. Cody Davidson, "Increasing FAFSA Completion Rates: Research, Policies and Practices," *Journal of Student Financial Aid* 43 no. 1 (2013). Also see Stephen Bahr, Dinah Sparks, and Kathleen Mulvaney Hoyer, *Why Didn't Students Complete a Free Application for Federal Student Aid (FAFSA)? A Detailed Look*, NCES 2018-061 (Washington, DC: US Department of Education, National Center for Education Statistics, December 2018).

6. William G. Tierney and Kristan M. Venegas, "Finding Money on the Table: Information, Financial Aid, and Access to College," *Journal of Higher Education* 80, no. 4 (July–August 2009): 363–388.

7. Ben Daley, *The $50,000 Prize: An Improvement Project to Increase Cal Grant Award Rates* (unpublished report, San Diego, CA: High Tech High, n.d).

8. National Center for Education Statistics, *Digest of Education Statistics* (Washington, DC: US Department of Education, National Center for Education Statistics, 2016).

9. See, for example, Alan Ginsburg, Phyllis Jordan, and Hedy Chang, *Absences Add Up: How School Attendance Influences Student Success* (San Francisco: Attendance Works, 2014); https://www.attendanceworks.org/wp-content/uploads/2017/05/Absenses-Add-Up_September-3rd-2014.pdf). They reported, using data from the National Assessment of Educational Progress, that about one in five students in fourth and eighth grade reported missing three or more days in the month before the test—or about 15 percent of the school year—and 3 percent reported missing ten or more days that month. This level of absenteeism was associated with the lowest scores.

10. It is, for example, a key component in the on-track indicator for school success

pioneered by the Chicago Consortium on School Research. See Elaine Allensworth and John Q. Easton, *The On-Track Indicator as a Predictor of High School Graduation* (Chicago: University of Chicago Consortium on School Research, 2005). See also Hedy N. Chang and Mariajosé Romero, *Present, Engaged, and Accounted For: The Critical Importance of Addressing Chronic Absence in the Early Grades* (New York: Columbia University, Mailman School of Public Health, National Center for Children in Poverty, September 2008).

11. See, for example, the Utah Education Policy Center's *Chronic Absenteeism in Utah Public Schools* (Salt Lake City: University of Utah, Utah Education Policy Center, July 2012). This study found that students who were chronically absent in any grade between eighth- and twelfth- grade were 7.4 times more likely to drop out than those who attended more regularly.

12. At High Tech High schools, the site manager sits at the front desk of the school and greets families and students. The site director is the principal.

13. For a further discussion on this improvement concept, see Anthony S. Bryk et al., *Learning to Improve: How America's Schools Can Get Better at Getting Better* (Cambridge, MA: Harvard Education Press, 2015), 203–206.

14. Bryk et al., *Learning to Improve,* chapter 1. The original concept of Triple Aims was developed in health care by the Institute for Healthcare Improvement. We are indebted to them as the resource for our adaptation.

15. For a further discussion of a system of measures see Bryk et al., chapter 5.

16. Everett M. Rogers, *Diffusion of Innovations* (New York: The Free Press, 1962).

17. The term *early majority* draws directly from Rogers's theory of innovation diffusion (see Rogers, *Diffusion of Innovations*). While a true majority has not yet coalesced, they were on route toward it. Ergo, the expression of an *early* majority.

18. Also noteworthy is that school and network leaders were also interested in expanding the improvement work for a very pragmatic reason: the charter school reauthorization process. Under California law, charter schools must present evidence of improved school performance every five years or risk losing their charter. HTH had been reauthorized four times by then, and also permitted to expand to new schools, but leaders knew that charter authorizers wanted quantitative evidence of performance gains. The move toward improvement was serendipitous in that it would create a reason and a new way to amass that evidence. So this external accountability press played a modest supporting role in its expansion into the HTH network as well.

19. Curtis A. Taylor, "How Can We Promote Mathematical Identity?" *Learning Deeply* (blog), edweek.org;http://blogs.edweek.org/edweek/learning_deeply/2017/11/how_can_we_help_promote_mathematical_identity.html.

20. https://hthgse.edu/crei/overview/.

21. See Bryk et al., *Learning to Improve*, chapter 4, p. 114.

22. Daley cited as an example their efforts to promote a "launch, explore, discuss" core practice in math classrooms. In some classes, the whole-class discussion lasted fifteen minutes, while in others, it lasted thirty minutes. Data from one classroom showed that the shorter discussions were more effective—students were more likely to get bored or distracted in the longer discussions—but that data was not sufficient to persuade some teachers to change their practice. As in the instance where the measured outcome is test scores, Daley noted, "Not everybody agrees that this [test scores] is something we should care about."

23. Dr. Seuss, *Oh, The Places You'll Go!*.

CHAPTER 5

This chapter should be cited as Anthony Bryk and Paul G. LeMahieu, "Advancing Instructional Improvement," in Anthony Bryk, *Improvement in Action: Advancing Quality in America's Schools* (Cambridge, MA: Harvard Education Press, 2020), 125–147.

1. For a rich and deep discussion of the promises and challenges in advancing deeper learning, see Jal Mehta and Sarah Fine, *In Search of Deeper Learning: The Quest to Remake the American High School* (Cambridge, MA: Harvard University Press, 2019).

2. On this account, see the *Language Arts Journal of Michigan* 34, no. 2 (special issue), April 2019.

3. James Gray, "Teachers at the Center: A Memoir of the Early Years of the National Writing Project," (Berkeley, CA: National Writing Project, 2000.)

4. Mark St. John and Laura Stokes, *Lessons to Be Learned from the National Writing Project* (Inverness, CA: Inverness Research, March 2008).

5. This practice of a shared induction experience forming a community of memory is a key characteristic of intentionally formed communities. For a further discussion about the concept, see for example, Robert N. Bellah et al., *Habits of the Heart: Individualism and Commitment in American Life: Updated Edition with a New Introduction* (Berkeley: University of California Press, 1996).

6. National Governors Association and Council of Chief State School Officers, *Common Core State Standards for English Language Arts and Literacy in History/Social Studies, Science, and Technical Subjects* (Washington, DC: NGA and CCSSO, 2010), 18.

7. Brad Phillips, "Teaching with the Lights On," *RE: Philanthropy*, September 29, 2011.

8. H. A. Gallagher, K. R. Woodworth, and N. L. Arshan, *Impact of the National*

Writing Project's College-Ready Writers Program on Teachers and Students (Menlo Park, CA: SRI International, 2015).

9. Throughout this case, we refer to the work of the C3WP hub as a support center for this effort. Such a hub did exist and exercised these functions. It operated in tandem with significant leadership and learning about these efforts occurring in the local sites. Many of the changes that the hub initiated often came about because local leaders learned things as the work proceeded in their sites and communicated issues "up" to the national hub. For simplicity in writing this chapter, we use the term hub to refer to both the deliberate actions taken by a central group and the more organic forms of social learning characteristic of a vital social learning web.

10. As a long-standing example of this, see David K. Cohen, "A Revolution in One Classroom: The Case of Mrs. Oublier" *Education Evaluation and Policy Analysis* 12, no. 3 (September 1990): 311–329.

11. See Mehta and Fine, *In Search of Deeper Learning*, for a discussion of *deeper learning*, which has now become a popular term. For an earlier exposition along these lines, see F.M. Newmann, *Authentic Achievement: Restructuring Schools for Intellectual Quality* (San Francisco: Jossey-Bass, 1996).

12. Joseph Harris, *Rewriting: How to Do Things with Texts* (Logan, UT: Utah State University Press, 2006).

13. Harris, *Rewriting*, 58.

14. For a discussion of the difference between leading and lagging outcome measures in the context of an improvement system of measures, see Bryk et al., *Learning to Improve*, 136–139.

15. Gallagher, Woodworth, and Arshan, *Impact*.

16. Gallagher, Woodworth, and Arshan, *Impact*.

17. For a further discussion of this idea specifically in the context of the National Writing Project, see St. John and Stokes, *Lessons to be Learned*. In elaborating this point, St. John draws on key ideas found in the writings of Douglas Englebart, the originator of the term *networked improvement community*.

CHAPTER 6

This chapter should be cited as Anthony Bryk and Ash Vasudeva, "Transforming a School District," in Anthony Bryk, *Improvement in Action: Advancing Quality in America's Schools* (Cambridge, MA: Harvard Education Press, 2020), 149–171.

1. School District of Menomonee Falls, 2018 Malcolm Baldrige National Quality Award application, p. 4.

2. No Child Left Behind Act of 2001, P.L. 107-110, 20 U.S.C. § 6319 (2002).

3. Recounted by Patricia Greco in "Healing Our Systems and Making Improvement Stick," *School Administrator* (blog), AASA website, March 2019, http://my.aasa.org/AASA/Resources/SAMag/2019/Mar19/Greco.aspx.

4. Christopher Kuhagen, "Menomonee Falls Schools Superintendent Pat Greco Announces her Upcoming Retirement," *Milwaukee Journal Sentinel*, February 23, 2018, updated February 27, 2018, retrieved from https://eu.jsonline .com/story/communities/northwest/news/menomonee-falls/2018/02/23/ menomonee-falls-schools-superintendent-pat-greco-announces-her-upcoming-retirement/368423002/.

5. Interview with JoAnn Sternke and Pat Greco, San Francisco, March 27–28, 2017.

6. Although Deming developed his ideas early in the twentieth century, his theories did not gain much traction in the United States until well after he had helped Japan rebuild its manufacturing industry following World War II. When Greco entered the superintendency, improvement efforts were alive at the Carnegie Foundation and in a few other educational organizations, but the crosswalk into the field of education remained largely untouched ground. The W. Edwards Deming Institute contains information on Deming's work and how his ideas remain salient today; see https://deming.org/.

7. Anthony S. Bryk et al., *Learning to Improve: How America's Schools Can Get Better at Getting Better* (Cambridge, MA: Harvard Education Press, 2016), 176–177.

8. The W. Edwards Deming Institute, "Where There Is Fear, You Do Not Get Honest Figures," *The W. Edwards Deming Institute Blog*, February 28, 2013, https://blog.deming.org/2013/02/where-there-is-fear-you-do-not-get-honest-figures/.

9. Matthew Bates, Lynne Mahony, and Stephanie Striepeck, *The Evidence Behind Evidence-Based Leadership* (Chicago: The Studer Group, October 6, 2016), https://www.studergroup.com/resources/articles-and-industry-updates/ articles-and-whitepapers/the-evidence-behind-evidence-based-leadership.

10. Wisconsin Budget Project, email message to Kathyrn Borman of the Carnegie Foundation, August 25. In 2017 dollars, Wisconsin spent $5.987 billion in general purpose revenue on K–12 education in fiscal year Big cuts to education funding started in fiscal year 2011. In fiscal year 2017, Wisconsin was budgeted to spend $5.395 billion in general purpose revenue dollars on K–12 education, or $592 million less than the state spent in 2011. These figures adjust for the cost of inflation over that period.

11. The American Society for Quality Control (ASQ), "The Define, Measure, Analyze, Improve, Control (DMAIC) Process," http://asq.org/learn-about-quality/six-sigma/overview/dmaic.html.

12. Cited in School District of Menomonnee Falls 2018 Malcolm Baldrige National Quality Award application.

13. See, for example, Quint Studer, *Hardwiring Excellence: Purpose, Worthwhile Work, Making a Difference* (Gulf Breeze, FL: Fire Starter Publishing, 2003).

14. See, for example, Studer Education, "9 Principles of Organizational Excellence," https://www.studereducation.com/nine-principles-solutions/. These principles closely mirrored Deming's original fourteen points but were stated in language that educators could embrace.

15. The training includes, for example, Certification in Project Management; and white/orange/green/black belt training. See Greco, "Healing Our Systems and Making Improvement Stick."

16. Bryk et al., *Learning to Improve*, PDSA (Plan-Do-Study-Act) is a pragmatic scientific method for iterative testing of changes in complex systems. Each cycle is essentially a mini-experiment where observed outcomes are compared to predictions and discrepancies between the two become a major source of learning.

17. The website of the Iowa State University Center for Excellence in Learning and Teaching, "Using a PLUS/DELTA Assessment Technique," http://www.celt.iastate.edu/teaching/assessment-and-evaluation/mid-term-formative-evaluation-using-a-plusdelta-assessment-technique/.

18. Studer Education,website, "Expect Excellence and Achieve at High Performance Levels—Teaching," *ALWAYS Actions* (blog), n.d., https://whatsrightin education.com/tag/teaching-always-actions/.

19. See Bryk, Gomez, Grunow, and LeMahieu, 114.

20. Continuous Quality Improvement, Policy 114, Board of Education, School District of Menomonee Falls, Wisconsin (April 23, 2014).

21. Alec Johnson, "Menomonee Falls School Board Recommends Corey Golla to be New Superintendent," *Milwaukee Journal Sentinel*, March 7, 2018, updated March 8, 2018); retrieved October 26, 2019, from https://www.jsonline.com/story/communities/northwest/news/menomonee-falls/2018/03/07/menomonee-falls-school-board-recommends-corey-golla-new-superintendent/405054002/.

22. Alec Johnson, "Falls Superintendent Pat Greco Named Wisconsin Superintendent of the Year," *Milwaukee Journal Sentinel*, November 13, 2017, updated November 18, 2017; retrieved October 26, 2019, from https://www.jsonline.com/story/communities/northwest/news/menomonee-falls/2017/11/13/falls-superintendent-pat-greco-named-wisconsin-superintendent-year/852980001/.

23. School District of Menomonnee Falls, 2018 Malcolm Baldrige National Quality Award application, p. 4.

24. P. Gores et al., "Top Workplaces," *Milwaukee Journal Sentinel* online, April 28, 2017, http://www.jsonline.com/business/top-workplaces-2017/.

CHAPTER 7

1. On occasion, they might also provide a measure attached to a primary driver. For example, if the overall aim of an improvement network is to increase the percentage of students judged proficient readers by the end of grade 3, one primary driver might be "accelerating the progress of struggling readers." Individual student trend data, based on progress-monitoring results, might be used to track changes on that particular improvement driver.

2. The formative work on this issue was led by David Kerbow at the Center for School Improvement at the University of Chicago, beginning in 1994. For a recent report on this from Chicago, see Melissa de la Torre and Julia Gwynne, *Changing Schools: A Look at Student Mobility Trends in Chicago Public Schools Since 1995* (Chicago: University of Chicago, Consortium on Chicago School Research, 2009).

3. These are typically defined as a ratio based on the number of students who move in or out of the school in a given year relative to the overall enrollment in that school.

4. The seminal framing for this work was anchored by a set of longitudinal qualitative case studies led by Melissa Roderick. The development of the on-track indicator grew out of this field-based inquiry.

5. Elaine Allensworth and John Q. Easton, *The On-Track Indicator as a Predictor of High School Graduation* (Chicago: University of Chicago Consortium on School Research, 2005).

6. For another example of developing a practical instructional improvement measure in the context of mathematics learning see Paul Cobb et al., "Design Research with Educational Systems: Investigating and Supporting Improvements in the Quality of Mathematics Teaching and Learning at Scale," in *Design-Based Implementation Research: 112th Yearbook of the National Society for the Study of Education*, ed. W. R. Penuel, B. J. Fishman, and B. Haugan (Chicago: National Society for the Study of Education, 2013), 320–349.

7. See Anthony S. Bryk et al., *Learning to Improve: How America's Schools Can Get Better at Getting Better* (Cambridge, MA: Harvard Education Press, 2015), 73–78.

8. These are examples of the kinds of questions that we would typically ask as PDSA cycles move into the testing of a change idea at larger scale: *Is the process actually happening? What local adaptations if any are occurring? And, what outcomes of this specific process should we expect to see?*

9. For a further discussion on this example, see Bryk et al., *Learning to Improve,*

103–110. The tests illustrated here closely align with the assessment of construct validity discussed in research on measurement. An assessment of a measure's validity depends on how it empirically functions within the nomological web of relationships hypothesized in a given theory. In improvement contexts, practical measures are referenced against a working theory of improvement. We examine whether the measure is behaving in ways we would expect given that working theory.

10. This comment assumes that the working theory of improvement includes both primary and secondary drivers, which is fairly common. In some applications, however there may only be primary drivers and change ideas. In contrast, complex improvement problems may also include tertiary drivers (or possibly even more detailed) drivers.

11. For a further discussion of the difference between a sharing community and a networked improvement community see Louis Gomez et al., "The Right Network for the Right Problem." *Kappan* 98, no. 3 (October 31, 2016): 8–15.

12. See Dean L. Fixsen, Karen A. Blasé, and Amanda A. M. Fixsen, "Scaling Effective Innovations," *Criminology and Public Policy* 16 no. 2 (2017): 487–499.

13. We are indebted to Elyse Eidman Adahl at the National Writing Project for suggesting this image.

14. The ideas introduced in this section draw heavily on a series of conversations that have been occurring among the staff and senior fellows of the Carnegie Foundation and through opportunities to convene with various leaders engaged in this work both inside the education field and more broadly. This project has been led by Christina Dixon and Simone Palmer, who have a longer white paper in preparation on the topic. Their efforts have informed the exposition presented here.

15. This proposition is anchored in my earlier experiences working with the Chicago Public School system, which spanned almost twenty years. During that time, I did not see a single school substantially improve without a strong individual in the principalship role. I maintain that this is equally the case for transforming a system of schools into a continuously improving organization.

16. Chip Heath and Dan Heath, *The Power of Moments: Why Certain Experiences Have Extraordinary Impact* (New York: Simon and Schuster, 2017).

17. For a detailed example of the use of a journey map during the process of chartering a networked improvement community see Sharon Greenberg and Anthony S. Bryk, *Initiating a Networked Improvement Community: The Chartering Phase* (Stanford, CA: Carnegie Foundation for the Advancement of Teaching, 2018).

18. Sandra Park and Sola Takahashi, *90-Day Cycle Handbook* (Stanford, CA: Carnegie Foundation for the Advancement of Teaching, October 2013).

19. The term was coined by Gerald J. Langley et al., *The Improvement Guide: A Practical Approach to Enhancing Organizational Performance* (San Francisco: Jossey-Bass, 2009). *Learning to Improve* made numerous citations to this text, but we did not adopt this particular term for reasons described here.

20. The seminal text on this is Clayton M. Christensen, *The Innovator's Dilemma: When Technologies Cause Great Firms to Fail* (Cambridge, MA: Harvard Business School Press, 1997). For a further discussion of efforts in this domain, see https://www.christenseninstitute.org/.

21. Clayton M. Christensen, Michael B. Horn, and Curtis W. Johnson, *Disrupting Class: How Disruptive Innovation Will Change the Way the World Learns* (New York: McGraw-Hill, 2008).

22. Danielle Allen, *Our Declaration: A Reading of the Declaration of Independence in Defense of Equality* (New York: W.W. Norton & Co., 2014).

Acknowledgments

THIS BOOK BECAME possible only because of the extraordinary efforts of a talented group of educators in the Fresno Unified School District, New Visions for Public Schools, Summit Public Schools, the High Tech High Charter Network, the National Writing Project, and the School District of Menomonee Falls (Wisconsin). I want to personally thank the leaders in these organizations who have generously given of their time to make their journeys of learning to improve visible to others. They, like so many educators around the country, work incredibly hard every day to advance the educational opportunities afforded to every child in their respective systems of schools. They each live the aspiration of every child succeeding. These leaders are: Michael Hanson, Jorge Aguilar, Vincent Harris, Christina Espinosa, Adam Bonilla, and Marlyn Gomez (Fresno and UC Merced); Bob Hughes, Mark Dunetz, Susan Fairchild, Jefferson Pestronk, Carl Manalo, Sandy Manessis, and Nikki Giunta (New Visions); Diane Tavenner, Adam Carter, and Kyle Moyer (Summit); Ben Daley, Stacey Caillier, and Ryan Gallagher (High Tech High); Elyse Eidman-Aadahl, Linda Friedrich, Robin Atwood, Mark St. John, and Tom Fox (National Writing Project); and Patricia Greco, Corey Golla, Faith VanderHorst, Elizabeth Sparks, and Melissa Matarazzo (Menomonee Falls).

I would like to extend a special thanks to Caroline Chauncey, senior editor at the Harvard Education Press. Her feedback on drafts of initial chapters strongly shaped the evolution of *Improvement in Action*. Thanks also to

Monica Jainschigg at Harvard Education Press, whose skillful copyediting helped to clarify and simplify the text at numerous points. I also owe a debt to Keicy Tolbert and Fernanda Martinez for their editorial and production assistance at Carnegie and for managing my calendar to create space to do the thinking and writing assembled here. They, along with Caroline, kept me moving forward to push this to completion.

I would also like to acknowledge the special contributions to this book from Sharon Greenberg. In addition to being lead author on the New Visions narrative, she read and commented on multiple drafts for all of the other chapters in this book. Her sense of good narrative, as well as her extensive critical commentaries, made each chapter better. My special thanks as well to Bob Rothman, whose background research, interviews with district staff and case notes afforded an initial scaffold and fact-check for each of the six case accounts.

I am also deeply grateful for the continued support and encouragement of the board of trustees of the Carnegie Foundation for the Advancement of Teaching. Beginning some twelve years ago, they embraced—and continue to do so—a person and a set of ideas. This book offers testimony to their staying the course with the Foundation's field-building mission of advancing more equitable educational outcomes through supporting schools to continuously improve.

Finally, my thanks to the terrific colleagues, both past and present, associated with the Carnegie Foundation. First, I am truly grateful to my coauthors and collaborators Paul G. LeMahieu and Ash Vasudeva. It is a joy to work with such thoughtful, creative, and dedicated colleagues every day. Senior Fellows Penny Carver, Don Peurach, Louis Gomez, and Jim Kohlmoos contributed valuable ideas in earlier efforts to spotlight the work of these six organizations. And lastly, many thanks to the wonderful staff of the Carnegie Foundation. Each of you, in your own ways, has been a valuable teacher to me. I am deeply grateful for the work you do, the questions you ask, the energy you bring every day in helping to advance improvement efforts all across our country and increasingly around the world as well.

About the Author

ANTHONY S. BRYK is the ninth president of the Carnegie Foundation for the Advancement of Teaching, where he is leading work on transforming educational research and development, more closely joining researchers and practitioners to improve teaching and learning. From 2004 until 2008, he held the Spencer Chair in Organizational Studies in the School of Education and the Graduate School of Business at Stanford University. He came to Stanford from the University of Chicago, where he was the Marshall Field IV Professor of Urban Education in the sociology department and where he helped found the Center for Urban School Improvement and the Consortium on Chicago School Research. He is a member of the National Academy of Education and the American Academy of Arts and Sciences. Bryk is one of America's most noted educational researchers. His 1993 book, *Catholic Schools and the Common Good*, is a classic in the sociology of education. His deep interest in bringing scholarship to bear on improving schooling is reflected in his later volumes *Trust in Schools* (2002) and *Organizing Schools for Improvement: Lessons from Chicago* (2010). In *Learning to Improve* (2015), Bryk argues that improvement science combined with the power of networks offers the field a new approach to reach ever-increasing educational aspirations.

About the Contributing Authors

SHARON GREENBERG IS a quality improvement adviser and a literacy and education consultant for groups including the Carnegie Foundation for the Advancement of Teaching, Amplify, Bellwether, the School of Education at Mills College, Room to Read, the Literacy Collaborative at Lesley College, Reading Recovery, Grade Level Reading, and the Philadelphia Leadership Academy. Greenberg started her career as a high school English teacher in the Chicago Public Schools. She is a co-founder of the Center for School Improvement at the University of Chicago and contributed to the development of the Consortium on Chicago School Research, the North Kenwood Oakland Charter School, and the Urban Teacher Education Program. She also served as a cabinet member and literacy consultant to the Chief Education Officer of the Chicago Public Schools. Greenberg's research and publications focus on school community politics, urban school reform and development, literacy as a lever for change, and teacher preparation and development. Greenberg has a PhD and MA from the University of Chicago, and a BA and MAT from Stanford University. She is also a reading specialist, and one of the first educators certified as an Improvement Advisor by the Institute for Healthcare Improvement.

PAUL G. LEMAHIEU is Senior Vice President for Programs at the Carnegie Foundation and graduate faculty in the College of Education, University of Hawai'i—Mānoa. LeMahieu served as Superintendent of Education for the State of Hawai'i, the chief educational and executive officer of the only state system that is a unitary school district. He has held a top research position in the State of Delaware as Undersecretary for Education Research and Policy. LeMahieu also served as Director of Research and Evaluation for the National Writing Project at the University of California, Berkeley, and Assistant Superintendent for Research and Evaluation for the Pittsburgh (Pennsylvania) Public Schools. He has been President of the National Association of Test Directors and Vice President of the American Educational Research Association. He served on the National Academy of Sciences' Board on International Comparative Studies in Education, and Mathematical Sciences Education Board. He is a Founding Director of the Center for the Study of Expertise in Teaching and Learning and served on the National Board on Testing Policy and the National Board on Professional Teaching Standards. LeMahieu's current professional interests focus on the adaptation of improvement science tools and methodologies for application in networks in education. He is a coauthor of the book *Learning to Improve: How America's Schools Can Get Better at Getting Better* (2015), and lead author of *Working to Improve: Seven Approaches to Quality Improvement in Education* (2017). He has a PhD from the University of Pittsburgh, an MEd from Harvard University, an AB from Yale College and an honors diploma from Pinkerton Academy.

ASH VASUDEVA is Vice President of Strategic Initiatives at the Carnegie Foundation for the Advancement of Teaching. He oversees the Carnegie Foundation's policy and communications teams, which enable and support field-based efforts to use improvement science (IS) and networked improvement communities (NICs) to reduce long-standing educational inequities. Vasudeva has catalyzed Carnegie's integration of IS and NICs into key field-building domains, including leading efforts to vitalize partnerships between local education agencies and schools of education through the use of improvement science, to build improvement-analytic capacity in research-practice partnerships and school improvement networks, and to develop and grow field-based leadership for improvement among practitioners, researchers, and policymakers. Prior to joining Carnegie,

Vasudeva was a senior program officer at the Bill & Melinda Gates Foundation, where he focused on supporting school systems to implement college and career ready standards and strengthen educator effectiveness systems. At the Gates Foundation, Vasudeva led portfolios of work that developed and tested college readiness indicator systems, measures of student-mindset and social-emotional learning, and instructional support systems for teachers and students. Previously, Vasudeva was Co-Executive Director of Stanford University's School Redesign Network, where he developed the LEADS network (Leadership for Equity and Accountability in Districts and Schools), which enabled superintendents and their cabinets to collaborate on systems reforms with faculty from Stanford's School of Education, School of Business, and School of Design (d. school). Vasudeva serves on the Learning Forward board of trustees and the research advisory board of Digital Promise. He has also served on advisory boards for the Alliance for Excellent Education and the Aspen Institute. Vasudeva taught science at Pasadena High School and entered the field through Teach for America. He received his BS degree from Carnegie Mellon University and his doctorate from the University of California, Los Angeles.

Index